W9-BKD-897

IT'S TRUE! IT'S TRUE!
KURT ANGLE

"This book is a recounting of my life and how
I see it. It is how life's triumphs and
shortcomings affected me."
Kurt Angle

CHAMPION OF BESTSELLER LISTS
EVERYWHERE—KURT ANGLE & WORLD
WRESTLING ENTERTAINMENT RULE!

"The latest in a relatively short but surprising line of
[WWE] best-selling writers . . . [It] shut[s] up the
naysayers who believe wrestling fans
don't know from reading."
Dayton Daily News

"At times achieve[s] a kind of poetry
of the grotesque."
Atlanta Journal-Constitution

"The world of pro wrestling is turning out
more best-selling authors than
the literary salons of 1920s Paris."
Philadelphia Inquirer

IT'S TRUE! ★
IT'S TRUE !

KURT ANGLE

with John Harper

IT'S TRUE!
IT'S TRUE!

ReganBooks

HarperTorch
An Imprint of HarperCollins*Publishers*

❧

HARPERTORCH
An Imprint of HarperCollins*Publishers*
10 East 53rd Street
New York, New York 10022-5299

First HarperTorch paperback printing: October 2002
First HarperCollins hardcover printing: September 2001

10   9   8   7   6   5   4   3   2   1

It is not the critic who counts; not the man who points out how the strong man stumbles, or where the doer of deeds could have done them better. The credit belongs to the man who is actually in the arena, whose face is marred by dust and sweat and blood; who strives valiantly; who errs, who comes short again and again, because there is no effort without error and shortcoming; but who does actually strive to do the deeds; who knows great enthusiasms, the great devotions; who spends himself in a worthy cause; who at the best knows in the end the triumph of high achievement, and who at the worst, if he fails, at least fails while daring greatly, so that his place shall never be with those cold and timid souls who neither know victory nor defeat.

— THEODORE ROOSEVELT

This book is a recounting of my life and how I see it. It is how life's triumphs and shortcomings affected me. This book is dedicated to the loving memory of my father, Dave Angle, who fought the battle of life each day and taught me its principles. During his life my father learned many lessons as he overcame life's hurdles. He may have stumbled a bit; however, with each misstep, a lesson was learned. Whether intending to or not, my father shared those lessons with me and passed on those experiences. This gave me the strength to conquer the battles life would present me with. It was his love, devotion, and teachings that molded me into the Olympic champion I became, as well the man I am today. I love you, Dad.

CONTENTS

ACKNOWLEDGMENTS

I would like to thank the many people who have made this book possible. First and foremost I would like to thank God for giving me the chance to live this life and meet so many wonderful people, as well as for giving me the talent and athletic ability that I have been so fortunate to receive.

I would like to thank my wonderful wife, Karen. We have had our good times as well as bad times, but, Karen, I know the best times are yet to come. Thanks for supporting me through my hectic schedule and constant travel. No matter where I have been in the world you were always on my mind. I live my life for you. You are my new family and mean everything to me and now I realize how much I mean to you. I love you.

To my dad. What else can I say that I have not already told you?

To my mom. Thank you for bringing me into this world. Thank you for your unconditional love and never-ending support. Thanks for being who you are and loving each and every one of us the same. You have taught and continue to teach me more than you will ever know. The simple lessons of life I've learned I owe to you. Thank you.

To my brothers David, Mark, John, and Eric, without whom I would not be who I am today. All of you have taught me the importance of family and what it means to stick together. You were there to watch me and encourage me to develop into the athlete and loyal brother I am today. Thanks.

To my sister and best friend, Le'Anne, who has guided me and nurtured me during the many years of abuse from our brothers. Thanks.

To the Angles and Barwicks. Thank you for caring. I am proud to be your relative and am honored to carry on the legacy of these two great families.

To the McMahon family, Jim Ross, and Bruce Prichard. Thank you for giving me the opportunity to become part of the greatest sports entertainment industry in the world. Thank you for confidence, for believing in me, and for constantly challenging me to go beyond my limits to make myself better.

To all World Wrestling Entertainment Superstars, agents, and writers. We have been a cohesive team that I am proud to be a part of and I thank you for letting me be a part of that greatness. I look forward to many more years ahead and to making World Wrestling Entertainment even stronger and more popular than it is today.

To John Harper. Thanks for your patience in listening to me tell the story of my life and making those words come to life. You are quite articulate and helped me put together a hell of a book.

To Ira Berg. Thanks for being the backbone of this project and making all the pieces come together and for being a good friend.

To Regan Books. Thank you for giving me the opportunity to express myself in words and to tell my *true* story. Remember, it's *true*, it's *true*.

To USA Wrestling and all of its wrestlers. You made our team the top wrestling power in the world and one that history will not forget.

To Dave Hawk. Thanks for all your hard work, for your neverending friendship, and, most important, for not taking too much of my money.

To Coach Lamprinakos. Thanks for having confidence in me and pushing me beyond my limits. Foremost thanks for being that second father.

To Coach Bubb and Coach Davis. Thanks for giving me the opportunity to wrestle for the Golden Eagles, thanks for your guidance, and thanks for a great college education.

To Dave and Nancy Schultz, the two people with the most passion for amateur wrestling that I have ever known, thank you.

To all the employees at World Wrestling Entertainment who helped me put together the book of my life, I thank you.

And finally, thanks to everyone who has supported me to help make my Olympic dream come true. God bless you all.

1

FROM HERO
TO HEEL

The silence was killing me. That's what I remember most about standing alone in the middle of the Olympic wrestling mat five years ago, waiting for a decision that would change my life dramatically in one way or another.

Was the gold medal mine or not? I didn't know. Nobody knew. But I couldn't believe that 7,000 people in the Georgia World Congress Center could be so quiet, because the place had been absolutely crazy only a few minutes earlier during my match.

Most of the noise was for me. I was the crowd favorite, the blue-collar kid from Pittsburgh trying to win the gold at the 1996 Olympics in Atlanta. Somebody decided to play the *Rocky* theme every time I entered the arena for a match, and it was fitting because I looked like the underdog in the 220-pound weight class. I only weighed about 210 pounds, and physically I was nowhere near as imposing as some of the fearsome-looking characters from the Eastern European countries. Yet time and again I had dazzled the fans during the two days of competition, winning match after match in dramatic fashion, with last-minute comebacks or overtime thrillers.

Matter of fact, I was such an inspirational figure at the time, overcoming serious injury and personal tragedy to make the Olympic team, that I never could have dreamed I'd become famous in the World Wrestling Entertainment a few years later as the red-white-and-blue-covered antihero the fans would love to hate.

Me, a bad guy? A heel? I was always the golden boy. The kid who stayed out of trouble. The guy that fathers wanted their daughters to date. I had dedicated my life to winning a gold medal in memory of my dad, who died when I was sixteen.

Hell, I wrestled in the Olympic trials with two cracked vertebrae in my neck because I wanted that medal so desperately. I was a real-life Disney movie, and the crowd in Atlanta was rooting hard for a storybook finish. At least the Americans were. For the finals, there were three thousand Iranians in the crowd, too, and they were rooting just as hard for their countryman, Abbas Jadidi. The atmosphere in the arena during the match had been electric as the two groups tried to outscream each other.

But now the place was deadly still, and it was terribly unsettling. You could feel the tension. The decision was in the hands of the three referees because Jadidi and I had wrestled to a 1–1 tie. Five minutes of regulation and three minutes of overtime, and neither one of us could pull off a move to win the match.

In my mind I felt I'd won. I was the aggressor, especially in overtime when Jadidi was exhausted.

Every time we rolled out-of-bounds he was lying on the mat, gasping for air, while I jumped up and hurried back to the center of the mat. Twice he faked being hurt to stall for time. Everybody in the place could see he was just trying to buy time to catch his breath. I was getting pissed and trying to intimidate him at the same time: I yelled at the ref to "get him in here" as I danced around on the mat, showing him I wasn't tired.

Actually, I was exhausted, too, but I had spent two solid years training eight hours a day, going to extremes like running 200-yard sprints up the hills of Pittsburgh carrying a training partner on my back so that I would never give in to fatigue. I loved being pushed to the limit like this because I knew that I was the best-conditioned wrestler in the world. If it had been up to me, we would have kept wrestling to settle it ourselves, because I knew Jadidi was completely out of gas.

As time ran out in overtime, I had been seconds away from a takedown that would have won the match. I had shot for his left leg and wrapped it up, but he was so strong that he was fighting me off, and I still had my head caught between his legs as the final seconds ticked off the clock. I was so close, but did the referees see it the same way? You can never be sure. And so as a minute passed, then two, while the referees huddled at the scorers' table, it seemed more like hours. As I stood, waiting, trying not to think the worst, I found myself pondering the long, difficult, and sometimes painful road that had brought me to this position.

So much had happened to transform me from a kid who cried often while losing as a young wrestler, from the youngest brother in a family of six kids who was haunted by a fear of failure, to a twenty-seven-year-old Olympic athlete.

My father's accidental death on a construction site had changed me forever. It gave me an inner strength that allowed me to rise above the life of brawling and partying that had destroyed the athletic dreams of my four older brothers in our hometown of Pittsburgh.

And now the memories came flooding down on me: the state championship in high school; the two NCAA Championships in college; the World Championship in '95.

There were the countless trips overseas to Russia, Turkey, and Bulgaria over the years, grueling odysseys that took as long as thirty-eight hours, one way, with connecting flights, all in search of the world's best competition. And there were all those insane days of training when I pushed myself to the brink of passing out, weeks and months and years when I was obsessed with winning a gold medal.

I had gone so far as to wrestle and win the Olympic trials just months earlier with what amounted to a broken neck, receiving injections of mepivacaine before every match despite warnings from doctors that I was risking paralysis. It sounds idiotic, I know, but I was blinded by my quest to become an Olympic champion. And now, finally, it was over and I was aching to let go of all the emotion I'd been storing over the years—for myself, for my late father, for my family members in the stands. And for

Dave Schultz, my friend and coach, who had been shot and killed months earlier by John du Pont, the crazed millionaire who sponsored the amateur wrestling club to which I'd once belonged.

I couldn't bear the thought of training four more years for another Olympics, and yet I knew that if the referees ruled against me, somehow I would try to convince myself to go for it all over again. Surely it wouldn't come to that, would it? I couldn't stop these thoughts from ricocheting around in my head as I stood, waiting helplessly for a decision. I was trying not to show my own desperation, but what was taking these referees so long anyway?

Jadidi was making it worse for me. While I waited in the center ring, he barged into the judging area, pleading his case and trying to convince anyone who would listen that he was the winner. People were trying to push him away, but he got a peek as one of the officials circled his name on a piece of paper as the winner, and he began jumping around in celebration.

"Oh no," I thought. "Does he know?" Finally, after the longest three minutes of my life, the lead referee marched toward me, calling Jadidi back to the center. In the tradition of wrestling protocol, he stood between us and took hold of a wrist from each of us, preparing to raise the arm of the winner. At that instant Jadidi's arm shot skyward, and I had a sickening feeling—instantly I envisioned four more years of torture.

What I didn't know was that Jadidi had raised his arm even as the referee was trying to hold it down. And suddenly the ref was raising my arm in triumph.

It turned out that Jadidi had seen the one official circle his name, but the other two had circled mine. I was the winner. The gold medal was mine. Finally, the silence in the arena was shattered as the crowd exploded in roars of applause from the Americans and boos from the Iranians. After the millisecond it took for the decision to register, I was so shocked that I jumped on the ref and hugged him. Then I dropped to my knees, overwhelmed by the moment.

I thanked God, I thanked my dad, sure that he was cheering somewhere. I broke down; I couldn't stop crying as my family rushed the mat to mob me with hugs of congratulations. I felt weak, dizzy from a feeling of euphoria. I could have died right there without regret, I was so ecstatic.

Jadidi, meanwhile, was enraged. He argued bitterly with the referees, and never did shake my hand. His coach practically had to push him onto the stand for the medal ceremony, and afterward he was quoted by reporters as saying, "That medal hanging around his neck should be hanging around mine." It wasn't very sportsmanlike, but I could understand his frustration. He'd had an unbelievable Olympics, dominating every wrestler he faced until the finals. In the semifinals he beat a Russian named Larry Khebalov, an Olympic champion and six-time world champion whom I had never beaten. Khebalov was one of the best ever in our sport, and Jadidi crushed him, beat him 8–1, which is like winning a football game 56–0.

The guy was on a rampage, and I'm sure he was counting on winning the gold. But I was able to negate his strength with my quickness, my balance, and my instincts, and we pushed and pulled at each other, neither one giving an inch. The match was unbelievably intense—maybe the most exciting 1–1 match in Olympic history. In the end, when it comes down to a referee's decision, you just never know what may have caught their eye to influence them. You're at the mercy of their judgment, and in a case like this, that judgment put me on a path that brought me to World Wrestling Entertainment.

I still wonder sometimes where I'd be right now if that decision had gone the other way. Would I be a World Wrestling Entertainment Superstar? I tend to doubt it. I never would have received the taste of celebrity life that came with winning the gold medal, a life I got hooked on pretty quickly. More likely I'd be coaching high school wrestling somewhere in western Pennsylvania, forever replaying that match with Jadidi in my mind. As it was, it took me two years, a short-lived broadcasting career, and quite a bit of soul-searching after the Olympics to make the decision to sign on with World Wrestling Entertainment. And that was after I earlier turned down a lucrative contract offer from World Wrestling Entertainment immediately following the Olympics because so many people around me advised against it—they told me I'd be selling out the sport of amateur wrestling.

I'd never really watched World Wrestling Entertainment until I turned on *RAW* on TV one night in 1998, and I loved it. I never realized what great athletes these guys were, and within a month I was in-

trigued by the thought of joining. At the time I was searching for a new identity, trying to find a career that would offer the challenge and the excitement of all those years of world-class competition, and keep me in the public eye. So I called Vince McMahon, came on board after a tryout, and skyrocketed to World Wrestling Entertainment stardom, winning the championship belt in less than a year. No one had ever moved up the ladder so quickly. Along the way I won over the skeptics, in Pittsburgh as well as in the world of amateur wrestling. My high school and college coaches, both wrestling purists, are loyal viewers now, and they appreciate the entertainment as well as the athleticism we display.

Of course, when I signed on I figured I'd be cheered the way I was all those years in amateur wrestling. But it doesn't work that way in the world of sports entertainment. These days you've pretty much gotta have some badass in you to be a good guy—or what is known as a babyface in the business. Fans love the rebellious guys, the guys who wear black. Like Stone Cold Steve Austin. People think he's the toughest SOB in the world. Same with Triple H. Those guys are great at what they do, but I wasn't going to be like them. Basically I was the perfect antihero, the red-white-and-blue Olympian who thinks everybody should be in awe of him. It seemed weird at first, but once I understood the concept I ate it up: Okay, I'm the nerdy straight arrow who's here to save the World Wrestling Entertainment from all the badasses.

I'm not going to say that's the real Kurt Angle. That's why Vince McMahon calls it sports entertainment. We're playing roles that are created to give the fans a great show, and I take that role as seriously as I took the Olympics. But I'm not really this goofy, self-absorbed character who's always showing off his gold medal, telling people they should appreciate what I've done. I've always been humble about my success. I liked proving that nice guys can finish on top. I make it a point to treat people the right way, and I'm aware that what I do as a celebrity can influence others.

But I adjusted pretty quickly to being a heel in the ring. It's fun, especially for somebody like me who was always so worried about being a good son, a good brother, a good guy. When I'm in character I don't have to worry about that. I'm willing to make myself look like a jerk to make it work. I'll do or say whatever it takes to get a reaction. I get on the microphone and make fun of every city we work in, as a way of baiting the crowd. I have to work hardest at it in my hometown of Pittsburgh, because I'm a local hero there. But I find a way, even if it's cracking on Mario Lemieux, who is my own sports idol. Last year I told the fans the state of sports in Pittsburgh was such a disgrace that if hockey superstar Mario Lemieux had any pride, he'd come out of retirement to save the Penguins. That did the trick. Then, when I went back this year, I told them they could thank me for shaming Lemieux into making his famous comeback, which actually did reenergize the city. Beloved as Lemieux is in Pittsburgh, I pissed people off like you couldn't believe.

By the time I won the World Wrestling Entertainment title at *No Mercy* in October 2000, pinning The Rock, I was hated by fans everywhere. I knew it pained people to see me beat The Rock, the People's Champ, and as they booed me that night in Albany, New York, I egged them on by spoofing my Olympic victory, falling to my knees and crying my eyes out, just as I had in '96 in Atlanta. I knew it would make the fans crazy. I had been planning it for five days, after Rocky gave me the news that I was going to win the belt.

But you know, I actually started crying for real because I was so happy. I just made it look more emotional than it was, like I was crying my eyes out. I was holding the championship belt to my chest and looking to the sky in thanks. And the fans were screaming at me as though I had murdered someone.

It's kind of funny, how different the reactions were to my show of emotion. When I cried in Atlanta in '96, the whole country cried with me. But that's the difference between sports and sports entertainment. Here, it's all about making your character work. My job is to make the fans boo me, so I said to myself, "Okay, people, the stuff you loved me for once, now I'm doing it again just to piss you off a little more."

But even with all the booing, winning the title gave me a feeling that was very much the same as winning the gold medal. I was ecstatic. I knew all along that I was winning, so there wasn't really any huge release of emotion at the end, but I felt like I was on top of the world—just like the Olympics. In World Wrestling Entertainment it's more about putting on the best show you can than about winning or losing. But

Vince McMahon and World Wrestling Entertainment decision makers aren't just going to give the belt to anyone. Winning the title labeled me as one of the top guys in the business, and to me that's every bit as good a feeling as being the best in the world at amateur wrestling.

Some people might laugh at the idea that I actually compare the two victories. But I'm in the sports entertainment business now. It's just as important to me to excel here as it was in the Olympics, so I don't want to hear that it shouldn't be as important. This is what I do now, and I'm going to be the best at it, too.

You know, I'll probably always look at winning the gold medal as the most important moment in my life. It was the culmination of so many years of dedication. It brought me a slice of fame and led me to World Wrestling Entertainment. I believe that winning that gold medal was my destiny, but in my heart, I enjoy the WWE even more than amateur wrestling. I love the spotlight. I love entertaining people. I think people love to hate me because they can see I'm funny, I'm good at being a heel. I throw myself completely into my character, which has evolved somewhat since I started.

Since I lost the World Wrestling Entertainment title in February 2001, nearly five months after I won it, my character has become a little more cynical, a little meaner in the ring. I get this crazed look of intensity on my face when I put someone in an ankle lock, which has become my trademark move, and I yank on that ankle like I want to break it off.

I even started backstabbing the guys I was teamed

up with in tag-team matches, because I wanted to be the one to get the glory. But at the same time I continue to preach that I'm the smartest, most ethical Superstar in World Wrestling Entertainment, the guy who lives by the three I's—intensity, integrity, and intelligence. And so the fans seem to hate me more than ever.

It's a long way from that memorable day in Atlanta. When the referees finally ended that agonizing wait and declared me the winner, I instantly became a national hero, with a big picture splashed across the front page of *USA Today*. For months I was treated like royalty in Pittsburgh—parades, banquets, commercial and corporate endorsements, you name it. I did the star tour on TV nationally with Regis and Kathie Lee, Jay Leno, Conan O'Brien. I loved all that attention and adulation; who wouldn't? Now I'm booed everywhere I go, and yet it brings the same sense of satisfaction. I've heard actors say that playing the villain in a movie is more fun than being the leading man, and I can relate to that. You can push the envelope, see just how far you can go to get a reaction from the crowd. At the same time I believe that eventually I'll win the fans over, and become one of the greatest babyfaces World Wrestling Entertainment has ever had. They can't hate an Olympic champion forever. Can they?

2

DAD'S DEATH

The first year I ever wrestled I won two matches and lost fourteen. And I cried every time I lost. I was six years old and I hated wrestling. I never thought I'd be any good because I was scared to be out on the mat by myself. I was afraid of losing.

The funny thing was, I excelled at team sports from the first day I started playing. Baseball, basketball, football—I played them all and I was always one of the best kids on the team. I loved contributing to the team, being part of the group. I guess it's because if we lost, I knew it wasn't all my fault.

I'm sure a psychiatrist would love to put me on the couch to analyze those feelings, but to me it wasn't much of a mystery. It was all about proving myself to my father and my older brothers.

I was the youngest of six kids in our family. We were a blue-collar family, living in Dormont, about ten miles south of downtown Pittsburgh. We had a ranch house with three bedrooms, which meant the house was very crowded. I slept in my mom and dad's bed until I was twelve years old. Eric, who was two years older than me, slept on a cot in their room, too.

My brothers were all good athletes, and they expected me to be the best of the family. I lived in fear of letting my dad and my brothers down. As a wrestler, I had no place to hide on the mat, and I didn't like that. I didn't have the mentality for it. I got better as I got older, but I needed a reason to believe in myself. I needed something to make me tougher. Unfortunately, it took the worst kind of tragedy for me to find it.

My father, Dave Angle, died when I was sixteen years old, and if I had to point to one crucial turning point in my life, that was it. In my mind I grew up and overcame my fears the day he died. I vowed right then and there to become a champion, to do whatever it took. And to do it for him.

Nothing was ever the same for me after that day. It was August 28, 1985, and my aunt Ruth Ann was waiting for me when I walked into the house after football practice. When she told me that my dad was in the hospital—it seems weird now but the words barely registered. Nothing could hurt my dad, I remember thinking. He was the toughest guy in the world.

And besides, football season started in two days. There's nothing bigger in western Pennsylvania than Friday nights in the fall, high school football under the lights. I was a junior, a starter at fullback and linebacker, and at the time nothing else really mattered to me.

I was actually annoyed that I even had to go to the hospital. When I got there I found out my dad, who was a crane operator, had fallen fifteen feet off his crane at work and landed on his head. But even then the seriousness of his accident didn't sink in. Maybe I

ANGLE
On Thurs. August 29, 1985 David Angle; beloved husband of M. Jacqueline Angle; father of David R., Mark A., John E., Mrs. Le Anne Graham of Virginia Beach, VA., Eric S. and Kurt S.; brother of Joseph, Jerome, Paul, Rose Ann Angle, Ursula Keefe, Gertrude Loerlin and the late Robert, Edward and John Angle; also seven grandchildren. Friends welcome at the **BEINHAUER MORTUARY,** 2630 West Liberty Ave., Sun. and Mon. 2-4 and 7-9 p.m. Mass of Christian Burial in St. Bernard Church on Tues. at 10 a.m.

Construction worker dies of fall injuries

David Angle, 55, of 101 Seneca Drive, Mt. Lebanon, died yesterday morning in Mercy Hospital, two days after he was hurt while working at the Liberty Center hotel-office construction project, Downtown.

Angle, an employee of the Mellon-Stuart Co., suffered multiple injuries Tuesday morning when he fell approximately 13 feet after losing his balance.

was in denial; I don't know. At the time it never crossed my mind that he might die. After we waited a while for news from the doctors, I asked if someone could take me home because I was tired and had to get up for school. My brothers looked at me like they couldn't believe the way I was acting. I remember one of my sisters-in-law looking at my mother like, "Doesn't he understand?"

The next day I went back to the hospital, and that's when the doctors told us my dad was in a coma and he wasn't coming out of it. He was brain-dead and we had to make a decision whether or not to keep him on life support. Finally, it hit me hard, but even then I think I was too numb to react. Not my dad. It still seemed incomprehensible to me.

He had always been there for me. From the time I was seven years old he had never missed one of my games, whether it was football, baseball, basketball, or wrestling, even if it meant leaving work early. My father demanded that you give your best in athletics, but he was very supportive of me. He never scolded me after a loss or a bad game—I think he recognized that I took a lot of pride in the way I played. Maybe he saw that I was the type of kid who needed a pat on the back more than a kick in the butt, that I would do anything to make sure I didn't disappoint him or my older brothers.

My work ethic is what eventually helped me win the gold medal at the Olympics, and I'm sure I got that from my dad. He never missed a day's work, and he often worked twelve hours a day. He never went to college but he wanted to be the best at his job, and he *was* the best at his company. He was the head crane operator for Mellon-Stewart, a Pittsburgh company that had a reputation at the time for being one of the best in the country but has since gone out of business.

At home my dad was a stern father, but I felt I had a special relationship with him, maybe because I was the youngest. I found out after he died that he was always bragging about me to his friends at work, saying I was going to be the best athlete of the Angle boys, that I was going to be something special. I used to love the mornings before school—that's when I'd get to spend time with my dad. He'd get me up early, before everybody else. We'd have breakfast together in the kitchen with the radio on, and we'd talk about sports and school and things before he left for work.

Unfortunately, I can't say life was perfect around my dad. He was what you would call a functional alcoholic. He never drank at work, and it never affected his job, but he depended on alcohol in his life. I saw it every day, and that's why I'm terrified of alcohol myself. Not that I never touch it, but I'm very careful on the few occasions when I have a drink.

My dad wasn't violent, thank God, because he was a big, strong man who could have been dangerous if he had been violent. But after work he needed his liquor. At home every couple of hours he needed to have two glasses of rum, and he'd just throw them down. I never understood it, but it was obviously a powerful force in his life, and eventually it ruined his marriage to my mom. They never separated, but their relationship just kind of drifted away.

There was a day when my mother said to him, "You either pick the alcohol or you pick me." My dad picked the alcohol, and their relationship was never the same.

It became very hard on my mother, but I was so young that I didn't really understand at the time. I just knew my mom and dad weren't getting along very well, to the point where they began sleeping in different rooms. As important as he was in my life, my dad had a problem, and as much as I hate to admit it, that problem definitely affected our family. When it was time to drink, after work, he had to drink and drink and drink and drink, to the point where he would just pass out at home all the time. On weekends my dad started his drinking earlier, usually at his neighborhood social club. If we'd go shopping, my dad would stop at the club for a few drinks on the way to the store or the mall, while my brothers and I played video games in the back. Same thing on Sundays: my father would take my brother Eric and me to church, and we'd always stop at the club, where he would drink with the guys while I took my Coke to the back and played video games.

As a kid at the time, it seemed normal to me. The club meant playtime. Eric and I would play those video games for hours. Sometimes we would be so competitive that we'd end up fighting. Once we got so wrapped up in this one video game that we started fighting and all of a sudden we were knocking over chairs and empty glasses. It got so bad that the head bartender had to kick us out. He told my dad and we were banned from going into an establishment that served alcohol. Boy, that pissed my dad off. But later he laughed about it and told all his friends and family that we were the first two to ever be kicked out of the club. But Eric and I were always competitive because we were brought up that way. My older brothers were more aware of my dad's drinking. After he died they told me stories about how he'd sit down at the bar in his club and order a Bloody Mary, a shot of vodka on the side, and a mug of beer as a chaser. He'd throw them all down in a matter of seconds and call the bartender back to order another round, and he would just continue, round after round.

When I hear stories like that, I don't know how my dad functioned as well as he did. But the drinking did take a toll on everyone in our house. My dad insisted that we have dinner as a family every night, and that

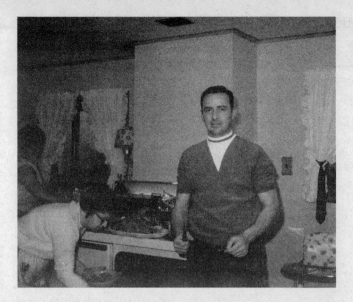

was a good thing. But we could never spend any time with him after dinner because he'd drink until he passed out. So my mom was the head of the house in the evening—she took care of everything with the kids. But if there was a problem, she'd go to my dad, and usually someone paid for it. If you did something wrong, like mouth off to my mom, you were going to get whupped for it. That's the way my dad grew up and that's the way he raised us.

It was worse for my older brothers. They tell me stories about the time before I was born, when they lived in a smaller house and all slept in the attic together. They'd be making noise when they were supposed to be going to sleep, and my dad would come up the stairs and use his belt on them.

They laugh about it now. They say that Mark, the toughest of all my brothers, seemed to take some kind of pride in how many licks he could take. My dad would be going back downstairs and Mark would giggle just to see if he could get away with it. Usually he didn't.

I took my share of lickings, too, but only when I deserved them. Still, as an adult, that's not my nature. I plan to have kids someday and I don't see myself disciplining them that way.

Maybe it's because of everything I saw as I grew up in our house. As much as I loved my dad, I saw how problems with alcohol can tear families apart. I don't know if it's why my older brothers rebelled, but they got into a lot of fights and trouble as they were growing up. My parents had to get involved—and by order of a judge they were forced to send Mark to a juvenile facility for a year to get him under control. Then my sister, Le'Anne, got pregnant and had a baby when she was just sixteen years old. I don't know if all the problems made my dad drink more, as a way of escaping them, but whatever it was, his addiction to alcohol caused some kind of tension in our house just about every day.

Sometimes I wonder if my dad was unhappy with his own life. He went into the army after high school, got married to my mom at age twenty-two, and worked hard his whole life to provide for six kids. He had a real private side to him; it seemed like he didn't want anyone to know what he was thinking most of the time. He wasn't a man to show his affection, even to his kids. I don't ever remember hugging him. He'd make me shake his hand and he taught me to be a gentleman, how to have respect for other people. But it was very formal. It was weird because my mom was just the opposite, always hugging us and telling us she loved us. But it was almost like my dad couldn't bring himself to show a soft side to anyone. He came from a family of ten kids himself, but he didn't seem to be very close to any of his brothers or sisters. Maybe because they all had big families and they had their own children to worry about. While my dad was alive I never got to know his side of our family very well. We were close to my mom's family, and my dad enjoyed getting together with her relatives. But we socialized with very few of the other Angles. It was only after my father died that my mother organized reunions with his family, and I got to know some of his relatives.

My dad came from a blue-collar upbringing himself, and I think he could have been a good athlete in a different environment. He played football for a team in the army, and he had a mean streak in him that was passed on to my brothers. They came to be known as some of the toughest guys in Pittsburgh, especially Mark. And they were all big guys, over 200 pounds. But when it came right down to it, they all backed down from my dad. I don't remember any violent confrontations, but my dad never hesitated to discipline my brothers, even when they were in high school. Big as he was, he seemed invincible to me. They did an autopsy on him after he died and they said he lived through two heart attacks in his sleep that he never even knew he had. I do remember one, I think—a night when he seemed to be flipping out on the couch. He fell onto the floor, holding his chest. Of course he had been drinking, and I thought he was just drunk. He just got up, got back on the couch, and went to sleep—never said a word to anyone about it. My dad never went to the hospital for anything, until he fell off his crane that day.

He was fifty-five years old at the time, building the Doubletree Hotel in downtown Pittsburgh. He was leaning on the gate, preparing to get into his crane, when the gate gave way, and he fell fifteen feet backward, landing on his head in a ditch. He got knocked out for a few minutes. Later we learned he cracked his skull in three different places and broke both of his shoulders. Yet he was so tough, he got up from that and walked to the hospital by himself. And they told us that all he cared about was making sure somebody called his wife and kids. Three hours later he was in a coma.

The next day, when the doctors told us he was brain-dead, we were all sitting there in his hospital room. It was extremely emotional for all of us. My mom and my sister were lying on each side of his bed, draped over him, crying and begging him, "Please don't die!" My mom was talking to him, hoping that somehow he could hear her, telling him that she would make things right between them again if only he would come back to her now.

We agonized over the decision to take him off the respirator. My mom didn't want to do it, but we talked about it as a family, and later that day we finally decided it was the right decision—even if it was the most painful thing anyone could ever imagine.

So my dad was gone, and everyone felt especially bad for me. I was the youngest, the only one still in high school. But I never did cry or become emotional that day. I don't know why. I didn't know how to react to such a terrible tragedy. I guess I was still in denial, still refusing to believe my dad could be gone. I just remember vowing to myself to become a champion, for my dad, because I knew there was nothing in the world that would have made him happier.

At sixteen, I was too wrapped up in my own little world to understand how my dad's death affected the rest of my family. But since then I've come to understand that each of my brothers, as well as my sister, had their own special memories of my dad, just as I did. And the good thing was that after he died we became closer as a family. My three oldest brothers and my sister weren't living in the house at the time, and we didn't see that much of one another. But after my dad died we started making a point of having regular family dinners, where everyone came over to the house. I'm sure my brothers felt it was partly their responsibility to look out for Eric and me, but as a family we all began to talk to one another more and enjoy one another's company. When we'd get together we'd always end up telling stories about my dad. We talked about the good side and the bad, and we always seemed to end up laughing and having a nice time. It's the same way these days when we get together, and I'm sure my dad would approve.

My dad's death was probably hardest on my mom. Even though their marriage had suffered because of my dad's drinking, I understood how much my mom cared for my dad when I saw the way she reacted in the hospital. She had old-fashioned values, and she believed in the commitment of marriage. I think she also believed they would be able to mend their relationship as the last of their kids grew up, and they could be happy growing old together. With my dad gone, I tried to make sure I was around to offer support for my mom. She was the main reason I wanted to stay fairly close to home for college. I used to come home quite a bit from college when I didn't really need to because I knew it was important to see my mom and let her know that I'd always be there for her. I wound up living with her until I was twenty-seven, and it was almost like we were a team, trying to make the Olympics together.

As for me, I held in the emotion I was feeling for losing my dad even when I saw my friends at school and they were asking me how my dad was doing. At that point I didn't let them know how I was feeling about it. I missed school that day, but I showed up to tell everyone that I was going to play in the season-opening football game that night. My friends, my coaches, and my family all tried to talk me out of it, but I felt that playing was the best way to let out the anger I was keeping bottled up inside. So I convinced everyone to let me play. We had a rule that if you missed two days of practice, you didn't start in the game that week, but this was a special circumstance, and I talked my coach into letting me start. Before the game I wasn't sure if I was ready to play. I was trying not to think about life without my dad. And then I went out and played the best game of my life. I believe that every bit of emotion I felt about my dad came out

that night, and it enabled me to do spectacular things.

I was reminded of it years later when I read about Dwight Gooden pitching a no-hitter for the Yankees the night before his father was having heart surgery, and then bringing him the game ball in the hospital the next day. I'm sure he would understand how I felt that night against Brashear High School and a great quarterback named Major Harris, who would go on to play college football for West Virginia and make them a national power while he was there.

I had sixteen solo tackles, two touchdown runs, two fumble recoveries, and an interception. Basically I kicked Major Harris's ass and won the game for us. It was the first game I ever started on the varsity, and while I went on to earn All-State honors, I never had another one quite like it. It's still hard to explain. I think I just wanted to prove to my dad, to everyone, that I was going to succeed as an athlete, even though he was gone. I always knew I had ability, but I needed more inner strength to deal with my fears. From that point on, everything seemed to click for me—in football, then wrestling, the Olympics, and now World Wrestling Entertainment. It was like my dad's death was the purpose for me to become a sports icon.

The way it worked out, I think my performance that night also helped our family get through a sad day. My brothers wound up going to the game, and the mood was lighter when we gathered at our house afterward. Everyone was talking about how well I had played, and then we started talking about the good memories of my father for the first time since the accident. There had been a lot of tears, and it was important for everyone to be able to laugh a little.

As for me, I think I refused to admit how much I was hurting inside. I didn't even cry during my dad's wake or his funeral. And I've always been an emotional person who cried in times of both joy and sorrow. I guess my vow to become a great athlete was my way of dealing with my dad's death, and it helped me block out the pain. I guess I wanted to believe he was still alive, perhaps living through me, and to this day I believe that. But I did start making it a point to visit my dad's gravesite every week, usually on days when I had a football game. I'd drive out to the cemetery and talk to him. I wouldn't even tell my family I was going. It was a quiet time for me to talk to my dad. It kind of calmed my nerves; I almost felt like he was listening to me, and I could open up and talk to him about how I felt about whatever was going on in my life.

Over the years I've continued to go and talk to my dad. It became a form of therapy for me to go visit his grave, when I was training for the Olympics, when I had a big decision to make, or when I was having some kind of personal problem. I still do it and I always come away feeling better afterward. It's like he's my best friend, even though he's not here anymore. It's kind of ironic because if my dad were still alive, I'm sure I wouldn't open up to him about my problems, my dreams, that kind of stuff. As it is, I feel like he's the only one I can talk to about certain things.

The strange thing was that even when I started going to his grave, a week after he died, I didn't cry. You always hear people say that you need to grieve when someone close to you dies, but it wasn't until about a month later that it hit me unexpectedly in the middle of the night. I was asleep, having a dream about my dad, when I woke up, startled, and sat up in bed. Suddenly I just started crying because I realized, once and for all, I was never going to see my dad again. And that's when I started thinking about all the important things that he told me, all the good times that we had, and how he was always there for me at every sporting event. As much as he liked his alcohol, he made sure he made time for me. I cried for about four hours and never did get back to sleep that night. But I haven't cried about him since then, unless you count that moment right after the gold medal match in Atlanta when I was too happy *not* to cry. Otherwise I've always been too busy living up to the silent promise I made to him.

3

BIG, BAD BROTHERS

Some people are inspired to be athletes by the games they see on TV—the fame and glamour of pro sports. I just wanted to be like my older brothers. From as early as I can remember, I was always sitting in the stands somewhere as a kid, watching my brothers in football or baseball or wrestling.

Sports meant everything around our house. Growing up in the 1970s in Pittsburgh, life seemed to revolve around sports. The city was in love with the Steelers. They won four Super Bowls in the seventies, and the Pirates were good then, too, winning the World Series in 1971 and 1979. Because '79 was also the same year the Steelers won their last Super Bowl, Pittsburgh was called the City of Champions that year. People took a lot of pride in that, especially since it was a time when steel mills were closing and a lot of people were being put out of jobs.

My dad was a big football fan, so I used to watch the Steelers game every week. We never went to see the Steelers or Pirates in person because we couldn't afford it. My parents were having enough trouble trying to provide for six kids. I did get to go see the University of Pittsburgh play, because my uncle Fred was a Pitt graduate and sometimes I'd go to games with him and my aunt Ruth Ann. That was exciting because Tony Dorsett was playing for Pitt back then and the Panthers won a national championship, too. Other than that, I never saw anything live. But if there was a game on TV, any kind of game, we'd watch it. I used to feel sorry for my mom sometimes because she got outvoted when she wanted to watch something on TV. If there was a game on, she had no chance.

What mattered most to us, though, were our games. If someone had a high school football game, or a peewee wrestling match, the whole family was there. I was barely out of diapers when Dave, my oldest brother, was in high school, so I don't know how many of my brothers' games I saw over the years. But I was always there, and then, when it was my turn, my brothers followed me everywhere, all the way to Atlanta for the Olympics in 1996.

Now we're all grown, but nothing much has changed. When I got married in 1998, I postponed my honeymoon and instead took my wife, Karen, on a two-hour drive to Clarion University, the college I had attended, to see my brother Mark's son, Mark Jr., wrestle in a big tournament. We stayed at a Days Inn that night. I asked for the honeymoon suite; I thought that was pretty funny, but I'm not sure my wife did.

The thing is, that's always what mattered to my family. At the dinner table we didn't talk about politics or current events. It was always sports, and usually whatever sports we were playing at the time. My four brothers, David, Mark, John, and Eric, were big, strong athletes and they were my inspiration. My sister, Le'Anne, was the captain of the cheerleading squad in high school, so our whole family life always revolved around local sports.

My brothers were my biggest supporters when I started playing sports, but they pushed me hard—harder than I wanted to be pushed when I was young. My dad was always supportive after I lost a game or a match, but my brothers were always telling me what I did wrong, what I had to do to get better. They saw that I had talent and they had high expectations for me.

They also saw to it that I cried a lot. They'd make me box or wrestle with Eric, who was two years older than me, just about every day, until one of us cried. Usually it was me. But that's the way my older brothers were. They could be viciously competitive, and just plain mean, on and off the ball field or the wrestling mat. As good as they were in organized sports, for a long time I thought fighting was their favorite sport. I don't mean boxing, either. I'm talking about street fighting, brawling, whatever you want to call it. If that kind of fighting were an Olympic event, there might be more gold medals in the Angle family today.

All of my brothers were constantly getting into fights as teenagers. I never saw or heard about them losing, either. It's not like they were bullies. My mom and dad didn't raise us that way. I don't know what it was, but my brothers were so competitive, and so tough, anything could set them off. Maybe it was some guy who picked the wrong time to make a wisecrack in school or challenge one of them at a party. I don't know what fueled their rage, but it's a good thing they grew up in the seventies and eighties, when kids fought mostly with their fists. I hate to think about what might have happened if they were growing up these days, with kids using knives and guns all the time.

For some reason, I wasn't like my brothers. I had a more easygoing personality, I guess, and I hardly ever got into fights. My mom thought I was such a good kid that when I was in my early teens she once asked me if I'd ever thought about becoming a priest. Even when I developed into a state champion high school wrestler, I really didn't have a mean streak in me. My brothers were always trying to get me to be more intimidating, and even my mom and my sister, Le'Anne, would tell me I needed to be a little meaner on the mat. They were constantly in my ear, saying, "Kurt, you've gotta be tougher! When you go out-of-bounds, shove that bastard you're wrestling in his face and stare him down. Show him you own him."

But no matter how many times I heard it, I had a rough time being a hard-ass. It wasn't my nature to intimidate or be macho. In a way, that was a blessing, because where my brothers would let their emotions get out of control, I found as I grew older that I had the ability to stay cool under pressure. In clutch situations, I wouldn't crack. I was able to keep things in perspective because I only worried about performing and winning.

Maybe my personality was some kind of reaction to being around my brothers. Their toughness was a mixed blessing for me. Sometimes I hated them for

treating me like a typical little brother, knocking me around and making me cry. Eric and I were the youngest by several years, and my three older brothers were always making us try to hurt each other. Every Friday night they would put boxing gloves on us and make us fight. They made it a show. They called it "The Friday Night Fights" and invited their friends over to watch. I'd come out in sunglasses and a robe. And then Eric and I would beat on each other. If one of us would take a shot to the nose and leave the room crying, my brothers would call out "Sissy, sissy" until Eric or I came running back in and started swinging again.

The thing is, I never wanted to hurt Eric. If I had the upper hand and got in a position where I could

It's True! It's True! ★ **35**

hurt him, I backed off and let up on him. Usually I'd pay for being too nice, because Eric had that mean streak in him as well. He wanted to hurt me, and if he got the chance, he usually did.

So there were Friday-night fights, and then Sunday was for football. Usually it was Johnny who would take Eric and me into the backyard. He'd be the quarterback. Eric would play running back and I'd play linebacker, or vice versa. Johnny would hand off, and then it was just the two of us. One on one. No pads. We'd crack heads and everything. Usually I'd end up crying.

Johnny watched us after school more than anybody, and he'd make Eric and me wrestle in the living room every day. Mark was my inspiration because he was the best wrestler among my brothers, but Johnny worked with me more than anyone when I was young. He'd move the furniture around in the living room and show me moves to work on every day. Of course, then he'd make me wrestle Eric, usually until one of us got hurt and started crying.

But as tough as my brothers were on me, they made sure that nobody outside of our family laid a hand on me. Eric was my worst enemy at home. He used to beat me up all the time—just torture me. But he was my personal bodyguard at school. I was in seventh grade when our family moved from Dormont to nearby Mount Lebanon. He was in ninth grade, and when he beat up a few kids who wanted to test him right away, he cleared a path for me. Eric let everyone know they'd have to answer to him if they messed with me. I remember once during a pickup football game, an older kid got mad at me for some reason and came after me. Eric stepped in and laid the guy out with one punch, just coldcocked him. He felt it was his duty to look after me and he never hesitated to use his fists to let people know it.

But the undisputed bare-knuckle champion in the Angle family was Mark, my second-oldest brother. He was such a brawler that he became kind of an underground legend in Pittsburgh. His name is still big there. It's funny, the Olympics and the World Wrestling Entertainment have made me more famous than I ever imagined—I'm recognized all over the United States, even worldwide. But in my hometown I'm still always running into people who look at me kind of funny and say, "You're Mark Angle's brother, right? How you doing?"

I'm constantly amazed at how far and wide the legend of my forty-five-year-old brother has spread over the years. These days he's just your basic workingman, a boilermaker who puts in his eight hours a day welding pipes and then spends most of his free time watching his kids play on various sports teams. He coached them when they were younger, and now he's like my dad was: he never misses one of their games. But sometimes it seems that everyone has a story they want to tell me about the guy who once was known around town as the baddest dude in Pittsburgh.

To this day I've never met anyone who had such an aura about him as a street fighter. He's still such an imposing guy; he's five-ten, 240 pounds, with eighteen-inch forearms, fists the size of cantaloupes, and an iron jaw. But it was his mentality that made

My brother Mark,
the fearsome brawler.

him so intimidating. Basically you had to kill him to stop him. Something would come over him when he got into a fight, sort of like Mike Tyson during his young and fearless days. When Mark was in ninth grade, he and David went at it in the garage one day. David was a senior in high school at the time and nobody messed with him at school, but that didn't matter to Mark. So one day they decided to settle the matter of who was the toughest Angle boy. I've heard different versions of how the fight started and how it went, but it sounds like Mark had the best of it. David says they were beating on each other when my mom ran into the garage and broke up the fight by hitting both of them with a baseball bat. Both of them were bleeding profusely—there was blood all over the walls of the garage. My mom remembers Mark doing the most damage. And Mark just laughed when I told him David remembers it as a draw.

"Then how come everybody wanted to try him after that?" Mark said about David. "He was one of the toughest at his high school, but after word got around about our fight, someone was coming to the house once a week looking for him. They said, 'He can't be that tough, if a ninth-grader beat him up.'"

All I know for sure is Mark and David never fought again, and that might say something about what happened in the garage that day. But anyway, it was later that same year when Mark's fighting finally caught up with him. You have to understand, he may have been a kid mentally, but physically he was a man by then. He already weighed 185 pounds, and he was just naturally strong as an ox. He was also very competitive, so anything could set him off. Finally, one day some kid accused him of stealing something. To this day Mark denies it, but anyway, they ended up in a fight and Mark beat the hell out of him at some event at the high school. The cops came and he got into some pushing and shoving with them. They knew about him because he'd been in so many fights, and they weren't going to let him just walk away from this one.

Local law enforcement officials came down hard on Mark and, with my parents' consent, sent him to a juvenile facility for a year. I was only three or four years old, but I remember we used to visit him on the weekends and it was never a trip that anybody looked forward to making. Mark was furious with my mom and dad for allowing him to be sent there, and he was always threatening to break out of the place. As young as I was, I remember being frightened by my brother's anger.

But somehow Mark did his time at the juvenile facility without any serious incidents, although he says he had a few fights there, too. So he went back to high school toward the end of his sophomore year, and as a junior, he went out for wrestling for the first time. It turned out to be the perfect sport to give him an outlet for his anger. He loved the intensity of the daily practices, the competitiveness of wrestling, and he picked it up quickly. He went to the high school state tournament that first year he wrestled, which was a major feat because Pennsylvania is known as one of the best wrestling states in the country. In the summer he won the freestyle state tournament, and he beat the high school state champion along the way. That tells you what kind of athlete Mark was. He also finished fifth in the Greco-Roman nationals that summer. In his senior year he missed going to the state tournament by a referee's decision, when the ref awarded a 1–1 match to his opponent in the regionals. It was a tough break because Mark probably would have at least placed in states. Then that summer he probably would have won the Greco-Roman nationals, but he got into a fight protecting my sister and her then-husband, and wound up getting stabbed.

The way my sister tells the story, a group of five guys had accused my sister's husband of having a buddy who stole something from them. He said he didn't know where his buddy was, so these guys tried to force him into their car. Mark came to the rescue and wound up beating the crap out of all five of those guys. But during the fight, one of them stabbed him with a knife. He was so involved with the fight that he didn't even realize he'd been cut until it was over. At that point my sister told me that Mark looked down and saw his own intestines oozing out of a gash in his stomach. He held them in his hands as he was rushed to the hospital for treatment. Later a doctor would tell us that the Volkswagen he rode in to the hospital saved his life, as it's small size kept him bunched up tight in the car.

I've heard so many stories like that over the years. Dennis Miller, the comedian and former *Monday Night Football* commentator, and his brother Jimmy, a successful Hollywood agent who manages celebrities like Jim Carrey, went to high school with my brothers, and Jimmy told me about a time when they saw Mark in action. Apparently, Mark stopped his truck on a narrow street to offer Dennis and Jimmy a ride as they were walking home. Jimmy said some teenagers in a car behind Mark were honking the horn, trying to go around him. Eventually Mark pulled over far enough, and as the kid drove by with his buddies, someone threw a full can of beer at Mark's truck and cracked the windshield. Obviously the kid didn't know who Mark was. Either that or he had a death wish. Mark told Dennis and Jimmy to hold on in the back of the truck, and sped off after the car, which turned down a side street and pulled up into a parking area behind some stores. Mark was so mad that he jumped the curb and rammed the front of his truck into the driver's side of the kid's car. I asked him about it once, why he would damage his truck like that. He said, "I had to make him pay for what he did."

After he rammed him, Mark backed up, got out of his truck, and walked up to the car. The driver couldn't get out because the door was smashed in. A guy got out of the passenger's side and Mark laid him out with one punch to the face. Then he went after the driver. The window was open, so Mark just started throwing uppercuts through the window, pounding on the kid's face. I guess the kid must have been a mess by the time Mark was done with him. Mark told me that a friend came to our house a few days later to warn him that the kid's father wanted to put out a hit on him.

It never happened, but those are the kind of stories that I still hear today about Mark. He developed a reputation that made him a target for every tough guy in Pittsburgh looking to earn his stripes in the street. And Pittsburgh has always been known as a shot-and-a-beer town full of tough guys. Mark swore he didn't go looking for fights. He said they always found him. I've yet to hear of one he ever lost, and that doesn't surprise me. He probably could have been a boxing champion—it's hard to imagine anyone with a combination of quickness, athleticism, power, and fearlessness to match what I saw and heard about over the years. Eventually Mark outgrew all the fighting and became a great dad to five kids, making a point of coaching them in various sports as often as possible. His son Markie was a three-time All-American wrestler in college at Pennsylvania's Clarion University, where I went to college. He's training for the 2004 Olympics, and I think he'll make it if he dedicates himself.

It's just too bad that Mark didn't fulfill his own potential as a wrestler. He was recruited out of high school by Arizona State, a top wrestling school at the time, but because his grades weren't good, Mark agreed to attend a junior college in Arizona for a year. But he never made it to Arizona State. Instead he got married that first year of junior college and his wife became pregnant. At that point Mark decided to give up on school and come home to Pittsburgh to make a life for himself and his family. He's divorced now, and as much as he loves his kids, I'm sure he still regrets that he never got the chance to live out his own dream of winning a national championship.

As I grew up I began to understand that Mark had

Posing with nephew Mark (Mark's son) at his college wrestling meet at Clarion University.

his shortcomings, but when I was young, he was the person I looked up to the most. He truly ignited the spark in me as a wrestler, and he wound up becoming my personal coach and wrestling partner when I was in high school. He'd go into work early during wrestling season so he could leave at four o'clock and come over to wrestling practice. I needed him because nobody else could give me much of a workout. We'd go at it hard, and it wasn't until my senior year that I could really hold my own with him. My mom says she knew I was going to be special when Mark called her one night that year and told her, "The little son of a gun is starting to beat me."

All of my brothers were there for me, especially after my dad died. I remember when I reached the high school state finals my senior year, Mark got me focused. When I got in those clutch situations, I always had a fear of losing. Doubts would go through my mind. I was wrestling the guy I had beaten the year before for third place in the states, but he was right there with me. Mark came down to the mat before my match and he could see that I was having doubts. He slapped me in the face a couple of times and said, "Do what you did last year. Go out there and kick his ass. Do what you did to me every day in practice this season. You kicked my ass." And that snapped me out of it. I went out there and handled the guy to win the state title.

As I moved on, to college and the USA team, my brothers stayed as close as ever, and I always liked having them in my corner, even though I had some of the best coaches in the world. In high school and college, my coaches were father figures and old-school guys. They were tough; they'd run three-hour practices, with two hours of live wrestling. And I loved that. The harder the better—I thought that was good for me. I liked to go way over the top when it came to conditioning. But my brothers pushed me more than anyone. I was the youngest in the family and I *had* to be the best. In a way they were living their lives through me, wanting me to go places they never did.

So they were always at my matches, and not only as spectators. Before every match, no matter where I was—the states, the nationals, the Olympics—they found a way to get onto the floor so they could talk to me and make sure I was ready. No matter what, they always had to be there before I started. I don't care if there were a billion security guards and it was impossible for them to get on the floor, somehow they did it. And after a while people accepted it. My USA coaches, my college coaches, they accepted the fact that my brothers were coming down on the floor to talk to me. That's the way it was with my brothers.

Somehow, Mark, Johnny, and David all got to me before my Olympic gold medal match. I don't know how the hell they did it, but they were on the warm-up mat with me. I was crying before they got there, emotional about the possibility of losing the last match of my career. My coach got to me before they did, thank God. If they had seen me crying, they would have kicked my ass. By the time they got to me, they saw I was focused, so they didn't have to say much. But they had to show me they were there supporting me. It was like a ritual we had.

Now they do it with my nephew, Mark's son. I do it to him, too. Most families, when you get to that college and Olympic level, let the coaching take over. But that's not the way my family does things. We let the coaches do their thing, "But you know what? You're still gonna hear from me." That's just the way it always was.

More than anything, my brothers wanted me to be better than them, to learn from their mistakes, especially when it came to school. I feel like my parents raised us the right way, disciplining us for getting in trouble. But if they had a flaw it was their laid-back attitude toward school. Maybe it was my dad's own background as a blue-collar worker, plus his drinking habits at night, but as kids we were left on our own when it came to schoolwork. And none of us ever really applied ourselves. My three oldest brothers grew up in that drug era of the seventies, and aside from sports, all they wanted to do was get high and hang out. To them it was more important in those days to be cool and enjoy life, not worry about school. So they wound up following in my dad's footsteps, going to work as laborers. Of the three oldest, Mark was the only one who even tried college, thanks to his wrestling ability, but when he started a family he gave up on school. My sister didn't even graduate high school because she got pregnant and had a baby when she was sixteen, but I give her a lot of credit because she got her diploma later through a GED program, and went on to graduate from a community college when she was twenty-eight years old.

I'm not saying there's anything wrong with putting

in an honest day's work with your hands. I'll always remember how much pride my dad took in his job as a crane operator, becoming the best at his company. He was so respected they put his name on the crane he operated. And my brothers are all doing fine now. David, forty-eight, is a crane operator and works for the County in Pittsburgh. John, forty-three, owns his own construction business, and Eric, thirty-three, has just signed on with the World Wrestling Entertainment after working for years as a personal fitness trainer. But they all wish they had done more with their athletic ability and their studies. They saw the talent I had in wrestling and they constantly encouraged me to make the most of it. They knew they had allowed their partying and fighting to interfere with their own athletic careers, and they made a point of telling me to work hard, study, get my college degree. "Don't end up like me," they would say, and I would promise that I wouldn't let them down.

Not that I was a great student myself in high school. I only did enough to get by, and I only went to college for wrestling. I didn't care about academics at the time—that was the environment I was raised in. Sports was what mattered in our family. It was only after a couple of years in college that I started to take an interest in my studies. I was named captain of the wrestling team my last three years at Clarion, and I wanted to be a leader and set an example for the other guys on the team. At the time I was thinking I wanted to coach wrestling in college after I pursued the Olympics, and I wound up getting a degree in geography, with the idea of eventually going to graduate school to become a college professor in that subject. The Olympics and World Wrestling Entertainment happened to me instead, but I am the first one in my family to get a four-year degree from college.

So I had to learn to become a good student, but I was always committed to excelling as an athlete, especially after my father died. I never got into trouble, and a lot of that was because of what I saw in my own house. My father's drinking scared me away from alcohol, and my brothers' wild ways left a huge impression, too. I remember one night when I was young and I saw Johnny come home absolutely wasted. I found out later he drank a bottle of vodka that night and messed around with some drugs, too. He was so out of it that my family couldn't control him. He was in his room ramming his head against the wall. Mark had to go in, beat on him, and literally hold him down on the bed as Johnny screamed at the top of his lungs. Watching that violent confrontation, I remember thinking that no one would ever have to worry about me doing drugs.

Johnny had just graduated high school at the time. Now he's married, he has two kids, he's a responsible adult who doesn't drink at all, let alone take drugs anymore. He's a great dad who loves his kids and he's very good to them. The contrast between now and then is really something, because he was wild as a teenager. That night I was sitting in the living room, scared to death of the way he was acting. His bedroom was directly across the hallway, and at some point he looked up, saw me, and waved for me to come into his room. I said no. He started chasing me around the dining-room table. When he couldn't catch me he ended up going back into his bedroom. All he had on was his underwear because he had puked all over his clothes. He was the nicest guy normally, only now the drugs were making him act like a madman. It was probably the best thing that could have happened to me at the time. The sight of him like that always served as a reminder to me of the power of drugs and alcohol.

In high school I hung around with the cool crowd—the athletes, the good-looking girls. But they knew what I was like. They knew that I didn't drink and I didn't take drugs. If they wanted to get high, they didn't call me. If they weren't doing that, they'd call me. I'm not going to say I never touched alcohol, but I made sure I never smoked dope or took drugs. Nobody ever tried to force them on me, either, because they knew how serious I was about what I was doing. You talk to people from my high school about what direction I was headed, and they'll say they knew I was going to do something special like win the Olympics. Years later a lot of them told me they used to say, "This kid's so focused. Nobody's going to stop him." Everyone knew I was special except for me. I just thought I was doing my thing. Some kids got straight A's; I won wrestling titles. That was important to me because it was important to my dad and my family. So my friends wouldn't put me in any situation where I could get in trouble, and I was always careful about it, too. I think all those lessons I learned from watching my brothers, the good and the bad, paid off. Without them I probably wouldn't have a gold medal and a career in World Wrestling Entertainment.

4

CROSSING THE TRACKS

It was only two miles, driveway to driveway, but when my family moved from Dormont to Mount Lebanon, I was devastated. I was in sixth grade. I had my friends, and we all thought the people from Mount Lebanon were a bunch of snobs. Cake-eaters, we called them. The houses were bigger there, the schools were nicer. Everybody thought of it as the rich side of the tracks. And I knew we weren't rich.

But my mom wanted to do it for Eric and me. The four older kids were finished with high school and she wanted to give the two of us the best chance at going to college. She looked into it and found out that Mount Lebanon High had a better precollege curriculum than Dormont, and since none of the older kids had gone to college, she really wanted us to go. It was hard on my parents financially, but my mom had been working for a few years as a secretary for the local AFL-CIO, and she had put some money away. She was saving for a new kitchen, but she decided we needed a bigger house and a better opportunity to make something of ourselves. Everybody tried to talk her out of it. Eric and I said we wouldn't go to school with a bunch of stuck-up kids—we tried every argument we could think of. But she was determined. So we moved, and it took about six months before Eric and I made friends and got comfortable in our new town. We found out the kids from Mount Lebanon weren't really any different from our friends in Dormont, and the move turned out to be good for us.

Still, when we moved in the other kids tested us right away. They tried to pick on us, but Eric quickly made a name for himself with his fists. He decked a couple of local bullies, and word spread fast. For me, it was easier to win people over with my athletic ability. You can make friends pretty quickly when you can help their teams win, and I could do that.

The more I played, the better I seemed to get at every sport, especially the team sports. I remember when we left Dormont, I had a basketball coach who wanted me to move in with his family until the season was over so I could keep playing for his team in the Dormont city league. He tried to talk my parents into letting him be my legal guardian for a few months, and this guy was the principal of our elementary school. That's the kind of ability I had, and I didn't even play that much basketball. My brothers were always entering me in wrestling tournaments at that age, but I was still the MVP of the basketball league. I could have been good at just about any sport, I guess. The only problem I ever had was that one-on-one thing in wrestling, being out there alone, scared to lose.

It's funny, everything always came natural to me in sports. You put me in any kind of athletic situation, and I'm just naturally graceful. Well, any sport but golf, anyway. I haven't conquered that one yet, and I'd like to someday because as a celebrity you get invited to a lot of golf tournaments. Mario Lemieux, who was kind of my idol, shocked me one time when I met him at a banquet in Pittsburgh after the Olympics by inviting me to play in his celebrity tournament. I couldn't because I had an appearance I had to make, but I started playing in some other charity events. And I was terrible.

I've never really worked at it, and it's a difficult sport that frustrates the hell out of me. I guess there's just not enough action for me in golf. But I really liked going out to play; that was what was so frustrating. I'd go to one of these charity tournaments and every time I'd get fired up to play. I'd tell myself this was the day I was going to concentrate and hit the ball straight. And after about four holes, I'd have a forty already and I'd say, "Okay, I don't want to do this." I couldn't take any more humiliation. Maybe someday I'll get serious about it, but I don't have the time to play these days, anyway.

Aside from golf, though, I've always amazed people with my skills in athletics. But around the house it was a different story. I was always a klutz. As a kid, I used to make everybody mad because I was always knocking something over in the kitchen. I used to spill something at the dinner table all the time. And I wasn't much of a handyman around the house, either. My dad or my brothers would give me jobs to do, and I was so helpless that they'd get disgusted with me. When I tried to help paint the house, I was so sloppy that they took my brush away from me. After a while they wouldn't even let me cut the grass. I was always slipping when I'd pull the mower backward to go over a spot, and they thought I was going to wind up cutting my foot off. One time I almost did cut my hand off. There were two levels to our yard, and you had to pick up the lawn mower and put it on the upper level. When I finished the lower level, I turned the mower off and I reached under it to pick it up before the blade even stopped. The blade sliced into my pinky finger and I yanked my hand out as quickly as I could. The cut was pretty deep and my finger was bleeding a lot. By the time my parents got me to the hospital, I was terrified because I could see that part of my finger was just sort of hanging there, and I didn't know if the doctors would be able to put it back together. But they stitched it up, thank God, and saved the finger. I still have nerve damage in that finger, and it bothers me sometimes, but at least I still have it.

Until that happened, my brothers thought I was always doing something stupid on purpose to get out of work. Actually, I wanted to show them I could do anything they were doing, but it seemed the only thing I was good at was playing sports. Even now, my brothers are all very good mechanically. They all take pride in fixing their own cars, fixing everything around their houses. But me, I have to call them when I need something fixed. Either that or my wife, Karen, fixes it. She's the handyman around the house.

She knows how I am, so she pretty much takes the responsibility herself when something needs to be done. I guess I never learned that stuff like other kids did as teenagers. My brothers had hobbies, cars and stuff like that. All I ever did was play sports. My hobby was sports.

Even when I got into high school, all of my friends used to get jobs in the summer, to save money for college or for a car. I never had a job. I felt like I didn't have time for a job, because even in the summer I was either competing in summer leagues or training to get in shape for football and wrestling. I couldn't understand why everybody didn't have the same attitude. I used to ask my friends, "Why put all your time into working some lousy job when you could be working out, getting ready for next season?" They probably thought I was nuts. My friends had cars, they had spending money that I didn't have. But it didn't bother me. All I really cared about was training and getting better, mostly in football and wrestling. I was also a hell of a baseball player as a kid. I set records for home runs in Little League, threw no-hitters, stuff like that. But I quit playing in high school because the coach told me I was doing too much weight training to be a baseball player. Now I look at guys like Mark McGwire and José Canseco, guys who are huge, and I realize that the coach was wrong, but at the time I let him talk me out of baseball.

That just made me hungrier for my other sports, though. I'd go to camps in the summer, do whatever I had to do to train harder. And I was really into weight training. I would gain forty to fifty pounds during the summer because I was doing so much lifting and eating to try and get bigger. I was always fast and I always had good agility, so I thought the bigger I got, the better I'd be, especially in football. But I got a little carried away. The summer before my senior year I bulked up to 255 pounds, but I found out quickly that size isn't everything. All of a sudden I wasn't so fast anymore. My coach actually got pissed at me when he saw how big I was—and how slow I'd become. I lost so much speed that he threatened to put me on the line instead of at fullback. So I dropped down to 235, but even then I didn't have my quickness. The year before I had played at 205 pounds, and I was all over the field as a linebacker. But not at 235. I remember picking up a fumble during one game, and after about forty yards, I ran out of gas while somebody caught me from behind. That convinced me to drop about another fifteen pounds and it taught me a lesson. I was blessed with speed and quickness, and if I was going to be a great athlete, I had to utilize it.

The more success I had in team sports, the more I began to develop some confidence out there alone on the wrestling mat. I stopped letting my fear of failure paralyze me, and my natural ability started to take over. I went undefeated on the freshman wrestling team at Mount Lebanon and made the varsity as a sophomore. In my first varsity match I wrestled a kid named Gary Horner. He was considered one of the top wrestlers in our region and he kicked my ass. He pinned me. I remember walking off the mat crying, thinking I'd never be good enough to wrestle varsity, and my coach grabbed me. George Lamprinakos was a real old-school coach, and he became a father figure to me after my dad died. He made me look him in the eyes that day and he said, "Listen to me, Kurt. You're gonna be a great wrestler. You're gonna win a state title by the time you're a senior."

I thought, "This guy's crazy. I just got my ass kicked."

But he knew. He saw my potential. Years later he told me he'd never seen anyone wrestle at the upper weights like I did, with the quickness and agility of a 135-pounder.

As that first varsity season went on, I did get better. I qualified for the state tournament as a sophomore, which was a great achievement in Pennsylvania, especially in the upper weights. I was wrestling in the 185-pound weight class and I only weighed 174 pounds. I was as big as my brother Eric, who was a senior and filled out a little later than me. Eric weighed 172 pounds. One of us was going to wrestle in the 167-pound class, and the other in the 185. I had enough respect for my brother that I let him wrestle the weight he wanted, which was 167.

That forced me up to 185. In amateur wrestling it's rare when kids wrestle above their weight. Most kids cut weight to wrestle at a lower weight class because they want to utilize their strength. But from that year on I never cut weight to wrestle. I didn't think it was healthy, physically or mentally. I remember watching guys who did it, and they were miserable. They weren't eating, and that affected their state of mind. A lot of days in practice they'd be lying around, tired and grouchy. The coaches were always yelling at them. And on top of that, they were getting mopped up on the mat by a second- or third-string wrestler who wasn't cutting weight.

But I know I was fortunate. I had a rare combination of speed and strength that allowed me to wrestle guys bigger than me. As a junior and senior, I weighed 200 to 225 pounds and I wrestled heavyweight against kids who weighed as much as 275 pounds. Same thing in college. And at the Olympics I won the gold in the 220-pound class and I only weighed 211 pounds. When I graduated high school, a lot of colleges thought I was too small for heavyweight. Some didn't recruit me, and others wanted me to drop down to 190. I said, "Forget it, I'm a heavyweight." And as it turned out, I was the smallest heavyweight in NCAA history to win a national title—I only weighed 199 pounds my senior year.

I was lucky, I guess, that I had the same kind of natural strength as my dad and my brothers. But I also started lifting weights as early as seventh grade, because I saw my brothers doing it. I don't know if that's what gave my body a boost, but I started growing like crazy. I went from 90 pounds in seventh grade to 115 in eighth grade to 138 in ninth grade to 175 in tenth grade to 200-plus in eleventh grade. I was making such dramatic jumps that some people thought I was on steroids. But I was just a growing kid who went through spurts every year, partly because I was training so hard and eating everything in the house.

But anyway, Coach Lamp turned out to be right

about me as a wrestler. The next year, my junior season, I took third in the states, and then, as a senior, I went undefeated and made his prediction come true by winning the state tournament. That's when I knew I had something special, my senior year. By then I knew I would go to college, but I still wasn't sure which sport, football or wrestling, would become my focus.

As much as I was enjoying my success in wrestling, especially after my early failures on the mat, nothing was bigger than football in high school. I loved those Friday nights under the lights. High school football is huge in Pennsylvania, and to me, there's nothing quite like a high school football game. I've been to college games and pro games, but there's something different about high school. There's this atmosphere, this electricity in the air, with the band playing, the whole town being there. I miss that feeling, that rush of excitement. I enjoyed the attention that came with it, too. On the field I was an All-State player as a middle linebacker, and off the field my girlfriend and I were the homecoming king and queen. I was very popular with the other kids, and their parents loved me, too, because they knew I didn't mess around with drugs or get in trouble.

Looking back, I feel like I could have played in the NFL as a linebacker if I had chosen football over wrestling. I won Defensive Player of the Year in western Pennsylvania as a senior. I had fairly good size and speed, and I had an instinct for the position that coaches say you can't teach. Somehow I just always ended up where the ball was going. I tied for most interceptions on the team. I had the most fumble recoveries and the most tackles. And I don't know what it was, but the football field was the one place where I had that mean streak my brothers were always trying to instill in me. I tried to play like Jack Lambert, the former Steelers middle linebacker, who seemed to be the nastiest guy on the field. He buried people and I tried to do the same. I was never into trash talking or any of that stuff on the field. I just let my hitting do the talking for me, and I had the size and speed to create a whole lot of force. My tackles are what people came to see. I had some vicious collisions.

One time I hit this quarterback so hard, he got up and walked to the wrong sideline. He had dropped back to pass on the play, so I dropped into my pass coverage zone. But I saw him searching for a receiver and I knew he was going to pull the ball down and try to run. I started moving toward the line of scrimmage, but he didn't really see me coming. He faked one way, ran right in my direction. I got a clean shot on him and just buried him. Cleaned his clock. I heard the crowd just kind of go "ooohhh." The kid popped up and tried to make it look like he wasn't hurt. But he had a little wobble in his legs and I knew he was out of it when he ran over to our sideline. My coach had to direct him over to his sideline.

That was the best feeling, hitting someone with a shot like that. One time I laid out Major Harris, the quarterback who went on to play at West Virginia. He was down for about fifteen seconds, and I was surprised at how good I felt about punishing somebody like that. I never wanted to hurt anybody seriously, but I loved ringing somebody's bell. That was better than scoring a touchdown. I played fullback and I averaged about eight yards a carry my senior year, but I only gained 480 yards because they used me more as a blocker or to pick up that tough yard on third-and-one. But I didn't mind because I really lived to play linebacker. I loved the contact.

My senior year our team made it to the semifinals of our region. We beat McKeesport in the first round of the playoffs and I had a tremendous game. I had 160 yards rushing and fourteen solo tackles. I was the Athlete of the Week in Western Pennsylvania. So we went into semifinals against Gateway. For two days before the game, it rained, and to make it worse, the sprinkler system went on by mistake the day of the game. We were playing a neutral field, Baldwin High School, and the whole field froze. Maintenance workers put salt and wood chips down. They did everything possible to make the field playable, and that should have been good enough.

But our team was spoiled. Mount Lebanon had an artificial turf field, one of the few in Pennsylvania. We were thought of as the rich kids from Mount Lebanon, playing on turf. And as soon as we saw the condition of this field, we started complaining: "Oh, this is horrible. We can't even stand up. This isn't fair." That type of stuff. And right there I think we were beaten. The other team wasn't complaining about the field. They were hungry to play in any conditions and they kicked our ass. We lost 22–6 and I was really upset about the way we handled ourselves. I'm convinced we could have won that game if we'd had our heads on right that night, and that's something I remembered for a long time.

It was my last game and it left a sour taste in my mouth. At the time I was still thinking I would play football in college. It turned out to be the toughest decision I made up to that point, choosing between football or wrestling. I wasn't being recruited as hard for football as I was for wrestling. A lot of people thought I was undersized. I was five-ten. It seemed like colleges didn't look at you unless you were six feet or taller. I learned later on it really doesn't matter what your height is. I see All-Pro linebackers in the NFL who are my size. If you can play, you can play.

Quickness and instinct are more important than size. But college recruiters are always looking for what they call "measurables," which means size and speed. They don't want to be wrong when they give out scholarships, and if a player doesn't cut it in college, it's easier to justify if they can point to his "measurables."

According to just about every All-State team I saw, I was one of the top four linebackers in the state. There was a local guy named Joe Butler who put together names for the recruiting services. He had me high on his list and he told me later he tried to push me to the college coaches, but said the coaches were always looking for that kid who was six-four, 230 pounds, who they thought had pro potential. That influenced my decision to wrestle. I believe I was meant to make that decision to wrestle. I believe everything happens for a reason, that God intended for me to wrestle. I guess that's part of the reason why football people overlooked me. It definitely had nothing to do with my play.

Most Pennsylvania kids who play football dream of playing for Joe Paterno at Penn State, and I was no different. I was told that Paterno loved the way I played, but he was one of those coaches who thought I was too short. He told my coaches he was willing to bring me in as a walk-on, but he wouldn't offer me a scholarship. Pitt showed some interest, but they wound up giving a scholarship to another linebacker who was six feet five. I did get a few Division I football offers—both North Carolina and North Carolina State recruited me. But it was very important for me to stay close to home, where my family could see me play.

So basically I had to choose between going far from home to play football or staying near home and wrestling. Penn State didn't offer me a wrestling scholarship, which really hurt me. Their coach felt I was too small to wrestle heavyweight for his team. But Pitt offered me a full scholarship and I thought that was the perfect situation. I made a verbal commitment to go there, but then the coaches from Clarion started calling me. I didn't know anything about the school because I didn't follow college wrestling, but as they recruited me I began to learn about its history in the sport. It's just this small school in Pennsylvania, a couple of hours' drive away from Pittsburgh, but their teams had a great tradition as a wrestling power. They were always ranked in the top ten nationally, along with big schools like Iowa and Oklahoma State.

The more I found out about the school, the more I became interested. They asked me to come up for a match and, ironically, it was against Pitt. I went, and I found myself sitting in this little gym that held about forty-five hundred people, and it was packed. The atmosphere in the place was full of intensity, and that turned out to be maybe the biggest reason I picked Clarion. They had a rock band behind the wrestlers, cranking out music to get the crowd even more pumped up. They had cheerleaders, guys and girls, like you see at the NCAA basketball tournament. I was sitting there and my head was spinning. I'd never seen anything like it at a wrestling match.

There were some kids in the stands with their faces painted blue and gold, others with their shirts off, each of them with a letter painted on their chest to spell C-L-A-R-I-O-N as they stood together. I was sitting there thinking, "Man, I could really enjoy wrestling at a place like this."

The match that night was close, and it came down to the heavyweights. The Pitt coach knew I was there, and I remember as his heavyweight took the mat, he looked over at me. They weren't strong at heavyweight, and I think he knew his guy was going to lose. So it was like he wanted me to know that "Hey, if you were with us, right now, we'd win this thing."

I gave him a nod, as if to say, "Don't worry, I'm coming."

And that was my intention. But I ended up being overwhelmed by the experience at Clarion. I met with the faculty advisers, and some professors, and they were all wrestling fans. They all seemed to want to take a personal interest in me, telling me they'd help me with anything I needed from an academic standpoint. The more I thought about it, the more Clarion seemed to be the school for me because they cared so much about wrestling. It was their claim to fame. At a school like Pitt they care more about football and basketball, sports that bring in revenue. Wrestling is almost an afterthought there. After a lot of thought, I wound up deciding to go to Clarion, and it was one of the best decisions I've ever made.

5

BIG MAN ON A SMALL CAMPUS

For some strange reason, I've been sur-
rounded by death at pivotal moments in my life.
Starting with my father, I've lost too many people
that I loved, but I've always seemed to respond by
raising my level of performance in athletics. I can't
really explain it. Maybe that's just the way I was able
to express my feelings about the people I loved, by
doing what I do best. Some people might be just the
opposite—they're affected to the point where they
have trouble concentrating on anything else in their
lives. I was always able to block everything out when
it came to competition, no matter how much I was
hurting inside.

Two days after my dad died I played the best football game of my life. When Dave Schultz, my mentor
when I was training for the Olympics, was murdered,
that drove me to train even harder and win the gold
medal. I had an uncle I was close to who died just before the Olympics started. And then there was my
grandmother on my mother's side. I was really close
to her, and when she died, I was only days away from

wrestling in the NCAA tournament my sophomore season at Clarion. I think it was the only time in my life when I let something like that affect me, and I nearly wound up losing a chance to win a national championship because of it.

She died a week before the tournament started. I was having a phenomenal season at the time. It was actually my third year at Clarion, but I was a sophomore because I red-shirted my second year. That's a term you hear associated more with college football than wrestling, but it's the same thing. The NCAA allows an athlete to sit out a year if he or the school chooses, and still compete for four seasons. Usually it's because of injury or a need to raise your grades, but in my case, I did it to improve my chances of winning a national title.

My freshman year had been disappointing from a team standpoint. I went to Clarion to be part of this little wrestling powerhouse. The school had ranked sixth in the nation the year before, and third the year before that. They hadn't had a losing season in twenty years. But seven starters graduated as I was coming in, and I guess the freshman class wasn't as good as our coach expected. We went 3–15 and it was a horrible experience.

Personally, I had a great year. I won twenty-nine matches and qualified for the national tournament, which was incredible for a freshman wrestling heavyweight. I wound up ranked in the top twelve heavyweights in the country, which was almost unheard of. So now I started thinking about winning a national title, and that year a junior named Carlton Haselrig won the title at heavyweight for the second straight year. Haselrig was a 290-pound monster who went on to play in the NFL as an offensive guard for a few years before getting involved with drugs and alcohol and ruining his career.

I thought I'd have no chance of beating him the next year, as a sophomore. As it turned out, we wrestled in a preseason tournament, before I had to declare I was red-shirting, and Haselrig beat me 4–3. I gave him a good match, and when I look back, I think I could have beaten him by the end of the season. But by then I had it in my head that I wanted to red-shirt.

I knew our team was going to need at least another year before we were a factor nationally. So I went to my coach, Bob Bubb, and told him what I wanted to do. He thought I was loopy. "Oh, one year and you've already got yourself winning the national tournament?" he said.

He was against me doing it, but I told him if he let me do it, I'd guarantee him that I'd win three national titles. As good as Clarion's wrestling program was, the school hadn't produced a national champion since 1973, and I knew Coach Bubb wanted to see one of his guys win another one before he retired. He was an old-school coach, just like my high school coach, and I felt I was lucky to have wrestled for each of them. They were great coaches for me, probably more for their personalities and the way they cared about their wrestlers than for anything they did technically. By the time I was in college, I was wrestling all over the country, and then the world, to learn technique. In the off-season I was always training with one of the club teams that prepared wrestlers for international competition. I'd work out at the Olympic wrestling training center in Colorado, or I'd go to the University of Iowa to work out in the summer with Dan Gable, the legendary coach there.

What my coaches did was give me support and guidance as well as discipline. As involved as my brothers were in pushing me as a wrestler, I needed that father figure who I could talk to sometimes. Coach Lamprinakos and Coach Bubb pushed me hard when I needed it, and I felt like I had a special relationship with both of them. I could talk to them about any kind of problems I was having, at home or in school, and they'd listen and try to help. It's funny, they were both near the end of their careers when they coached me, and both of them wound up retiring when I left. Coach Lamprinakos retired after thirty years in coaching when I graduated from Mount Lebanon, and Coach Bubb did the same thing at Clarion. My last year there was his thirtieth year in coaching, too, and he decided to retire. I guess my timing was perfect. They were old-school guys and I loved to work hard, do the extra things that would make me a champion.

So Coach Bubb finally agreed to let me red-shirt, but only when I promised him one other thing—that I'd gain weight. He was always on me to try and put on weight, because he felt I'd need it to beat the bigger heavyweights. Well, I never did gain any weight. By then I was convinced that my quickness and my

Kurt with state championship medal posing with high school coach, George Lamprinakos, after signing with Clarion University and Coach Bob Bubb.

technique, my positioning, were the keys to how far I'd go. So maybe I fibbed about gaining weight, but I was determined to keep my promise about winning three national titles.

The year I red-shirted, I did everything possible to make myself a better wrestler. I started doing more wrestling with Team USA, competing in tournaments overseas for the first time. I went to Turkey that year and finished second in a major international tournament. I started learning how to eat right because I took a couple of nutrition classes. All my life I thought I just had to eat as much as possible to get big. But now I started to eat high protein, lower carbohydrate, lower fat, and learn how to make my body operate better as a machine. Rather than eat three big meals, I was being taught to eat eight smaller meals. It worked for me. I looked better and felt better. My training became more productive. I felt like a machine because I was eating those smaller meals all day long. Dieting right became an important part of my everyday training regimen.

So finally, after that year off, I came back for my sophomore season more mature on and off the mat. And it showed. I went through the season undefeated, and I was the favorite to win the NCAA title at heavyweight. But then, about a week before the national tournament—that's when my grandmother died. Everyone in my family had been close to her, and like my parents and my brothers and sister, she made a point of going to my matches. But my grandmother saw something very special in me. In fact, all her life she never attended any of her children's, or even her other grandchildren's, functions, whether they were athletic functions or whatever. But she took pride in watching me compete. We had that special kind of relationship.

My mom called me at Clarion to give me the sad news, and the next day in practice I injured my knee. Looking back, I'm convinced it was because I wasn't into the practice mentally that day—I wasn't really focusing on what I was doing. Somehow my left knee got twisted while I was wrestling and I tore cartilage and sprained the medial collateral ligament. I had it checked out and a doctor told me I was done for the season, that I wasn't going to wrestle in the nationals, which began in four days.

I was devastated. But I wasn't about to give up that easily. I had to go back to Pittsburgh for my grandmother's funeral, and while I was there I went to see Dr. Freddie Fu, one of the most renowned orthopedic doctors in the world for treating sports injuries.

When he examined me he agreed with the team doctor. He said, "Kurt, you're out at least six weeks. You can't wrestle."

I had the highest respect for his opinion. But I just couldn't give up on the nationals that easily. I remember thinking, "I've come this far, I'm 30–0–1, I've gotta at least try, for my dad, for my grandmother, for my family, and for myself." I've always been a spiritual person, a believer in God. I think God intended for me to wrestle. So I decided to try. I got a knee brace shipped within twenty-four hours, and I had a trainer come out to the nationals with me. I taped my knee and wore the brace. I was very limited in what I could do, and I was in a lot of pain.

But the knee didn't give out on me, and I was able to wrestle. I was as careful as I could be. I wrestled a very conservative tournament, and in a way that was good for me. I was a very aggressive wrestler, and under normal conditions I probably would have been overexcited, since this was my first legitimate chance at winning a national title. Maybe I would have made a mistake being too aggressive. Instead, my knee slowed me down, and I didn't make any mistakes.

I kept telling myself to take it one match at a time, and every match I just barely pulled it out, usually by a point or two. I was amazed that I kept winning. Before I knew it I was in the national finals, ironically, against the heavyweight from Penn State, Greg Haladay, the guy they recruited over me. I beat him 3–2 to win my national title. I couldn't believe it. I'd gone into the tournament just hoping my injury would allow me to get into the top eight, and here I was, Clarion's first national champ in seventeen years. Overcoming that injury showed a lot of character, especially at that age.

After the tournament, I let my knee heal for five weeks, then I resumed training. I wasn't going to be satisfied with one national tournament. But the victory made me a full-fledged celebrity at Clarion. People gawked at me. They knew I was the best, and wrestling was so big in that town, I was treated like someone special. I was the Mario Lemieux of Clarion. Everywhere I went I ate for free. I got my haircuts for free. If I went to a football game, I got in for free. Everything was set on a silver platter for me because I was this great wrestler. I have to admit, that's one of the reasons I went there. It was one of the few colleges in the country where wrestlers are treated the way football players are treated at most big-time athletic schools. I got a lot of attention just being recruited there, so I knew what it would be like if I won. And the more I won, the more attention I got. If

Kurt with wrestlers from Iran and Russia at an international competition in Moscow, Russia, during college.

I was struggling in certain courses, professors made time to work with me. Not that they ever gave me anything; they made me work for the grade, but they always had an avenue for me to make sure I stayed eligible. It was important to have that kind of support, and know that people cared about me.

As much as I enjoyed the celebrity treatment, I didn't let it go to my head. I wasn't a flashy guy. I wore sweats around campus all the time, and I didn't go out much. I had such a busy schedule every day that I didn't have time for a social life, especially from October to March during wrestling season. I'd get up early, go for a six-mile run, then go to my classes from about eight in the morning to one in the afternoon. From there I'd go to lunch, and then I had practice from two-thirty to about six. Then it was on to dinner, and at night I either had Student Senate, which I was on for two years, or meetings for the Fellowship of Christian Athletes. I was the president of the FCA, and those meetings would last a couple of hours, from seven to nine. Usually I'd lift weights from nine to ten, then study until midnight. So I had a very full day, but it seemed like the busier I was, the better I did with everything. Usually everything revolved around how I felt about wrestling. There were times when I was injured, or I'd take some time off from training after the season, my grades would drop, I wouldn't eat well. When I stayed on schedule, and everything was going well with wrestling, I was getting A's in my courses, winning my matches, eating right, and feeling good.

What I really liked about being a celebrity on campus was just the idea that people knew who I was. They were nice to me and I was nice in return. It's not like I walked around like a hotshot. I liked being nice to people. I like people saying, "Man, that Kurt Angle, he's a nice guy. He could be a jerk, he's a national champion, but he's not." It was always real important for me to show that I had time to talk to people. Whether they were old couples or little kids, I've always been very considerate that way. It's the way I was raised. I always want kids to know that nice guys do end up on top. You don't have to be a jerk. And I think people appreciate that. I hate it when I see some professional athletes acting like idiots, whether it's turning down kids for autographs or complaining that they're not making enough money. It was always important for me to act a certain way in public, and it still is.

By the time my junior season started, my knee was fine and there were huge expectations for me. Everybody was talking about how I might even break Dan Gable's record of 119 consecutive wins in college. I won my first thirty-three matches, and I had gone sixty-eight matches without a loss when I came to the NCAA All-Star match toward the end of the season. I was whipping everybody and I was starting to feel the pressure of my winning streak. The All-Star match brings together the number one and two ranked wrestlers in each weight class from around the country, and I was wrestling John Llewellyn from Illinois.

I was leading 4–3 late in the match. I thought I was about to win, but with five seconds left in the match the referee called me for stalling. I disagreed with the call, but it gave a point to Llewellyn and sent the match into overtime. Mentally, I let the call get to me and in overtime I just cracked, and I let him take me down to beat me. Athletically it was the biggest blow of my lifetime. I was shocked, more than anything, and devastated. This was a showcase match, and after all this talk comparing me to Dan Gable, the biggest name in the history of amateur wrestling, I lost. And the worst part, which I came to realize as time went by, was that I lost because I let a referee's call affect my concentration.

Afterward I went back to Clarion and I stayed in my room for three days. I didn't talk to anybody. I didn't go to practice. I didn't feel like doing anything.

Finally Coach Davis, the assistant coach who had been responsible for recruiting me to Clarion, called me in my room and said, "Hey, you're part of this team. Get in here and train."

And he was right. I knew it, but I was still bitter about the loss. I went to practice that day, but I went with this nasty attitude, like I didn't really want to be there. And sure enough, I blew my other knee out. In a different way, it was like the day I went to practice after my grandmother died. Both times my mind wasn't really on what I was doing, and both times I wound up getting hurt. This time I tore two ligaments in my knee, the medial collateral and the posterior collateral. And I tore some cartilage again, too.

Once again the doctors told me I was finished for the season. And this time there was more pain. I had about a month before the nationals, so I worked hard at rehabbing the knee, hoping it would heal enough for me to compete. A couple of times late in the season I tried to practice, but every time I tried to do anything, my knee hurt so much that I'd roll around with tears in my eyes. But I kept rehabbing and working on the knee. I wouldn't give up.

By the time I went to the national qualifiers, my knee had improved just enough to at least let me try to wrestle. I felt like I was dragging my leg around, but when the adrenaline kicked in, I didn't feel the pain so much. I was wrestling on guts, but somehow I kept advancing. I was barely winning every match, but I made it through the qualifier. My knee was still killing me, and I couldn't train even when I returned to Clarion after the qualifier. But I went to the na-

tionals to defend my title, and by this time all those days away from the mat were catching up with me. I wasn't anywhere near top shape. I weighed 215 pounds and I should have been about 205. I didn't have my usual stamina.

But I kept telling myself to take it match by match, period by period. And somehow I was winning again. It's weird. I felt like I wasn't beating these guys so much as they were beating themselves. I was wrestling very conservatively because I couldn't move much on my knee anyway. But I think my reputation was enough to intimidate the guys I was wrestling, because it seemed like each one would make a critical mistake, and before I knew it I was in the finals.

It blew my mind that I got that far. I really never

expected it, but there I was, facing John Llewellyn, the guy who snapped my winning streak at the All-Star match. And all of a sudden I was playing head games with myself.

I remember thinking, "Okay, I'm content. I can take second. I shouldn't be here anyway, so whatever happens is fine."

I don't know if there was some psychological fall-out from the All-Star match or what, but it was almost as if I talked myself into believing it was okay to lose. It was so out of character for me, and it was a fatal mistake. I wound up losing 6–4, and when I look back now, I'm convinced I could have beaten that guy even with one leg. It's all about confidence and believing in yourself, and that was one day where I beat myself mentally. I learned from it, but it was a costly lesson.

Afterward I went back to the hotel and Coach Bubb sat in the room with me. I sat there for two hours and I barely said a word. He said, "What's wrong with you?"

"Coach, I gave up," I said. "I didn't even try to win. I was content with second, and now I feel like I threw every dream I had down the drain."

I felt like I was a failure. Not because I didn't win, but because I wasn't ready to compete. I went out there prepared to lose instead of desperate to win. That haunts me to this day. I'm pretty sure of one thing, though: It made me obsessed with winning again my senior year. Along with everything else, I'd let Coach Bubb down. I'd broken my promise to win three national titles.

I had surgery on my knee that spring, then rehabbed all summer long and came back with a vengeance. I was killing people all season, just mowing them down. I went 26–0 during the season, and I wanted to prove to people that I was one of the best college heavyweights ever. At the national tournament I had a huge challenge, though. In the finals I wrestled this 275-pound mountain of muscle named Sylvester Terkay from North Carolina State. He had seventy-eight pins during his college career. During the tournament he pinned every opponent in an average of just over a minute. Basically he just went in, tied 'em up, and pinned 'em. This guy was an animal. Meanwhile I was the lightest I'd been during my whole college career. I was worn down a little by the long season, and I weighed in at the nationals at 199 pounds. I was puny compared to Terkay and I was worried that he might just be able to overpower me.

But my body type and my wrestling techniques always worked for me against big guys. I was short for my weight class, and very stocky. People could not get me out of position. My legs and hips were always underneath me. If I was attacking somebody, I'd never get overextended. I was very good at that. Terkay couldn't attack my legs. Every time he shot I was there to jack him up or snap him down. He never got to my legs. He was the type of guy that, if he even touched one of your legs, he was pulling it in with one hand and taking you down.

In the final period, the match was tied 1–1. With eighteen seconds remaining, I slicked him. I faked

one way, ducking under his left armpit, and he sprawled, thinking I was going that way. Instead I went all the way across, under his right armpit, and ducked behind him. I burned him badly with that move. He went from his feet to his stomach trying to push me away, but I was behind him in one tenth of a second, controlling him for a takedown. It blew everybody's mind because it was so quick, and I held on for the final seconds. That quickly, I'd done it. I dropped to my knees and cried that day, the same as I would in the Olympics. I guess I put so much emotion into matches like these that when they were over, crying was the only way I could release the emotion. It was a match people in amateur wrestling still talk about: the day that David beat Goliath. I was the focal point of a story in *Sports Illustrated*. Iowa won the team title, but they wrote mostly about my match with Terkay.

So at least I won two nationals, if not the three I promised Coach Bubb. And I was finished with college wrestling. The next step was to take the experience I'd gained during my summers wrestling with the USA national team and try for the Olympics. It was the spring of 1992, and the Olympic trials for the '92 Barcelona Games were coming soon. I knew it would be a tough task because I didn't have a lot of experience in freestyle wrestling, which is the international style you see in the Olympics. It's different from high school and college wrestling. The biggest difference for me was learning to wrestle more cautiously, because in freestyle you can't even roll across your back or it costs you two points. In college wrestling the other wrestler has to put you in a pinning position to get back points, but not freestyle. I was real aggressive in high school and college, always shooting for takedowns, and rolling through sometimes to escape trouble. I couldn't do that in freestyle, so I had to learn to wrestle a little differently.

I adjusted eventually, but mentally I just don't think I was ready for the commitment it would take to be at the top of my game again so soon. All I'd thought about for a year was redeeming myself by winning the college nationals. I needed a little more downtime to recharge my batteries. But I also had a problem at school that spring.

I'd gone out one night several months earlier, before wrestling season, and that night I wound up sleeping with a girl who was visiting a friend at the college. It just sort of happened, and neither one of us made an effort to turn it into a relationship. I didn't even see her the rest of the year. One night sometime later, after I won the national tournament, I decided to go out with my buddies, and I ran into this same girl at a local party. I said hello and I didn't think much of it. Pretty soon my friends and I went to a different party.

I found out later that after seeing me that night, she went over to her boyfriend—who she wasn't dating at the time we slept together—and told him that I had gotten her drunk and raped her. It wasn't even close to being true, but it stoked her boyfriend up. He came looking for me with a screwdriver. He didn't find me, but he found my car. I had this Suzuki Sidekick with racing stripes on the side, and everybody knew it was mine. He took the screwdriver to it and ripped it up good. I don't know if someone called the cops, but they showed up, and he told them that "Kurt Angle raped my girlfriend."

Now, that's big news around Clarion, especially after I'd just won the nationals. So the police wanted to investigate and I had to get a lawyer. I called John du Pont, the millionaire who wound up murdering Dave Schultz four years later. He ran Team Foxcatcher, a club I had been wrestling with for a couple of years. He was always considered a little eccentric, but at the time no one knew he had the potential to kill someone for no apparent reason. I just knew he'd take care of it. He did just about anything he could for his wrestlers. So he got me a lawyer, but I didn't really end up needing one.

When the cops investigated they must have decided she had no case, because nothing came of it. But I was left with the stigma of the accusation, and I didn't like it.

I had already graduated and I was going to leave Clarion that year. But I felt it was my responsibility to clear my name. So I took a job as an assistant coach for the next school year. I wanted people to see me. I wanted to let them know I didn't do anything and I wasn't going to be accused of rape. I was well liked at Clarion, but there are always people who are going to be jealous about the kind of attention I received in that town. So I stayed to let people know: I don't care how you feel about me, I'm not going to let people call me a rapist.

But I can't say the whole thing didn't leave a scar. I was never formally charged with anything, but you don't forget something like that. I learned that I had to be more careful, that my local fame could make me an easy target for something like that. And the stress really affected me at the Olympic trials. Every night I was lying in bed, trying to remember every detail of the night in question, writing things down on a notepad. Looking back, I don't think I was ready to win a gold medal that year, because I didn't have enough international experience, but I might have been able to win a spot on the U.S. Olympic team if my head was clear. I was young and I did want to make the team. I felt I was in my best shape. I was just out of college and you can't get in better shape than in college wrestling, the hours of practice and training you put in every day.

But I didn't make it, and for the next year or so I wasn't sure where I was headed. The '96 Olympics seemed to be a long, long way off in the distance, and suddenly I wasn't a celebrity anymore. I didn't have all of Clarion cheering for me at matches anymore. It's a long, hard road to the top in freestyle wrestling, and you have to be completely self-motivated because nobody outside of the sport cares even a little bit until the Olympics come along every four years. The change was difficult for me, and the wrestling was a lot tougher, too. I was getting my butt whipped at times in some of the tournaments overseas, and I was starting to have some doubts about whether I could beat some of these guys. I was wondering if all the work and travel was worth it anymore. I guess I was a little burned out on wrestling. For a while in 1993 and '94 I thought hard about giving it up and starting a new career.

I even managed to get a tryout with the Steelers in February of 1994. I hadn't played football since high school, but I knew I had ability, and I knew I was in great shape. I had a couple of people in Pittsburgh call the Steelers for me, and they were willing to take a look. They knew that Carlton Haselrig, the heavyweight who convinced me to red-shirt at Clarion, had made the conversion from wrestling to become a good NFL player. He never played football, but he had the size and speed to adapt to professional football, so the Steelers probably thought, "Why not?"

I wasn't as big as Haselrig, so I wasn't going to

make it as a lineman at 220 pounds. When I told them I could run a 4.65 in the forty-yard dash, they decided to take a look at me as a fullback. So I went down to Three Rivers Stadium one day in February. Bill Cowher, the Steelers' coach was there, and we talked for a few minutes. He said he hoped I made it, and that was kind of cool. It wasn't a great day to be showing off fullback skills, though, because it was snowing. But they took me outside anyway, and they make you wear their turf shoes, I guess so they know they're getting times in the forty that they can accurately compare to their players. The problem was they did not have my shoe size. I wear size 11½ and all they had were size 10's and 12½'s. I took the 12½'s, but I felt like I was sloshing around in them. And the snow made me slip a couple of times when I was doing the shuttle runs. All in all, I still had a pretty good tryout. They wanted to see me catch the ball coming out of the backfield like a fullback. I ran fifteen pass routes, and I caught the passes from one of the coaches on fourteen of them. They told me to catch a few of them with one hand, and I did that without a problem. I had great hands, and when I was a kid my brothers used to make me do drills catching the ball with one hand. The only pass I didn't catch was a bad throw I had to dive for and couldn't reach.

So I think I impressed them that day. But I didn't have a good time in the forty-yard dash, and that killed me. NFL teams put a lot of stock in those times. They're always looking for speed, and if you're

a raw talent like I was, you have to have it. I ran a 4.8, which wasn't good enough to even get a second look. I really think the shoes had something to do with it, because in training for the tryout I had been running 4.6 to 4.68 consistently. I knew they weren't going to take two looks at me. I knew I had to run a 4.6 because I hadn't played college ball. They should have had me indoors somewhere, but maybe they were just giving me a courtesy look, I don't know. As it turned out, I'm glad that's all there was to it, because even if I had made their team, I'm sure I wouldn't have played for more than a few years as an average NFL fullback. I never would have become an Olympic champion, and my gold medal is something I wouldn't trade for anything in the world. I wouldn't be in World Wrestling Entertainment now either, and that's something else I wouldn't trade.

Still, I was disappointed, and I had to make a decision again. Was I willing to make a total commitment once more to wrestling? Was I ready to overcome my doubts about being able to beat some of the guys who had been handling me in freestyle? I did some soul-searching and finally decided I'd give it one more shot. But I knew if I was going to do it, I had to go all out. I had to dedicate myself more completely than ever. And I did.

6

WRESTLING ALL OVER THE WORLD

Anybody who ever wrestled knows that no other sport tests your will to win quite the same way. Five minutes on the mat in a tough match can seem like an hour of hell. I played other sports growing up and nothing pushed me to the limit of my endurance and conditioning like wrestling. In some sports you hear people say they won because they "wanted it more" than the other guys, but in wrestling you're not going to impose your will on somebody in those final, exhausting minutes unless you've paid the price with your training.

And nobody paid the price like I did for two years leading up to the Olympics. I'd always trained hard, but once I recommitted myself after my Steelers fantasy, I took it to another level. Because the nature of freestyle wrestling forced me to tone down my aggressive style, I decided the only way to beat some of these guys was to wear them down, break their will with better conditioning. So for two years I trained morning, afternoon, and night, just about every day. I'd take maybe one full day off a month, and maybe another half day somewhere. I was determined to make myself the best-conditioned wrestler in the world. I felt it would give me an edge, physically and mentally, that I needed.

No matter how much conditioning you do as a wrestler, everybody gets exhausted, especially at the elite level. But when I'd get to that point where my body was telling me to quit, it was so used to being in that numbing state that it didn't affect me. I could work through it. My secret was what I called "fatigue training." I trained to the point where I was fatigued and didn't want to do any more. And that's when I'd just be getting started.

A lot of guys train until they're fatigued, then quit. I learned to train through my state of fatigue, and when you do that, you don't lose your mind-set, your strategy, or your game plan because you're worried about being exhausted. Your mind works through it. I'm a firm believer that your body is capable of doing 100 times more than what you think you can. So much of it is in your head.

So here was a normal day of training for me when I was home, living with my mom in the condominium she had moved into after the other kids had moved out of our old house: I'd get up in the morning, go to the workout facility there at the condo complex, warm up for twenty minutes on an exercise bike, and do some stretching. Then I'd go on a four-mile run through the hills of Pittsburgh. Every hill I'd hit, I'd sprint as hard as I could, usually for about 200 to 300 yards. I'd do that run in about twenty-eight minutes—seven minutes a mile. When I got done I was pretty tired, but that's when my training was just beginning.

My manager, Jim Perri, would come over to be my partner and I'd grab him and do about fifteen sprints up this steep hill that was about 200 yards long. Jim weighed about 185 pounds, and I'd run up the hills carrying him on my back, and that was a killer. That's a lot of weight to be carrying up a hill at full speed. We'd both jog down the hills, and then I'd do it again. And again. And again. Only I'd change the way I carried him. One time I'd hold him in front of me, the way you would carry your wife over the threshold when you get married. That's even harder, on your back and thighs. Then I'd carry him piggy-back. Then I'd put him in a fireman's carry. I'd get to the point where I felt like I was going to fall over, completely exhausted. And then I'd move on to the hardest carry drill of all.

I would wrap a bungee cord around me, and my partner would hold me back, so I'd be running against resistance—like Rocky Balboa pulling that sled in the snow in the movie *Rocky IV* over in Russia. It would take me a minute, a minute and a half, to get up the hill because the guy was pulling so hard to resist me. I'd do about ten of those, to the point where I could hardly stand.

If it sounds like torture, it was. And I was doing it faithfully every day. I could see it starting to pay off in a matter of months. I began to see that if I wore down some of those huge heavyweights that had been beating me for a couple of years, I could do whatever I wanted with them. By the time I got to the

Olympics, I wasn't the strongest wrestler there, or even the most technically sound. I can't say I was smarter than other guys, but I was the best conditioned. You can turn a giant into a mouse just by getting him fatigued. That was my whole game plan. All these horses, these studs who were six four, 240 pounds, I was going to make these guys feel like they were mice. That was the attitude I took into my workouts every day.

So that was my morning session. Altogether it lasted about two hours. Then I'd go in and warm down, do some stretching, go sit in the sauna for a half hour. I'd have a little lunch and then I'd do my wrestling training for about two and a half hours. If I was on the road, at Team Foxcatcher, or the U.S. Olympic Center, or with Dan Gable at the University of Iowa, I could usually find someone to give me a real good workout. At home I had to be a little more creative. I'd go down to the wrestling room at Pitt or Duquesne University to find some bodies to wrestle. Sometimes I'd wrestle an assistant coach, sometimes I'd call guys I knew in the area to come down. None of them gave me much of a match, so I'd have three guys rotate in on me. They'd just keep taking turns, keep coming at me to wear me down, so that I got used to having to wrestle when I was dead tired. That's what my high school and college coaches had done with me. I was such a force that they'd use three or four guys to give me the workout I needed, and raise my intensity. Ideally you want someone of about equal ability to really make you work. At that level, wrestling is like a chess match, each guy trying to find the right move to put the other guy in trouble. But at times it's good to beat up on guys, too. Then you can work your technique all the way through. You don't have somebody stopping it all the time, so you can complete your moves. Either way it would turn out to be a very intense workout. I'd warm up, do some drills for about a half hour, then wrestle live for about an hour, and finish off with some conditioning work on the mat.

After dinner I'd go lift weights in the evening for a couple of hours. So I was doing three-a-days every day, putting in an average of about seven hours a day of conditioning. I logged all that stuff in notebooks, and every once in a while I'll look at those notebooks and it still amazes me that I stayed on that routine as long as I did. I think back to running those hills with Jim on my back; those hills were so steep! I don't think I could do that now, and I don't think I'd even want to do it now. A lot of things I did, I can't imagine doing anymore. I used to take eighty-pound dumbbells and do 100 jump squats. I wouldn't be able to walk when I was finished. My training was so crazy. I've yet to meet or hear of a person who trained harder than me. I've met people who trained just as hard, but not harder. The training was sacred to me.

People had respect for what I did. I almost felt like my training became a part of Pittsburgh's culture, like something to be pointed out on a sightseeing tour. I'd be doing my hill sprints, and people would be driving by, waving at me, because they knew who I was and what I was doing. I'd be down in the Pitt wrestling room or the Duquesne wrestling room, and people at the school would just wander in and watch me practice. Or I'd be at the local gym training, and people would stop their own workouts and watch me: it was like they were thinking, "Look at this SOB. He's an animal."

I don't blame them for thinking that way, either. I was relentless. When I got tired, I'd have these frightening facial expressions. And when I got so tired that I couldn't stand up, I'd get mad and I'd try to psych myself out of being tired. Sometimes I'd start punching myself in the head just to get the message across: You're *not* tired. That was my whole philosophy: "You think you're tired? The hell you are."

You punch yourself in the head a few times and you're going to stop thinking about being tired. People looked at me like I was a weirdo, but that was just my way of trying to keep myself from falling short of my goals and giving less than the 150 percent that I demanded. I didn't like just having a decent workout. I never felt good about walking away unless I'd done everything on my checklist. I had daily goals, whether it was a certain time for my sprints, or how much weight I wanted to lift, and or how many reps I needed to burn out my legs.

In the weight room I used to do crazy stuff, too, stuff no one else did, as a way to combine strength and endurance and intensity. I would squat 225 pounds as many times as I could. Once I did it 77 times. To an athlete who lifts weights, 225 pounds isn't a lot of weight to squat, but I guaran-damn-tee you that the strongest man in the world—somebody who can squat 800 or 900 pounds—can't squat 225 pounds 77 times without stopping. You can't believe how heavy 225 pounds gets after 30 or 40 reps. My brother Eric can squat 720 pounds, but he can't squat 225 pounds more than 40 times. I couldn't walk when I was done, but that was the idea. I'd burn my legs out, then I'd do my power-clean and my dead lifts with very heavy weights.

It was all about fatigue training. I was always changing my routine, pushing myself to the max. I'd change the weight on those squats each week. The week after I did 225, I'd do 315 pounds—41 times was the most repetitions I ever did without stopping. The following week I'd do 405 pounds—did 28 reps with that weight. Then one week I'd drop down to 135 pounds. I remember doing 136 reps once with that. And this was at the beginning of my workout. My legs would be completely gassed, and I still had a whole routine to do.

People had always told me that you should just lift for maintenance during your season; use light weights, just to keep your strength. But I didn't believe in that. To me, if you're just maintenance training, you're actually losing strength. I always went in with the idea of lifting heavy, getting an intense workout. And I was able to keep my strength, sometimes even improve during the season. So I'd start with those squats, then do a series of lifts, doing different parts of the body on different days. And at the end of each workout, I did plyometrics. I'd hold sixty- or eighty-pound dumbbells in my hand, squat down, and jump as high as I could. I'd do about fifty

to one hundred of them. Then I'd do the same thing on one leg. I'd lunge up on a bench and come back down on it—twenty-five each leg. Then I'd grab thirty-pound dumbbells and hop back and forth over a bench. Those types of exercise really helped my explosiveness.

And I did some variation of this whole regimen every day. There were plenty of days when I didn't feel like getting up in the morning for another day of torture, but if I didn't get up I'd feel guilty. I'd start thinking about my dad. Sometimes I'd turn that alarm clock off and roll over in bed. But then I'd be lying there thinking, "What would my dad think? Would he be okay with me going back to sleep, or would he want me to get my ass out of bed and get back to work to accomplish my goal?" And before I knew it, I'd be out on the street running. That motivation of doing it for Dad was always there, and some days I needed it.

But there were other times when I needed others to push me. That's why I'd travel every few weeks or so, change my training routine to include more live wrestling. I would go to the Team Foxcatcher facility in Philadelphia and work with Dave Schultz. I'd go to the U.S. Olympic Training Center and there would always be guys there to give me a workout. Or if I really wanted to punish myself, I'd go to Dan Gable's wrestling facility in Iowa. I think Gable is the most famous name in amateur wrestling. He is a legendary NCAA and Olympic champion, and coach of the University of Iowa wrestling team. He's known for holding the most intense practices in the country. I worked hard on my own, but Gable had a way of pushing you beyond what you thought you were capable of doing. As a coach, he'd pound you into the mat to where you couldn't walk, and then he'd pound you some more.

He'd put us through a series of drills, then have us do some live wrestling. Then we'd do sprints, climb ropes, a series of calisthenics. And then we'd wrestle some more. It was nonstop for two and a half hours, with nothing but a thirty-second break for a drink once in a while. I remember one day, in particular. I had been there for nine straight days and I was dying for a day off. So Gable comes in and says, "We're gonna take it easy today. After we warm up, we're just going to have one match."

Everybody was relieved. Of course the warm-up itself is enough to kill you—forty minutes of drilling and sprints. After the warm-up, he said, "Okay, grab a partner. One match."

A college match is seven minutes long—periods of three minutes, two minutes, and two minutes. So we started wrestling and I was going at it pretty good with this college heavyweight. We're wrestling and wrestling, and after about ten or twelve minutes, I'm thinking, "What the hell is going on?"

After a while I started looking at the other wrestlers. But they're all scared to death of Gable. He's got that aura about him. They're like, "Just keep going." After thirty minutes, he stopped the clock. We're all dead. I'm ready to fall over. Finally, one guy gets up the courage to say, "I thought you said it was one match."

"It is one match," Gable said. "But I didn't tell you how long the match was." Then he smiled this wicked smile. "It's not three-two-two. It's thirty-twenty-twenty."

I wanted to die right there. I had nothing left and I had to wrestle for another forty minutes straight. But that was typical Dan Gable. Guys know what they're getting into when they go wrestle for him. His teams are probably the best conditioned in the country, and year in and year out, he makes them believe they're the best in the nation. They're always in contention for the NCAA title, and they've won it a bunch of times. He was '94 world team head coach for Team USA, when I was number two in my weight class, and he was gone in '95 when I was number one on the world team. So I was never coached by him directly, but I got to know him well enough where I could call him and he'd tell me to come on out. I'd go out there for a couple of weeks at a time when I felt like I needed someone to kick my ass.

As I said, I don't train like that anymore. I don't think I could take it anyway. Now I train to look good, not for strength. And I need to save myself for my World Wrestling Entertainment matches, because I take a pounding with all the flying and hitting the canvas that we do. But I'm convinced that my training was what won me the gold medal in the Olympics. I won so many matches by scoring points late in the match, or in overtime, when my opponent was exhausted. I used to love it when a match went into overtime. I'd say, "Okay, I own this guy." Most guys got into overtime and they were worried about making a mistake because they were tired. To me it was just like I'd finished my four-mile run and it was time to run the sprints up the hill. I could be more aggressive in overtime because the other guys were too tired to make me pay for committing myself to a move.

Sometimes a guy would take a time-out, and that's when I knew I had him. If I could see a guy was tired, I tried to intimidate him with my conditioning. If we went out-of-bounds, I'd run back to the center. If my opponent took even a few seconds to catch his breath, I'd point at him and tell the ref, "Get him back here." It was a strategy to make him look bad, and it forced the ref to be ready to call him for a penalty point if he stayed down trying to regroup. I had some key matches, including the gold medal match, come down to a referee's decision, and I never lost that way. I'm sure my conditioning influenced the judges. They saw me as the more aggressive wrestler, and that's why those decisions always went my way.

So all that training paid off, but it was obviously a full-time job, too, which meant that I had to find ways to support myself. It's a problem for a lot of Olympic athletes. Unless you're Michael Johnson in track and field, someone like that who has a big endorsement deal, nobody is knocking your door down offering to pay your way to the Olympics. Some athletes manage to work a job and still do their training, but the way I was training, that was impossible.

What I did instead was start my own Kurt Angle foundation. I went out and found some great sponsors. Coca-Cola stepped forward to help me. A local steel company, Copperweld, donated money to live on

while I trained. I found a bunch of local sponsors—
Versamatic Pumps and Fireplace & Patio were two of
the most enthusiastic—but I had to hustle and do
whatever I could to raise money. I made my own
brochure and gave copies of it to friends, who gave
them to their friends—that type of thing. People
would sign up to sponsor my Olympic training.
Whether they donated ten dollars, fifty dollars, or
one hundred dollars, it added up. We put out two
thousand brochures and I got one thousand two hundred back from people willing to donate something,
and that really helped.

I hired Jim Perri, the same guy I carried up those
hills during my conditioning workouts, to be my
manager. He was one of my closest friends, and I

gave him a small stipend every month to represent me. He set up meetings with corporations, anybody who might be willing to donate money, and I would go with him and give a little presentation about myself and my Olympic hopes. It worked out really well. We actually wound up raising enough money to fly my family and friends to Atlanta and pay for their hotel and their food. Jimmy did a real good job so everybody could enjoy my Olympic experience.

All in all, I had a lot of help from people in Pittsburgh, and I really appreciated them supporting my cause. But training was still kind of a no-frills existence. I was completely dedicated to my training, and consumed with making the Olympic team. I had a girlfriend, but I didn't spend very much time with her. When you're an Olympic athlete you have to be selfish. You can't live a normal life. At least I couldn't.

Besides the conditioning work, I was making trips overseas every year, mostly to the Eastern-bloc countries, and that was crucial to being ready for the Olympics. That's where most of the best competition was, in Eastern Europe, especially Russia, and nobody knew it better than me. I was developing a complex about Russian wrestlers, because from 1988 to 1994 I wrestled against Russians eleven times and I never won. I used to go on USA wrestling tours during winter and summer breaks from college, and the international experience was really valuable in making me a better wrestler. But I was letting the Russian thing get in my head.

So when I recommitted myself to going for the Olympics, I knew I had to overcome that feeling. I think it was part of the reason that I took a break from wrestling. For years I was convinced that I couldn't beat those damn Russians—they were too good. They were the best, the very best. For a while I was actually telling myself, "Okay, maybe winning a gold medal is impossible, but you can win a silver." I felt I could beat everybody else, but not the Russians.

Then, when the Soviet Union was dissolved after the '92 Olympics, it was a nightmare for me. Because now I wouldn't have just one Russian to deal with if I made the Olympic team, but more like sixteen, because I knew they would be fleeing to represent different countries. It was real discouraging because I thought it might prevent me from winning an Olympic medal.

But in January of 1994 I had a breakthrough when I won the 1994 Krasnoyarsk tournament, which is held in Siberia and basically considered the toughest tournament in the world. Some people think it's tougher than the Olympics because you have twenty Russians in it as well as wrestlers from other countries. The guys I considered the best Russian wrestlers got knocked off before I met them during the tournament, but I did beat three Russians in that tournament, and that ended about six years of frustration against them. The win was a huge boost for my confidence. I was only the fourth American wrestler ever to win at Krasnoyarsk, and it came at a perfect time because I felt like I'd come to a crossroads in my wrestling career right about then.

I had been getting discouraged and burned out, thinking about giving up on my dream because I couldn't seem to beat the best guys. I had already

committed myself by then to the tryout with the Steelers, which I had a month or so later. But if I hadn't won at Krasnoyarsk, I don't know if I would have returned to wrestling after I took that break to get ready for my football tryout. It gave me a big confidence boost that I needed at about that time. I started thinking that maybe I could win the gold after all.

Eventually I think all of that experience overseas paid off. It was intimidating at first, wrestling in places like Russia and Bulgaria and Turkey. There

were a lot of times I had to push myself to go, just because I knew the trip would be so grueling. USA Wrestling was paying for it, and they were on a tight budget, so there were times it took me thirty-eight hours to get there. I'd fly from home in Pittsburgh to New York. I'd have a layover there, then fly New York to Germany. Another layover. Then Germany to Bulgaria. Bulgaria to Moscow. Moscow to Siberia. And then we'd have a four-hour bus ride in Siberia to the tournament site. It was pure hell. You could barely sleep, so then, when you got there, you felt terrible, and usually you had to compete a day later. But you got used to it. You had no choice.

Wrestling in some of those countries really made you appreciate the United States. They're not big on comfort over there. At the Krasnoyarsk tournament in Siberia that I won, it was unbelievably cold outside—the temperature was like thirty-five below zero. And it didn't feel much warmer than that inside. They kept the thermostat—if there was one!—at about forty degrees. To them that's not cold, but to an athlete trying to warm up and break a sweat, then stay loose, it was brutal. But there were a million inconveniences to deal with in places like that. That's why every time I'd come back to the United States from one of those trips, I'd literally get on my knees and kiss the ground, the way they do in the movies. Put it this way: We didn't get treated like kings in any of those countries. It seemed like there was always one problem or another for us to handle.

I had my worst overseas experience in Russia in 1995. I'd just won the world championships in Atlanta and I flew to Vladivostok for a tournament that matched all the New World champions against Russia's best team. It was one of those long trips and I was feeling sluggish when I got there, so I went for a run along the river. I was running and all of a sudden this river dog was running alongside me. It was dirty and disgusting, foaming at the mouth. The dog started barking at me, so I squared off against it to make sure it didn't get anywhere near me. It barked at me some more but then ran away, so I started running again. A minute or so later the dog came out of nowhere. I never saw or heard it until it had leaped at my leg and I felt a sharp pain. I dropped to my hands and knees, and when I looked at my leg, the dog had taken a big chunk of skin off of my thigh. It bit a hole about three-quarters of an inch into my leg, and then it attacked me. I fought it off by kicking it until it finally got tired and ran away.

When I finally got rid of the dog and got a look at how deeply it had bitten me, I became concerned that it had rabies. I ran back to the hotel. Dave Schultz was there, and when I told him what happened, and he saw my leg bleeding, he knew we had to go to the hospital. There were some Russian wrestlers in the lobby of the hotel at the time, and Dave, who spoke Russian, said something to them about getting me to the hospital. They laughed. As Dave translated it for me, they said, "If you're not howling by midnight, you'll be okay."

They said it wasn't serious because dogs in their country don't have rabies. We weren't buying that one. Dave found a guy who was affiliated with the Russian team to take me to the hospital. Dave couldn't go himself, so the translator for our team went, along with two of the Russian wrestlers. Now, I didn't tell the driver to rush me there or anything like that. But he got out on the highway and he was going so fast I swore we were going to take off like a plane. He was going 100 to 120 miles per hour on the freeways, and I knew he wasn't worried about getting pulled over by the cops. The police there don't mess with the wrestlers. Wrestlers are the kingpins over there. They get special treatment. Wrestling is that big over there. It's the number one sport in most of those Eastern-bloc countries. It's so popular there that it's like football, baseball, basketball, hockey, *and* wrestling combined in the United States. The Russian wrestlers have higher profiles than any football or baseball player has in our country. They're considered national heroes.

So this guy was not only going 120 miles per hour—and from the backseat I could see the speedometer, which read 180 kilometers per hour—but he's going the wrong way on a highway because the traffic was heavy on the side he should have been on. He's flashing his high beams at oncoming cars and I can see people yanking the steering wheel to get out of the way. I told our translator to tell the guy to slow down because I didn't want to die, and he slowed down to about 90 miles per hour. By the time we got to the hospital, my heart rate was about 190. I went into the emergency room and my leg was still bleeding a lot. The cut was so deep that I couldn't stop the bleeding. So someone took me to this doctor's office. The doctor was a woman and she gave me a cold look, then went back to reading a book at her desk. I sat there for a half hour and she still hadn't gotten up from her desk.

I said to my translator, "What the hell's going on here? Why won't she take care of me?"

"She's upset," he said to me.

"About what?" I said. "I'm the one with a big hole in my leg."

"Well," he said, "this is her break time."

I don't know if that's the way the old idea of socialism works or what, but I had the feeling that my leg could have been hanging by a thread, and she still wasn't going to do anything for me until break time was over. I waited another twenty minutes or so, at which point, finally, she put her book down, and even then she acted like it was a pain in her ass that I was there. She cleaned me up and gave me rabies shots, but the technology was from the 1960s. I had to get a prescription for a series of shots to be taken over a three-month period. When I got home a doctor told me that with today's technology I only needed one shot. It was just one more reminder that there's no place like America, and there's no way I would want to live in another part of the world.

When I've traveled to Western Europe, places like France, Germany, and Italy, the living conditions are much better than what I found in Eastern Europe. But even there they don't have the hotel accommodations we do, or the food we do. You can't just walk down the street and find a 7-Eleven convenience store. I guess we get used to convenience in the United States, and maybe we're kind of spoiled. But if that's the case, I like being spoiled.

I was shocked by the conditions in some of the Eastern European countries. I remember going to Istanbul, Turkey, when I was in college. I know the United States has pollution problems, but for the whole week I was there, the pollution was so thick that I don't know how people live with it. You could smell it every day, the sulfur in the air. You could smell the smoke, see the dust on the buildings. There were smoke clouds all around the city.

The food was so bad that I brought my own on every trip. I rarely ate anything in Russia or anywhere else. All Russia had was cabbage, and some kind of cruddy, high-fatty meat. They had these stews, but I was never sure what was in them. I majored in geography in college and we studied the Russian transportation system, how long it took to transport food like chicken and beef and get it into stores. I wasn't about to take a chance eating their meat. I'm pretty strict about what I eat anyway: I like chicken and rice, baked potatoes and steak, fruit and vegetables. They didn't seem to have a lot of that kind of stuff. So I'd eat my own food, except when I'd treat myself to Pizza Hut over there once in a while.

I'd bring one whole suitcase just filled with food. I'd pack a hot pot and cook in my room. I brought canned chicken, tuna, noodles, rice, oatmeal, peanut butter, bagels, and hard pretzels. That type of stuff. If I was over there for a week, I knew I would not order room service or eat out. In fact, I would be eating in quite a bit.

The hardest part was getting enough to eat on the trips. I remember on one trip to Siberia, we stopped in Moscow, and the food on the plane was so disgusting. You got a piece of stale bread, half of a rotten cucumber, and an empty plate. Then the stewardess came down the aisle with a huge pot that had dead-looking chicken legs on it. They'd pick out a chicken leg and drop it on your plate. I sat there thinking, "You've gotta be kidding." So for about thirty hours straight we didn't eat, except for snacks you might have brought with you. Sometimes we were so hungry by the time we got to Moscow that we'd say the hell with our fitness plans, and we'd run to McDonald's and order about five Big Macs each.

In my ten years of freestyle competition, starting in 1987, I probably went on forty international trips, and I thought I would see dramatic changes in countries like Russia after the Iron Curtain came down in 1992, but I really didn't. We were always watched pretty carefully when we were there. They had guards around to keep an eye on us, and they always knew where we were and what we were doing. They had our passports all the time. We had to get permission anytime we wanted to go somewhere. You never really had the feeling that you were in a free country.

There was more emphasis on money after the Iron Curtain fell. We used to go to these bazaars where everyone was selling stuff. All that mattered was money. People were rushing around, trying to make money for their families. They wanted to sell you stuff, but it was sort of on the side. They didn't want the Russian Mafia to see them. You had the feeling the Mafia became much more powerful there after the Iron Curtain fell. People had that look like they were scared to death. I guess the change in the system was hard for some people because they had to find ways to make money. You go to Russia now and it seems like every car on the street is a taxicab. All you have to do is flag down a car and they'll take you wherever you want to go for a buck. It's amazing. If

you have American money, a dollar or two, they'll take you on a forty-five-minute drive, wherever you want to go.

In other ways they try to take advantage of Americans. At the Pizza Hut in Moscow, there are two lines for ordering pizza—one for Russians and one for Americans. In the Russian line, you pay for the pizza in rubles. It costs the equivalent of $2.25 for a large pizza. If you go to the American side, it costs you $22. Fortunately, the Russian wrestlers would let us go on the Russian side. Even when the old system broke up, the wrestlers were still a powerful force. Someone told me that some of the wrestlers in Russia have Mafia connections and are powerful because of that. Watching them operate was like watching the *Godfather* movies. They're like twenty years behind us in a lot of ways. But the wrestlers are still a powerful group. They also have a lot of influence politically in Russia.

One thing that never changed after the breakup of the Soviet Union was Russia's elite status in wrestling. Americans knew that if they were serious about succeeding on the international level, they had to make the sacrifice and go there to learn the technique and style of the Russians and other Eastern European wrestlers. But those trips were depressing. After a while those places all started to look the same. They all seemed to have depressed economies, and the majority of people were poor. That's probably why wrestling is so popular in those countries. You don't need much to compete in wrestling. It's the oldest sport in the world and it's a sport for the common man. I think wrestling is also the best form of self-defense, because it teaches discipline and balance and leverage, everything a person needs to learn to protect themselves. That's not a reason kids usually think about when they decide to wrestle, but it's something to consider in this day and age when fewer and fewer kids seem to be wrestling, at least in the United States. In countries like Russia, Bulgaria, Czechoslovakia, Turkey, and Iran, wrestling continues to be the number one sport or very close to it.

The United States has always been a world power in amateur wrestling, along with the two or three best Eastern European countries. But the sport has begun to spread to other countries and become more popular worldwide while it's suffering in our country. Title IX has taken a toll on college programs. Title IX is the law passed years ago that guarantees equivalency for women's athletics. But the problem is that colleges have started to drop men's programs to balance things rather than add women's programs. Because wrestling is not a moneymaker at most schools, it's always a candidate to be dropped. It's the same reason men's gymnastics has been turned into a club sport in college, and I'm afraid the same thing could happen to wrestling.

Without strong college programs we won't be able to continue to be a world power. In the 1980s, there were over two hundred NCAA Division I wrestling programs. And there were over four hundred programs between NCAA Division I, II, and III as well as NAIA schools. Now there are only about ninety Division I programs in the country, and as that number gets smaller, it's bound to affect us in international competition eventually.

As it is, countries like Russia have always had much more depth than us. The teams in those Eastern-bloc countries were always about twenty deep in each weight class. In the United States, guys wrestle in international competition because they're all trying to win a gold medal in the Olympics. In Russia, it's enough just to be on the national team. They take great pride in that, and if they get to be number one in their weight class, they become national heroes.

It was always very intimidating wrestling the Russians, especially in their country. They're all so skilled and they act like robots—kind of like the Russian fighter in *Rocky IV*. That's the way they are. They don't show any emotion. You look a Russian wrestler in the eyes and he'll make you feel like you don't belong on the mat with him. It's like, "This is nothing to me. I'm gonna kick your ass and there's nothing you can do about it."

But if you can beat them in their own country, you feel like you're ready to take on the world. And that's what happened to me. After that first win at Krasnoyarsk in 1994, I began to have more and more success with the Russians. I shocked everyone by winning the World Championship in 1995, which is basically the same as winning the Olympics, except in a non-Olympic year. Nobody outside of the wrestling world knows or cares about it. It was a great achievement, but in some ways it made my goal of winning the Olympics more difficult because now I was on top.

And everybody was gunning for me, internationally as well as nationally. Now the pressure was really on, and it's rare when you see guys win the World Championship one year and then the Olympics the next. There's such a tiny difference in talent between the top wrestlers in the world, usually it's hard to make things go your way two years in a row.

I had another problem after I won the World Championship. Everybody was talking about me and a lot of people seemed to be accusing me of being on steroids. They saw a difference in my structure from college to Olympic style and they thought I must have been cheating. But it was simple, really. It was because I learned how to take protein supplements, and how to eat right. That plus the lunatic level of my conditioning program.

To some people it doesn't matter what you say, though. They're going to believe what they want to believe. For a while there was a rumor going around that one of my brothers was a doctor who came up with a steroid that no one could detect. That was a good one, since my brothers are all laborers. It seemed like it was the guys in my weight class making up those stories, too. Whatever it was, after I won worlds in 1995, I think I became the most drug-tested athlete in Olympic history. People on the Olympic committee were testing me every month. A guy would show up at my door every month to get a urine sample.

They said it was random, that my name just happened to be popping up every month. I think it was because I came out of nowhere and won the worlds in '95. All I know was the rumors started to follow me around. In '96, I got tested at the Olympic trials and people were telling me there were stories on the Internet saying I'd tested positive for steroids. I was in a rage. I called my USA coach, Bruce Burnett, and told him about the Internet stuff. He said, "Relax, I've got your tests in my hand. You're clean."

The whole thing bothered me because I never, ever, messed with steroids. I never wanted to win by taking something that was considered illegal. I know some athletes have done it and gotten away with it. Besides the random testing, everybody who wins a medal gets tested. But some guys get off the stuff in enough time to get away with it; others have used substances that mask the steroids and allow athletes to pass the test.

You don't see it often in wrestling, though. I think most amateur wrestlers develop a work ethic and a respect for their conditioning that won't allow them to mess with steroids. To me, anytime you mess with any kind of drugs, you're putting a stress on your body which can be dangerous. After the rumors started, it was just one more thing I had to overcome to win the Olympics in 1996.

7

DAVE SCHULTZ

I'd made the same phone call dozens of times over the years. It was January of 1996 and I wanted to tell Dave Schultz that I'd be coming to work out at the Team Foxcatcher wrestling facility the next day. I got his answering machine, so I left a message and I didn't think anything of it until later that night. I came home from lifting weights and I was channel-surfing when I saw my good friend's face on CNN. The guy on TV was talking about a shooting. It took a minute or so for me to figure out the voices were saying that John du Pont allegedly had shot Dave Schultz for no apparent reason. The words sent chills down my spine. It was shocking, but at the same time, in a weird sort of way, it wasn't.

I never expected John du Pont to shoot anyone, especially Dave, who worked for John as one of the coaches of Team Foxcatcher. But I had heard the stories, especially in the weeks leading up to the murder. John was always considered eccentric by some, and just plain crazy by others, but people were saying he was acting more and more bizarre. I had known John for about six years. I lived off and on at the Team Foxcatcher facility just outside of Philadelphia for about six years, using the club's state-of-the-art facilities to train for international tournaments. John was a great friend to amateur wrestling and he was a personal friend to me, helping me out anytime I had a problem. But for a long time afterward I was shaken by the thought that I could have been killed just as easily as Dave. Who knows how much danger I was in during all that time I spent at Foxcatcher? What if John had picked the next day, when I was on the grounds, to shoot somebody? Those are still difficult questions for me to think about. But mostly I can never forgive John for killing Dave.

Dave Schultz might have been amateur wrestling's greatest ambassador. He had been traveling the world for nearly twenty years, he spoke eight languages, and he made friends everywhere he went. He won a gold medal in the 1984 Olympics and there probably wasn't a better technical wrestler in the world. He was also the only guy who weighed less than 170 pounds that ever kicked my ass on the wrestling mat. I remember coming out of college, I weighed 225 pounds, and Dave was about 169 pounds. I wrestled him a lot that summer at Foxcatcher, and he handed my ass to me more times than I care to remember. I thought, "Man, if I can't beat this 163-pounder, what am I gonna do at 220?"

But that's how good Dave was. His execution was so perfect, he just chewed me up, and I was already a two-time NCAA champion. But this was freestyle, and Dave was a master of the international style. He had cutting-edge moves, unconventional stuff that you never saw anyone else use. He had some judo tricks that would blow your mind. That's why he learned eight different languages—he wanted to be able to talk to wrestlers all over the world, study and learn their techniques. He wound up combining them into his own technique, and it worked for him. It took me a couple of years until I could actually beat Dave, and when it happened I knew I was making strides toward becoming a world champion.

Dave had been a personal mentor for me since my sophomore year in college. I won the Espoir freestyle nationals for wrestlers under age twenty and earned a spot on the Espoir world cup team. The team had a camp at Northwestern University that summer, and that's where Dave first saw me. He took a quick liking to me, I think, because he appreciated my work ethic and he knew that if someone taught me right, I could be something special. I had watched him on video and I thought he was the greatest ever. As nice a guy as he was, he had a mean streak on the mat like I've never seen. He would inflict pain. Rumor has it, he broke this Turkish wrestler's arm in 1984 at the Olympics, and it caused such hard feelings that Dave received death threats from some of the Turkish fans. The guy was Turkey's best wrestler, so people told Dave if he ever came to Turkey to take part in a tournament, they would kill him. But Dave took it in stride. He didn't change his style. That's how he was; when he got into the heat of the moment, he was vicious.

Still, I found out just how serious those threats were. When I went to Istanbul for a tournament in 1989, the people who were assigned to us as translators and tour guides were worried for my safety because they thought I was Dave's brother, Mark, who also won a gold medal in 1984. When they asked me if I was Mark Schultz, I said, "No, but thanks for the compliment."

They said, "It's not a compliment. But you look so much like Mark Schultz that we're worried for your safety."

I wanted to get the hell out of there right then, but they assured me that nothing would happen. They said they would keep security tight and inform everyone that I wasn't related to the Schultz brothers. And nothing did happen, but that was the kind of reaction Dave could cause because he was so ruthless on the mat. That incident, as well as a few others, earned him a reputation for being the bad boy of wrestling. Guys used to shoot for a takedown on him and he'd get them in a front headlock. He found a way of choking guys. They'd go limp, and he'd whip them over and pin them real quick. By the time the ref would see the guy was out, it was too late. By the time he got to the '84 Olympics, everybody was watching him closely. Dave would give somebody a front headlock and the refs would stop the match. They were on him all the time. And he still won the gold that year with a phenomenal performance.

When he died he was thirty-seven years old. He was obviously past his prime, but he was trying to make the Olympics one last time. He was still great—he was ranked number one in the USA in his weight class in 1995. Kenny Monday, the 1988 Olympic champion, was making a comeback and the two of them would have met in the '96 Olympic trials if Dave hadn't been killed. Kenny was the only American to beat Dave in the 163-pound weight class over a span of twelve years, from '84 to '96, and he wound up going to the Olympics and finishing sixth, but there's no doubt in my mind that Dave had a good chance of beating Kenny in the trials.

It was du Pont who had hired Dave and Greg Strobel to run Team Foxcatcher. John was heir to one of the largest family fortunes in the world, but he wasn't your typical CEO-in-waiting. As much time as I spent around him, I never saw anything myself to believe he was mentally unbalanced, but obviously John had problems. I knew that he had been through alcohol and drug rehab, and he wasn't good with personal relationships. He was married once and the woman left him after two months. I think the only person he was close to was his mother, and when she passed away, it was very difficult for him. People told me he became more eccentric after that.

He was involved in athletics for years, both as a competitor and a sponsor. He sponsored triathletes, pentathletes, and swimmers. His parents thought wrestling was too barbaric and they wouldn't allow him to sponsor wrestlers, but after they died he decided to get involved in the sport. He built the Team Foxcatcher facility on a farm in Newtown Square, just outside of Philadelphia, and turned it into the best wrestling club in the United States, not to mention the rest of the world. He also donated nearly a half-million dollars a year to USA Wrestling. We won the world championships for the first time in 1993 as a team, and a lot of it was because of the money John spent to make USA Wrestling a world power. The best wrestlers could continue to train and get paid a stipend as they got older, instead of being forced to retire and go make a living, as had been the case for years.

John had a passion for the sport and even competed himself in senior-division tournaments when he was in his late forties and early fifties. He wasn't very good, but people around the world came to know how much he cared about wrestling. John invited certain foreign wrestlers to train at Foxcatcher, even though they competed against our team in tournaments. He became especially fond of a Bulgarian wrestler named Valentine Jordanov, who was a seven-time world champion. John even made Valentine a coach at Foxcatcher for a while. Valentine paid him back by arranging a special match for John when we were wrestling in a tournament in Bulgaria. It was billed as the "main event." At the end of the tournament, John wrestled this retired Bulgarian wrestler who was maybe in his late thirties—younger than John. The fans over there loved John because they knew he paid for some of the Bulgarian wrestlers to come over and train at Foxcatcher, and they knew he and Valentine, who was their national hero, were close friends.

So they cheered for John as the match began. What Valentine didn't tell John was that he fixed the match for him to win. It was Valentine's way of thanking John for everything he had done, and John believed it was for real. We were sitting there watching this match, and John was so bad, he would actually lose points by accident, even though the other guy was trying to let him win. The guy would try to give away points and John would fall on his back and score points for his opponent. It was a riot because you never see a fixed match in amateur wrestling. It was almost like watching John compete in the World Wrestling Entertainment. He ended up winning, like 15–14, and the Bulgarians lifted him up in the air, carried him around the mat. He always believed he'd legitimately won the match and he was proud of it.

But that's how far John's reputation in wrestling spread around the world. And in the United States, just about every top amateur wrestler wanted to wrestle for Team Foxcatcher. The Foxcatcher facility was heaven for wrestlers. At the time there were maybe six to ten wrestling clubs in the United States that signed wrestlers and paid some of their expenses to travel and compete internationally. But no other club compared to Foxcatcher. John spent $800,000 to build the facility and it had everything you could want. The weight room had every imaginable weight machine as well as free weights. There was a computer you could use to study and learn wrestling techniques. It was all so high tech, we couldn't believe it. There were four full-size wrestling mats, a swimming pool, and a kitchen with all of the best nutrition supplements. A full-time masseur and a full-time trainer were on the staff and always available to the wrestlers. And John was a hands-on presence. He lived on the grounds and oversaw the entire operation.

After I won the national title my sophomore year at Clarion, the top wrestling clubs around the country all invited me to join. Foxcatcher seemed to have the best of everything, so I went there to meet with John. I remember sitting down with him in his TV room. He lives in a beautiful mansion on a farm. He built small cabin-type houses on the farm to house the athletes. He took great pride in the place. So he sat me down in a spot where I could see all these awards he'd won as a pentathlete when he was younger. For some reason, wrestling had become his passion. There was a spot on the wall that was bare and John pointed to it. He said, "You're a national champion, Kurt. We'd like you to sign with us, and I think one day you can be on that wall right there as a world champion."

I'm sure he did that with every athlete he wanted, but I was impressed. At the time I thought his place had the facilities and the coaching to help make me an Olympian, so I took the carrot. John was well-known throughout amateur wrestling. He funded about forty wrestlers with his club and we were treated like kings there. He had the place fully stocked with protein supplements, nutrient drinks, fruit, food; whatever you wanted, it was there for you. Nobody had ever done this for wrestlers, and so it became almost like a status thing to wrestle for Foxcatcher.

I was there off and on for about six years, and during that time I only heard stories from people there about John's strange behavior. Once, he drove his tank across his farm and crushed everything in sight—all the corn, trees, everything. One time he used dynamite to blow up one of the barns on the farm for no apparent reason. There were all kinds of stories, but John never had any trouble with the local police. He had a shooting range on the farm and he allowed the cops to come and shoot there, so they were good to him.

I never heard of him causing any trouble outside of his farm. But he was liable to do anything on his own property. There was a story about the day he had the head guy from FILA, which is the world governing body of wrestling, in for a visit. Supposedly John asked the guy to go for a ride with him in his new Lincoln Town Car. John loved being able to have some influence in the world of amateur wrestling. He was in his early fifties by then and still wrestling. FILA had senior-division wrestling competitions for wrestlers in their thirties and forties. John decided to create a fifty-and-over category. He figured he could wrestle in it and nobody else that age would show up. And he was right. He had his own world championships, and he was a three-time world champion because nobody challenged him in that age group.

Not that John was a good wrestler, as we witnessed in Bulgaria that time. But he was always working with wrestling coaches, trying to get better. I don't think that's eccentric so much as I just think that's a guy with the money to chase after his dreams, a guy who wanted to be somebody special in the sport of wrestling. I respected him for that. But if he didn't get what he wanted, you never knew what he might do. I don't know if he had a disagreement with the guy from FILA, but he had this guy in a Lincoln Town Car and he came down a hill on his farm and drove right into a lake at the bottom of the hill. As the limo started sinking, John, who was a great swimmer, got out and brought the guy to safety.

People weren't sure if John wanted to give this wrestling bigwig a scare or what. But the guy was furious. I was working out in the wrestling room at the time, and he came into the room, cursing John up and down in French. The thing is, John had done the same thing with a different car four days earlier, only nobody was in the passenger seat for that one. Nobody knew what the hell was going on with John. Nobody thought he was crazy, but people were starting to think he was back to doing drugs.

At some point everybody knew that John had started carrying a gun. I never heard about him pulling it out or pointing it at anyone, but he was very paranoid that people were trying to get to him. One time he thought I was haunting him from inside his walls. I think it was a time when he was doing a lot of drugs. He never said it to me, but other people told me they were in his office when John started shouting, "Angle, if you don't get out from behind my wall, I'm gonna shoot it." People didn't know what to make of him when they saw things like that.

There was more and more talk around the club that something wasn't right with John. Still, I don't think anybody felt threatened by him. If they did they didn't say anything. As far as the wrestlers were concerned, nobody wanted to mess with a good thing, and I think everybody just figured they could live with John's quirks. But later everybody agreed there had been signs that John was losing it.

Only about four days before the murder, John fell down in his house and banged his head on a chair or table. He got knocked out, and when he came to, he thought that one of the wrestlers had hit him in the head with a bat. He's looking for this wrestler, he's all pissed off. This was like four days before Dave was killed. He went around threatening various guys for knocking him out, and threw some of them off the farm because of it.

A week or so before that, John had kicked Fox-catcher's only three black wrestlers out of the club. John used to tell people that he felt the color black was evil, that it represented death. It had nothing to do with black people. It was the color black that scared him. When he seemed to start to deteriorate, John told the black wrestlers they had to leave. At that point he had to be losing it mentally.

Until then he had treated the black guys as if they were his own brothers. So it was shocking when he let them go. Especially since one of them was Kevin Jackson, who had won an Olympic gold medal while wrestling for Foxcatcher. Kenny Monday, who wasn't training there at the time, was really pissed and he spoke out against John at the time. I didn't blame him. If I were African-American and I heard that shit, I'd think it was racial, too. But I didn't feel that way because I knew enough about John by then to believe that in his mind, he needed to get every-thing black out of his life. Obviously, African-Americans are really brown-skinned, but I guess to

John all that mattered was that they were called blacks. It tells you he was probably cracking.

Dave had been living on the farm with his family. John paid him a salary to coach the wrestling club team, but Dave wasn't there for the money. His life was wrestling. He loved working with other wrestlers, and he was trying to make the Olympic team. He had kids in school in the area, but he was planning to move off the farm after the Olympics.

Who can ever know what was in John's mind the day he killed Dave Schultz? But you wouldn't think he planned it, because he had a retired FBI agent in the car with him when he drove down to Dave's house that day. John had hired the guy for security because he thought somebody was out to get him. The way the story was told to me by people close to Dave, he was outside working on his car when John pulled up to the house. Dave walked over to John's car, and from the driver's seat, John pulled out the gun, and *boom,* he blew Dave away. The former FBI agent didn't know what the hell to do. John pointed the gun at him, so he jumped out and hid behind the car. John got out, pointed the gun at Dave's chest, and shot him again. Dave's wife, Nancy, came running out of the house. John pointed the gun at her and told her to get back in the house. She ran into the house and called the cops. Dave rolled over, started crawling away, and John shot him again, this time in the back. Then he got in the car and drove back to his house. He was holed up there for about sixty hours before the cops got him. The story was that they tricked him into coming out of the house to turn the generator on because he had no heat in the house, but John was too smart not to know he was going to get caught if he went outside. I think he just decided to give up, but he didn't want to admit he was giving up.

Ironically, Dave was really the only guy that John would listen to sometimes. Obviously, John cracked, but when that was I don't know. I found out later that Dave was worried enough about the way John had been acting that he had talked to some people about trying to get him some help. I still get asked if I thought John was crazy, and it's hard to say. I've never been able to conclude anything definitive except that maybe he was and maybe he wasn't. Every time I talked to the man, he seemed sane. The John du Pont I knew had to know what he was doing when he killed Dave. I just think he was very sinister. Other people who saw him do some of those weird things on the farm might have different opinions. He might have gone back to doing drugs. But sometimes I think he had this little make-believe world. As much as I hate him for what he did, I felt bad for him in some ways. Even with all that money, he was never happy with his life. His parents expected a lot of him and he didn't deal with that well.

He was convicted, but he's not in jail. He's in a mental home, so in a way I really think John won. He's eligible for parole in five years and it hurts me to think of him ever getting out. I guess we'll never know for sure what drove him to kill Dave. The only thing I could ever figure was that John must have thought Dave was out to get him. Whether it was drugs or something wrong in his mind, people said he had begun talking like he thought everybody was out to get him.

After the murder, the du Pont lawyers tried to blame it on the wrestlers. They said USA Wrestling used John, that its people knew John was crazy but they wanted his money. It was such bullshit. If anything, I considered Dave a hero. When John du Pont became harder to deal with those last few months, Dave could have left and gone a lot of places to train for the Olympics. He had that kind of reputation. Any club in the United States would have loved to pay his way. Dave stayed there and put up with John's crap so that all of the rest of us could have an opportunity to keep competing, and it cost him his life.

Obviously, Dave's death was hardest on his family—his wife, Nancy, and their two kids; his brother, Mark; and his parents. But it affected a lot of wrestlers, too, especially me. Dave had been my coach, my mentor, and one of my best friends. Of course, Dave had a lot of best friends because everybody wanted to be close to him. When I rededicated myself in 1994 to going for the Olympics, I spent as much time at Foxcatcher working with Dave as I could. He understood the tricks of the international style better than anyone. Working with him, I learned how to work strategies where I could move guys, turn them in ways that would let me score on them. I learned how to control the tempo of a match, how to slow it down at times and yet stay active to avoid getting called for stalling. He showed me so many little tiny things that are important, things that maybe I'd done instinctively but I hadn't really thought much about—like always keeping your back to the center of the mat. That way you were always pushing the other guy out-of-bounds, and never backing out-of-bounds yourself and leaving yourself open to a stalling call. He knew so many little things that could make the other guy look bad and maybe make the difference in a match if it was tied after overtime and decided by a referees' decision. I had no way of knowing then that my gold medal match would be decided that way, but I knew that working with Dave was taking my preparation for the Olympics to a new level.

So from a wrestling standpoint alone, losing Dave just crushed me. But after the shock wore off, I had to make a decision. It was an important time for any wrestler with hopes of making the Olympic team, and our lives revolved around our training. Foxcatcher continued to operate, and some guys stayed on because they didn't have anywhere else to go for funds.

Personally, there was no way I could stay on at the club. It wasn't right. I was the first wrestler to quit Foxcatcher. It was important to me because of Dave. I admit I had to think about it. I was walking away from a stipend of $1,000 a month, plus all of my expenses, and that was a lot of money for a wrestler. But when I found myself thinking that way, I said, "What's wrong with you? This guy killed Dave Schultz. Screw that. You're not wrestling for him." So I called my manager and told him to get on the phone and find some more sponsors. And that's what we did.

When I quit, Nancy Schultz called me to thank me and said I was now an official member of the Dave Schultz Wrestling Club, which she formed immediately after Dave's death. The club wound up paying my expenses to the Olympic trials, and since then Nancy has turned it into one of the top clubs in the country. All these corporations donated money toward the club, and Nancy offered USA Wrestling the chance to get involved and help the program grow. But USA Wrestling didn't want any part of it. I think they were afraid to get involved because at the time du Pont's lawyers were making a lot of accusations, criticizing them for taking money from du Pont.

I think that's why Foxcatcher didn't shut down completely. It wasn't running as a workout club, but it continued to pay the bills for any wrestlers who wanted to stay. I think it was because the lawyers felt it was good for John's case to do it—to show he really cared about the wrestlers. Their whole defense was built on the idea that the athletes were taking advantage of John, so maybe they wanted people to think, "Look, Dave Schultz was killed, and they're still taking money from John. They're fucking vultures."

They tried to make John look like the victim. But I was there enough to know better. John called the shots all the time. John said yes or no to everything. He sat me down and told me how much I was getting paid and when I was getting paid. It wasn't like I said, "Hey, John, this is how much I want," or somebody else said, "I'll get you this much from John." He was a businessman. He'd sit you down, tell you what he expected of you. There was nothing unstable about the way he handled business decisions. He knew what he was doing. He knew what he was getting into in every aspect of the wrestling club.

Anyway, Nancy sued and wound up getting about thirty-four million dollars from the du Pont fortune. It's not a replacement for her husband but at least she's set financially, and it helps keep the Dave Schultz Wrestling Club going strong. I was proud to be the first Olympic champion for the Dave Schultz Club. I remember seeing Nancy after I won the gold. I had this big press conference and I saw Nancy in the crowd, crying, and I just decided to let everybody in the world know I'd been thinking of her late husband.

I said, "Nancy, I just want you to know Dave had the greatest impact in the world on me. That one was for Dave, too. I want to thank you for everything you did for me and I especially want to thank your husband for helping me win the gold medal."

I meant it, too. Dave went out of his way to work with me. He used to always grab me and work on technique, show me moves I might want to use. I think he knew I had the ability to be the best. So anytime I was around he'd say, "Come on, come on, I want to show you something." I was still a nobody then, at least in the world of freestyle wrestling, but he treated me like I was something special. He became my idol in wrestling, and he left a legacy in the sport that is being carried on by his club. Today it's one of the strongest clubs in the United States. Nancy did a tremendous job getting contributions from corporations and I'm sure Nancy is putting her own money in it, too. I guarantee that Nancy is not being selfish with that thirty-four million dollars she was awarded. You talk about good people and what's keeping wrestling in America strong enough to compete internationally, and it's because of people like Nancy Schultz. Wrestling was Dave's life, and I'm sure he would be proud.

8

ON THE ROAD
TO ATLANTA

I'll always remember 1996 as the year that changed my life forever, but it started with a catastrophe. Put it this way: You never want to land face-first on the mat, but that's what I did in the semifinals of the U.S. Nationals, and the mishap nearly wiped out my year before it started.

I was only about five months away from the Olympics, and I was wrestling a guy named Jason Loukides, from the New York Athletic Club. The tournament was important because the winner earned a pass right into the finals of the Olympic trials in two months. So if I won, the other top nine wrestlers in my weight class would have to wrestle off in a mini-tournament for the right to wrestle a best-of-three match against me for the berth on the Olympic team.

I had beaten Loukides before, but he surprised me this time. He hit me with an arm throw when we first tied up at the start of the match. When I went to reach in, he turned his body, grabbed my arm, and whipped me over. My lack of caution was about to cost me. Right away I was thinking about the three points he was going to get for taking me right from my feet to my back, which is the rule in international freestyle. And usually, if you get behind by three points in freestyle at this level, you're pretty much dead. The other guys are so good that they can protect that lead by using their size and strength to keep you away from their legs, keep you from taking them down. And then you start chasing, trying to make a spectacular move to get the points back, and you make mistakes.

So I was determined to avoid the three points. He had my one arm as I was flying through the air, and I was trying to get the other arm out in front of me, but I couldn't. So I'm vertical and I put my face up, trying to block the move with my face, still hoping to avoid the back points. I should have just ducked my head and surrendered the points, but I was too stubborn. And, man, was that a bad decision.

Not that I had much time to consider the possibilities. The whole move took only a second or two. *Boom,* I slammed onto the mat right on my head. I felt everything crack, crunch, and pull in my neck. And the force of the throw still carried me onto my back, so almost immediately I also heard the ref say "Three," and that sickened me more than the sound effects my neck was making. That quickly, I was behind by three points in the semifinals of the nationals and basically I had just broken my neck. I would find out later that I had bulged and herniated two disks, cracked two vertebrae, and pulled four muscles in my neck. At the time I only knew that I was in excruciating pain, and to make it worse I might have blown my shot at the Olympics. I called for an injury time-out because I couldn't move my neck. It was killing me. I stood up and looked over at my brother Mark, who was coaching me, and he isn't the sympathetic type.

"Get your ass back in there and get those points back," he said.

I had wrestled in pain before, disregarding doctors' warnings when I sprained my knee two different times in college. But this was something entirely different. I went back to the mat and I couldn't do much of anything. Every time I tried to make a move the pain in my neck was too severe. But I kept wrestling. Finally, there was about a minute left in the match and I was saying to myself, "You've gotta score."

So I shot in and got one of his legs. I'm hanging on as he's trying to push me off. About thirty seconds went by and finally I was able to get around his waist and control him from the back for a point. But now I had to turn him or I lose. I'm working and I'm working, and I finally got him in a gut wrench and turned him to expose his back to the mat for two points. So it was 3–3 and I let him up so I could go for a last-second takedown. There were only fifteen seconds left and my neck was throbbing. But I hit a quick duck-in and got behind him—my trademark move. I took him down right at the buzzer, and I won 4–3.

I still don't know how I did it, the pain was that bad. Afterward the doctor on hand for the match checked me out and said he thought there might be some permanent damage to the disks. I had about six hours before the finals later that night, so I went to a chiropractor, and then an acupuncturist, who was soon sticking needles in my head and neck, trying to make the swelling go down and give me a chance to wrestle in the finals. Nothing really helped and I was seriously thinking about defaulting, just taking my chances at the Olympic trials. But it's such a huge advantage to win the nationals and avoid the mini-tournament at the trials. Even if I finished second in the nationals I knew I would have to wrestle all these guys again, and they were all talented enough to win the trials. So I decided I had to at least give it a shot in the finals.

I was wrestling Kerry McCoy, this young stud just out of college who was a great technician as a college heavyweight. He was quick and agile and strong. He was six five, 240 pounds, but he cut 20 pounds for this tournament to wrestle in my 220 weight class. Once he made weight, the day before the tournament, he put the 20 pounds back on by the finals, so he was at 240, and I was at about 209. Before the match I had second thoughts. I told my brother my neck was killing me.

"Just go out and try," he said.

So I did. But all I could do was wrestle defensively, trying to hold off McCoy. He'd make a move and I'd underhook him, jack him up, and push him around the mat. Basically I just tried to outposition him the whole match because I knew I couldn't score on him. My neck was hurting that badly. Neither one of us scored a point during the five-minute match or the three-minute overtime. So it came down to a referees' decision. He had more stalling calls, because I was pushing him around, and so they awarded me the national title, but it was that close. To hold that guy scoreless in my condition—it still seems kind of unbelievable.

I must have a higher tolerance for pain than other people because I've always been able to overcome injuries and wrestle when doctors told me I shouldn't or couldn't. The only time in my life when I did absolutely nothing but rest was during my freshman year in high school, when I got a real scare with a strep infection that could have destroyed my athletic career. I was diagnosed with this infection after my buddies and I did a stupid thing. One night after a spring football game we went over to my buddy's house, and we all went swimming in his pool. The only problem was, it was thirty-five degrees outside. Within a few days I was feeling extremely tired all the time, and I was even passing out from time to time for no apparent reason. I had all sorts of CAT scans and blood tests done; my white blood cell count dropped very low and eventually the strep infection was diagnosed. When my condition wasn't improving after a couple of months, doctors told me it could lead to rheumatic fever and keep me from playing sports ever again.

So I wound up taking four months off after wrestling season my freshman year. I had to rest to give my body a chance to heal, so I didn't play baseball that spring. It was a very difficult time, sitting around doing nothing and worrying about whether I was going to get better. Doctors were telling me I might not be able to go back to football in the fall, and that in the worst-case scenario the infection could even be fatal. I think I was too young to comprehend the possibility of dying; all I was worried about was returning to sports, and when I felt better after the four months off, I started training for football again. The doctors were against me going back so soon, but I felt strong again and my family knew how much playing sports meant to me. So I came back and proved the doctors wrong by staying healthy. From then on, I've always felt, as a well-conditioned athlete, that I could push my body beyond what doctors recommended for me, and it became a pattern throughout my career in dealing with any type of physical setbacks.

When I won my very first national wrestling title, at the junior nationals the summer after my senior year in high school, I tore three ligaments in my ankle in the match before the quarterfinals. The ankle swelled so badly that I wanted to withdraw from the tournament because I couldn't even stand on it. But my coaches and my brothers convinced me to get it taped and give it a shot in my next match, and once I limped out onto the mat, it was like a light switch went on. I seemed to have this remarkable power of mind over body. The adrenaline would kick in and somehow the pain wasn't quite so bad. Maybe it's because I was always incredibly focused on winning; years of watching my brothers lose control of their tempers during matches had taught me to keep that focus, no matter the situation, and I've got to believe that overcoming pain was a result of that poise and focus. My brothers always teased me about being too

nice, but my way of proving my toughness was refusing to allow anything to stop me from winning.

I fought through the pain in my ankle to win the junior nationals that year as a heavyweight, and that was a great accomplishment. You had to win eleven matches in that tournament against the best high school wrestlers in the country, and I did it as a heavyweight, beating guys who weighed as much as 295 pounds. But it was also the first leg of the grand slam—junior nationals, NCAA nationals, world championships, and Olympics—I would win, something only four American wrestlers have ever done. And perhaps most important, it was the first of many times I amazed myself by winning big matches when I thought I might not even be able to wrestle.

Still, nothing compares to gutting out a win in the 1996 nationals when my neck was throbbing with pain. The next day I went home and had an MRI done. The results were as bad as I feared: my vertebra was cracked in two places; two disks were sticking directly into my spinal cord; and I had four pulled muscles in my neck as well. The doctor told me I would be at a high risk of paralysis if I didn't rest it completely and allow it to heal. He said, "You're done, son. You're done. There's nothing you can do."

I was devastated. I sat there crying my eyes out in the doctor's office at the hospital. He said I needed six months to heal. I only had two and a half months before the Olympic trials. I had defied the doctors before, but this was my neck, not a knee. Still, I was dumb enough to try. But I couldn't do any wrestling whatsoever because the pain would just bring me to my knees. I was able to do some running and even a little bit of weight lifting, but nothing on the mat. So I went to a second doctor, and then a third. Both of them agreed that I had no chance of wrestling.

Finally, my brother Dave said he had one more doctor he wanted to examine me. I didn't really see the point, but Dave said this doctor knew how much this shot at the Olympics meant to me, and he might be able to help. After I told him how this was my last shot at the Olympics and how it meant the world to me, he said that maybe we could try something. He said I could try getting injections of mepivacaine in my neck before I wrestled, to make my neck numb so I couldn't feel the pain, but he warned that there could be serious side effects. I get chills just thinking about it even now. I ask myself, "What the hell was I thinking?" But I was completely obsessed with making the Olympics, so I agreed to try it. I was getting injections to see if I could do drills in practice, about two weeks before the trials.

The mepivacaine worked. It dulled the pain enough for me to wrestle. My neck still hurt, but nothing like it did without the injections. After two weeks of this, I was at the point where I thought I could wrestle in live competition again. I continued to train and go through strenuous physical training and began to ready myself for the trials. Since I won the Nationals, I did not have to wrestle in the mini-tournament and only had to wrestle a best-of-three series against Dan Chaid, the mini-tournament winner.

At the trials, I decided to scout the mini-tournament, which took place in Spokane, Washington, anyway, and that felt as intense as wrestling in it myself. I watched every match to learn as much as I could about each of the ten wrestlers, and it was nerve-racking, waiting to find out who I would have to beat for that precious spot on the Olympic team. My body was twitching as I sat in the stands, as if I was reacting to every move on the mat. My brothers kept telling me to relax, but I couldn't. I was one step away from realizing my dream, and watching it unfold in front of me made me more nervous than I'd ever been on the mat.

I thought the two favorites to win the mini-tournament were Mark Coleman, a former Ultimate Fighting champion and world silver medalist, and Mark Kerr, a former Pride Fighting champion in Japan and three-time national champion. However, since my weight class was so competitive, both Kerr and Coleman were eliminated early and Chaid surprised the field. There wasn't any doubt that Chaid was the hottest wrestler in the mini-tournament. He pinned a couple of former national champs and then in the finals he handled Kerry McCoy fairly easily, the guy I beat to win the 1996 nationals. At the time I felt I'd have my hands full with Chaid even if I were completely healthy; a year earlier I'd beaten him 1–0 in the semifinals of U.S. Nationals. It was a very, very tight match that could have gone either way. Before that, he'd kicked my ass many a time during practice with the USA wrestling team. He was a powerful guy who tried to intimidate you with sheer brutality, and even tried to hurt you if he had the opportunity, so you know he's a warrior. He wasn't the guy to be wrestling at less than full strength. And the truth was, because of my neck, I had no idea if I could even be competitive against him.

Before the first match with Chaid, I received injections of mepivacaine, since the pain was as persistent and severe as before I left for the trials. And I know that in the big picture, it was stupid. I've always wanted to be a good role model to kids, and I'd never want to see anyone else try what I did. Getting those injections was probably the stupidest thing I could ever do. I truly was risking possible serious injury, but at the time I couldn't give up on my dream. I wasn't going to let anything stop me.

So I went out there and shocked myself by dominating Chaid, beating him 7–0. I didn't feel any pain in my neck, thanks to the mepivacaine, and I felt fresh on the mat because I really hadn't wrestled live in months. It was almost like I had a burst of new energy. But it helped that Chaid seemed more determined to take advantage of my neck than wrestle his normal match.

Everyone at the trials was aware I'd hurt my neck at the nationals. No one knew the extent of the injury, but I had called the USA coach, Bruce Burnett, a few times and pleaded with him to push back the date for my best-of-three series. He said he couldn't change the rules for me, so everyone knew the neck was still a problem for me. And sure enough, the first thing Chaid did was go after my head, trying to pull on it, give me a front headlock, wiggle it, yank it, anything to make it hurt. Thirty seconds into the match I was so mad that I start throwing punches at him and he's throwing them right back.

The referee jumped in and broke it up. "What the hell is going on here?" he asked.

I didn't say anything. The ref warned both of us that he'd penalize or disqualify the guy who started it the next time. I knew what Chaid was trying to do, but I was actually feeling good about it for two reasons. I hadn't felt any pain in my neck, even with him yanking on it, and also, I remember thinking, "This SOB is so worried about my neck, I'm gonna pick him apart."

Within seconds I took him down and turned him for a 3–0 lead. He was never in the match and I took him down left and right. Chaid had been a national champion himself, but I was handling him so easily that about halfway through the match I was thinking I could tech-fall him, which means to get ahead by ten points and end the match automatically. But once I went ahead 7–0, I decided not to take any chances with my neck, so I just wrestled conservatively and held my ground to keep him from scoring. He had given me some easy points by being too aggressive in going after my neck; otherwise I'm sure it would have been a tight match.

But since it was a best-of-three format, I needed to beat him again and I knew he probably wouldn't make the same mistake. We had about six hours before the second match and I knew my neck would stiffen up, so I took more shots. This time the match was tight. Chaid stuck to his normal strategy, but I was able to score a couple of points early and hold him off to win 3–0. Afterward I was in a dazed state of celebration. It didn't seem real, making the

Olympic team with a broken neck, but I'd done it. I'd really done it.

Once again, I wouldn't want any young wrestler to follow my path and take the risks I took. You have to keep sports in perspective. But at the time I felt like it was my whole life. I'm sure it had something to do with wanting to win it for my late father. I used to think that it would have been worth it if something happened and I did get injured, as long as I made it to the Olympics and won the gold medal. I know there's a lot more to life, but for whatever reason, that was my mind-set at the time. I feel fortunate now that nothing did happen to me. As it is, I know it could still catch up with me. I went to get an MRI on my neck just last year, because I still get a lot of stiffness there, and the doctor said, "Your neck looks like it's eighty years old." He said there was no fluid around it as there should be, that the bones were pushed together, and that I better be careful as I get older.

But anyway, I was on my way to Atlanta. Finally, I had some time to let my neck heal. I took five or six weeks off before I went to Olympic training camp in Chattanooga, Tennessee. I still had about a month to prepare for the Games. The cracks in my neck healed by then, but I still had a lot of pain and stiffness. By the time I reached Atlanta, it still bothered me some, but not enough to affect me on the mat.

As the defending world champion, I should have been the favorite to win the gold. But in the eyes of the rest of the world, I had come out of nowhere to win the world title in 1995, and people were skeptical about whether I was good enough to do it again.

It was my first Olympics, and there were a handful of guys in my weight class who had previous Olympic experience, including a few who had medaled and one previous Olympic champion.

I was excited about going to the Games, but it wasn't until I lined up for the opening ceremonies that the feeling of being an Olympian really grabbed me. All the athletes from around the world were lined up in the old baseball stadium in Atlanta, waiting to march across the street into the new Olympic stadium, which was filled with 100,000 people, while another 3 billion people worldwide were watching on TV. I was looking around at people like Michael Johnson and Shaquille O'Neal, and I was thinking, "Wow, here I am with the best athletes in the world, some of the best athletes in U.S. history." And knowing the world was watching on TV, it was just a wonderful feeling. I think every Olympian would tell you that aside from winning a medal, the opening ceremonies were the most memorable part. You walk into that stadium, especially in your own country, and they announce the U.S. Olympic team while the fans are roaring in appreciation . . . it was the most memorable experience in my life to that point.

It was also the only time I really was able to relax and have fun during the Olympics. I had worked too hard to get to Atlanta and lose my focus because of the magnitude of the event. But we had a week before the wrestling competition started, so that night I just soaked in the atmosphere and totally enjoyed myself. Meeting all these world-class athletes and just enjoying your Olympic status, it was a feeling that would be awfully hard to match.

As we waited to make our entrance, I happened to be standing next to the Dream Team, Shaquille O'Neal and the other NBA players. Even among all these great athletes, these guys were celebrities. It seemed like every athlete from every country in the world was trying to get over to shake hands with Shaq. I introduced myself and shook hands with him. He seemed pretty cool.

The next day it was back to work. The American wrestling team flew back to the Olympic training center in Chattanooga and worked for a few days there. Then we went back to Atlanta to stay in the Olympic Village. The only athletes who weren't there were the U.S. gymnasts and the Dream Team. They were staying in a hotel, for security reasons, I guess. But I wouldn't have wanted to miss the atmosphere in the village. Because our sport gets so little media coverage, wrestlers aren't exactly high-profile athletes, but at the Olympics every competitor is made to feel like a star. And our team did have some celebrity starpower in the name of Garth Brooks, who was our honorary team captain. Garth had gone to Oklahoma State, which is perennially one of the top wrestling programs in the country, and he's a big wrestling fan. He donated money to USA Wrestling to help the Olympic cause, and posed with a few of us for a poster that was sold nationally to raise money as well. He does a lot to help promote amateur wrestling, and I became good friends with him in Atlanta, which was just one more cool thing about the whole experience.

There was only one drawback to being in the Olympic Village: it was hard to relax because it was so crowded. We had eight wrestlers in our apartment. I was sleeping on a bunk in a room the size of a jail cell. It was probably harder on other athletes, though. As a wrestler you learn to adapt, going to tournaments all over the world and sleeping in beds that are a lot smaller and less comfortable than your own. The real hard part was just counting down the days until the wrestling competition began.

Finally, it was time for weigh-ins, the day before the match. That's always an event in itself for the guys who starve and dehydrate themselves to make weight. There were guys who could barely stand that day, they were so weak because they hadn't been eating. One of our guys, who went on to be a medalist, practically passed out after he made weight. The medical people put him on a stretcher and put an IV in his arm to fill him with fluids because he'd throw up when they tried to give him water. That's the brutal side of wrestling that I don't think is good for the sport. I've never cut weight because I don't think it's healthy. All my life I've been into training hard, eating right, and using my natural ability. Some of these guys will do anything to get themselves down to a weight class where they believe their size becomes an advantage.

It worked for the guy. He was tall and rangy and was able to beat smaller, shorter guys in his class. I didn't know how he'd wrestle when I saw him being taken to the hospital after the weigh-in, but his body recovered quickly. They probably put about 10

pounds of fluid in him and then slowly he started to eat. Once you make weight, you can eat anything you want because you're not weighed again during the competition. By the next day the guy looked like a different person. He weighed himself in the locker room and he had gained 23 pounds in twenty-four hours, which tells you how dehydrated his body was at the weigh-in. They really ought to make these guys weigh in the day the competition starts. That would cut down on some of the starving, because if guys didn't have time to regain their strength, they wouldn't go so low.

As for me, I was just the opposite. When I weighed in, I didn't want the other heavyweights to see how light I was. I didn't look light, because I had a thick build, but at five feet eleven, I was shorter than most of the guys in the 220-pound weight class. A lot of these guys would do the same thing—they starved themselves to get down to 220 for the weigh-in, then went back up to 230, 240 the next day. I only weighed 211, and I had eaten a huge meal right beforehand to try to bulk up. They announce your name and weight, so everybody knows. When I turned around to step off the scale, I saw a couple of the Russian wrestlers with smiles on their faces. I'm sure they were thinking they were going to throw me around on the mat the next day.

After you're weighed, you pull a number from a barrel to determine your spot in the brackets. The various Olympic trials and qualifying tournaments throughout the world produce thirty-two wrestlers for the Olympics, and there is no seeding. It's luck of the draw, so the top two guys in the world could wind up wrestling each other in the first round.

I was the defending world champion, but I knew that a bunch of these other guys were good enough to win, and I was hoping I wouldn't draw a real tough opening match because it always seemed like I never wrestled my best in the first round. I wound up getting a pretty good draw. I drew a young Mongolian kid in the first round who I felt I could beat. Best of all, the one guy I didn't want to face in the first round, Larry Khebalov, a seven-time world champion and former Olympic champion who had come out of retirement after two years off, was on the other side of the bracket sheet. I wouldn't meet him until the finals. The guy I feared most on my side of the bracket was Arawat Sabejew, the 1994 world champion defector who now wrestles for Germany and who dominated the 220-pound weight class for two years until I beat him in the finals in '95 to become world champion.

Finally, it was time to wrestle, and I was so pumped that I had to throttle back emotionally before my first match. I didn't want to be too aggressive and make mistakes. I had a plan to wrestle conservatively, use my positioning, and wear down my opponents. It worked, but not without some nervous moments. I had three matches the first day, and every one was frighteningly close. I won my first two matches in overtime, first against the Mongolian and then against a Cuban who was six feet eight inches tall. Then I needed the comeback of my life to survive my third match.

I fell behind 3–0 early in that one against a wrestler from Russia named Sahid Murtazaliyev, and that was big trouble. When you're down 3–0 in freestyle, usually you're going to start making mistakes because you've got to try to score. The Russians are very good at taking advantage of mistakes, and that's where they're going to make it 4–0, 5–0, 6–0. It was exactly the reason my game plan was to wrestle cautiously. But this guy surprised me. When I first tied up with him, I went to dig an underhook underneath his arm. He knew I was going to do it; he must have been watching films on me, because he was waiting. He dropped his head under my armpit real quick, and— *boom!*—he hit me with a fireman's carry, and I landed right on my back. As I bellied out to my stomach, I looked up and saw the ref holding up three points and I said, "Oooh, shit."

My first thought was that I'd just blown the Olympics, because this guy was a Russian, and nobody comes back from 3–0 against a Russian. But I didn't panic. He couldn't turn me on my back, so they let us both back up. I felt sure I could get this guy, but I had to be patient and wait for an opening. Two minutes later I shot in and hit a really slick low single-leg takedown on him. He fought like hell for at least forty seconds. He fought it and fought it and fought it, and really made me earn that point. By the time I finally took him down, we fell out-of-bounds, but the ref said I was in control and gave me a point.

Because I took him down out-of-bounds, I had the option of starting from a standing position, or the referee's position with me positioned on top of him. I opted for the referee's position so that I could try to turn him on his back. I knew I had to turn him right there, because there was only a minute and a half left. It's funny, because throughout my career I was always at my best on my feet. My greatest asset was my quickness, my ability to shoot for a takedown and surprise even the best wrestlers in the world with my speed.

That's basically how I stunned the wrestling world and won the world tournament in 1995. I remember thinking how great I was after that win, only to have my world team coach, Bruce Burnett, sit me down afterward and bring me back to earth. At the time he told me that I had better learn how to turn someone and not just rely on my takedown ability so much. I remember him saying, "You're not going to win the Olympics just by taking people down. You're not gonna win a referees' decision that way. Some of these guys are going to get ahead of you next year; you're going to have to turn them to win."

I listened to him, and that's what I worked on for the next year, all year long. It paid off in a big way, too. At that '95 world tournament I had a total of six takedowns, but I didn't turn anybody to get back points. Two guys took me down, but nobody turned me, either. Then, at the Olympics, I had five takedowns, and five turns in my five matches. Without the turns I wouldn't have won the gold, so Bruce couldn't have been more right.

And this was the match where his advice paid off the most. I worked and worked and finally I got Murtazaliyev with a gut wrench. I locked my arms around his lower hips, then I faked one way and went the other way and put him on his back. The ref gave me the two points to tie the match 3–3, and when I looked up at the Russian, he put his hands on his face like "I blew it." Basically he was telling everybody he'd made a crucial mistake, and I said to myself, "I've got him. Whether it's in regulation or overtime, I've got him."

Anytime I got this deep into a match with the score at least tied, I felt like I had a huge edge because of all that insane conditioning I'd done for two years. So we both got up, and I started attacking him because I knew he was tired. I wasn't really taking full shots at his legs. More like half shots, just enough to make him react and have to work to keep me off him. Finally, time was about up in regulation, and I could see in his face that he was panicking. He didn't want to go into overtime because he was exhausted. So I knew he was going to take a shot at me, and when he did I was ready. He shot in, bellied out, and I spun in behind him right when time ran out. I got the point to go ahead 4–3, and the match was over, just like that.

Afterward I was really proud of myself because I never panicked when I had fallen behind. I stuck to my strategy. I knew I could wear him down, and that really ignited my whole tournament. It was the first time I ever came back to beat a Russian after falling behind. That's when I knew I was on. The guy I beat, Murtazaliyev, was having an impressive tournament. He had beaten Sabejew, the guy I beat in the '95 world finals. I watched that match and Murtazaliyev fell behind 5–0 against Sabejew, and it looked like an easy win for Sabejew. But Murtazaliyev reversed him and leg-laced him about seven times in the space of thirty seconds. He locked up Sabejew's legs and kept turning him over on his back, getting two points each time. That quickly, he was ahead 15–5 and the match was over by tech-fall—a margin of ten points ends the match. It was a shocking turnaround, but as dangerous as Murtazaliyev looked with that leg lace, I felt I caught a break by escaping a meeting with Sabejew. I know I could have beaten Sabejew, and after '95 he probably knew it, too. But his experience made him a dangerous opponent.

So I wrestled three matches that first day, and I felt I was getting more comfortable with every match. I was into the semifinals, which were held the next day. I had to wrestle a guy who looked like Homer Simpson, a Russian named Konstantin Aleksandrov who was wrestling for Kirghizstan. To look at this guy, you'd never believe he was a world-class wrestler. He was bald, short, and fat. But the first time I ever wrestled him, in a tournament in Italy, he beat the hell out of me. When I came home from the tournament, I had pictures and I showed them to everybody. When my brothers saw pictures of Aleksandrov they laughed at me for a week. They wanted to know how the hell I lost to Homer Simpson.

But the guy was deceptively quick on his feet. He might have been the quickest guy I ever faced. He was having a great tournament, too, but I handled him pretty easily. He made a couple of mistakes at the beginning that I capitalized on. He hit me with an arm throw and knocked me on my ass. But here's where my quickness and instincts paid off. When he went to jump on me, my reaction was to turn to my stomach and kick in a circle. I surprised him with my quickness, and as he was lunging for me, I was able to spin behind him and take him down. From there I was able to turn him on his back for two more points, so I was leading 3–0, and I controlled the match from there to win 4–1. He got tired in the last couple of minutes, and didn't really attack me with any force, so it was an easy win for me—the only easy match I had during the Olympics. Everything just clicked for me, but there was one problem: I popped my hip flexor during the match.

It happened when I took back-to-back shots trying to get a takedown. On the second one, I went to come up from the shot, and my hip popped. It didn't bother me much during the match because I never gave it a chance to stiffen up, but afterward, in the hours before the finals, it got tighter and tighter. I was concerned because Jadidi has a hell of a leg lace. A leg lace means that you pull your opponent's knees together, straighten his body out flat on the mat, put your shoulder in his butt, and straighten his legs out underneath you. You go under one leg, over another, and end up in a leg lace where you hook the legs together, then turn him over on his back for points. The defense for the move is to bring your knees to your chest when he tries it. Whenever I tried, I couldn't do it because my hip and groin area was so sore. So I knew if this guy got me in a leg lace, I wouldn't be able to lift my knee up.

I had about six hours before the finals to try and

do something about it. The trainers there alternated ice and heat packs for a couple of hours, but there is not a lot you can do for an injury like that. It was one more thing I was going to have to overcome, but by this point I felt that nothing could stop me. The way I saw it, a hip flexor was nothing compared to a broken neck. And that was the mentality I took into the finals.

9

GOOD AS GOLD

I was warming up for the gold medal match, and instead of focusing on how I was going to beat Abbas Jadidi, I found myself reminiscing about my own career. I knew this was my last match, win or lose, and the finality of it hit me hard. I was out on the warm-up mat, warming up with the other wrestlers, and suddenly I got a little panicked, with tears in my eyes right there in front of all these other guys. I think I was reflecting back on my childhood, how my fear used to overcome me. I started breathing quickly, almost hyperventilating. My coach, Bruce Burnett, came over to me and said, "What the hell is wrong with you?"

I told him that after all the work I'd done my whole life to get to this gold medal match, I didn't want to go out there and blow it. I couldn't even look at him, but Bruce slapped me in the face and made me look him in the eye.

"Let me ask you something," he said. "Did you cry at the U.S. Nationals?"

"No."

"Did you cry at the Olympic trials?"

"No."

"Did you cry before any of your other matches in the Olympics?"

"No."

"Well, don't start now," he said. "Do the exact same thing you did in these other matches. Don't think of it as a gold medal match. Just go out there and treat it like every other match you've had. Do what you did these other matches because, Kurt, you're the best."

I'd heard people say that before, but no one had ever really told me that right before I went out to wrestle. And it got through to me. He didn't really say anything out of the ordinary to me. It was the kind of speech you hear from every coach, but the timing of it was perfect. I realized he was right: just do your best. I quit crying, and it was like a big weight fell off of me.

I knew I might have to wrestle the match of my life to beat Jadidi, especially after he had dominated Larry Khebalov, the six-time world champion, in the semifinals. Jadidi seemed to be on a mission; he had been suspended from international competition for two years because he tested positive for a banned substance, and I'm sure he was out to prove something to people once he was reinstated. At twenty-seven years old, he was the same age as me, and he was at his peak physically. He was difficult to wrestle because he was tall and rangy, with long arms and legs, and I knew that I had to be very careful not to be too aggressive and give him opportunities to use his leverage against me.

But after I settled down emotionally I knew I'd be

all right. I had stuck to my conservative game plan for all of my matches, even when I fell behind 3–0 in the third round against Murtazaliyev. So I thought Jadidi and I would have a close match. He might have beaten Khebalov 8–1, but nobody ever scored a lot of points against me, because of my positioning and my quickness. And that's how the match went. I was able to handle his strength with my quickness and my instincts, and we pushed and pulled at each other for eight minutes. Neither one of us was giving an inch.

The score was 0–0 about three minutes into the match, and this SOB goes for a leg lace, the move I feared because of the injury to my hip flexor. I couldn't block it. I had to let him get me in a leg lace, then fight it so I wouldn't get turned. I fought it with my legs instead of my hip flexor and he ended up turning me once. He received a point because I went hand-to-hand instead of over my back. If you turn across your back, post your hands out, instead of rolling across your back or your elbows, it only costs you one point instead of two. When I rolled I said, "Oh, shit, I just gave him a point," and the SOB went for it again. On the second one, I blocked it purely on guts. I used every bit of strength I had. I almost blew my knees out because my legs were straight and he was twisting my ankles. My hip flexor was on fire, but I was able to hold him off the second time, and that was crucial. He led 1–0, but I was able to take him down in the last minute to put the match into overtime at 1–1.

In the overtime I was trying to hang on, because I

had only one passivity call against me, and Jadidi had two. Passivity is the formal term for stalling, when they decide a wrestler isn't making any attempt to initiate action. If the overtime ends tied, the first tiebreaker goes to the wrestler with fewer passivity calls. So I was trying to keep him locked up, not give him any openings, but then I got called for stalling with about a minute left in overtime.

Now I had to make a move. I didn't want to wind up tied and leave the decision for the gold medal up to three referees. With about forty-five seconds left in overtime, a voice inside of me was saying, "You're gonna lose this match if you don't do something now." It sounds corny, but I swear it was like I heard my dad's voice in my head, telling me to make my move. I had waited the whole match for a chance to use my favorite move—a misdirection low single-leg takedown. He hadn't given me an opening, so I hadn't tried it because I was worried that if I missed he could spin on me for his own takedown. But now I had to try it.

What I did was circle to my left, making him think I was going to attack his right leg. When I was ready to shoot, I took a hard step toward it like I was going for it. He pulled that leg back, and just as he did that, I crossed over and shot for his left leg. And I got the leg. I pulled it in and knocked his hip to the mat and I covered both of his legs. So I had him. One ref gave me a point, but the other two said no because I still had my head caught between his legs. Most referees won't give you the point until you get your head on his right or left hip to score.

He was pushing down on my head, trying to fight me off, and I was trying to get my head out from between his legs when time ran out, and I didn't get the point.

But I've gotta believe that final move left an impression with the referees, or at least the two out of three who voted me the winner. And so, after that long, agonizing wait in the middle of the ring over the next couple of minutes, I was awarded the gold medal via the referees' decision, and my tearful celebration seemed to last for hours.

Jadidi's bitter reaction to the decision bothered some people, especially some of the 300 friends and family members who had traveled from Pittsburgh to root for me, but I didn't let it bother me. I had no doubt that I deserved the gold medal; nobody had worked harder than me during the previous two years, and I was going to enjoy it. I felt good that I was able to win it while representing the Dave Schultz Club, too.

Throughout the Olympics our wrestling team, and the wrestling competition overall, received more coverage than usual because of Dave's murder. The national media suddenly found wrestling interesting, but only because of the sensational nature of John du Pont's killing of Dave Schultz.

As much as wrestlers were always starved for attention, the media blitz caused some hard feelings because some of the wrestlers got tired after a while of answering questions about the situation. I didn't mind because I was always willing to talk about Dave, but some guys found it distracting. The media

was also reporting that there was a split on the U.S. team because a few of the wrestlers had stayed with du Pont's Foxcatcher club after the incident.

I didn't really see it as an issue within the team. Some guys may have felt they didn't have a choice because they needed the money to continue their training. I never could have lived with myself if I had done that, but I didn't feel it was my place to tell anyone else what to do. If other people felt more strongly about it, I never heard about it while we were in Atlanta. I think everybody was too wrapped up in their own preparation to worry about what other guys were doing.

But anyway, more media coverage meant more attention for me when I won the gold medal. I never answered so many questions in my life as I did that day. Finally, after I posed for all the pictures and the press conference ended, I took my gold medal off and put it around my mom's neck. I wanted her to have it for everything she'd done for me. As much as I've always credited my dad and my brothers and sister for being an inspiration in wrestling, my mom did more for me than anyone throughout my life.

I felt bad for my mom at times in my life because she had gone through a lot of heartache. She wasn't happy with her marriage, and there always seemed to be some kind of crisis in the house either with my sister or one of my brothers. After my dad died I became closer than ever to my mom. Eventually everyone else was out of the house, and I felt a responsibility to be there for her. She was the main reason I had wanted to stay close to home when I went to college. By the time I graduated college, she had sold our old house and moved into a condominium, so I moved in with her. I couldn't afford a place of my own anyway, because I was training full-time for the Olympics. She made life easy for me when I needed it by cooking for me, doing my laundry, and acting as my personal secretary—helping me in a million ways. It was nice because we were like a team, going for the Olympics, and she felt like she was a big part of it—and she was. That was the hardest part after the Olympics was over: I didn't need her doing everything for me anymore, and I think she missed it. We both cried when I finally moved out, but I knew I had to get on with my life.

Eventually I entered my relationship with my wife, and my mother became secondary. But she adjusted to it and she's still there for me. It was nice that she could play a role in helping me win that gold medal. In one way or another, everyone in my family did. When I gave her the gold medal, that was my way of saying thanks. She always kids me because I had to ask her for it back the next day to wear during my TV appearances, and I always seem to need it for one reason or another. But I know it meant a lot to her that I gave it to her to wear right after I won it. It was a proud moment for my whole family.

We celebrated together when we went back to the hotel, and for me the party just kept going. I even got drunk for one of the few times in my life. All

my high school buddies were there and they felt it was their duty to take me out and give me a celebration night. So I was drinking and drinking, celebrating old times, and all of a sudden it's morning and I had to go on the *Today* show with Bryant Gumbel. NBC was televising the Olympics, so they were doing the *Today* show from there. It was exciting, going on national TV to do an interview, but I don't remember much about it after being up drinking all night.

From there, the whirlwind began. I called it the Kurt Angle Appreciation Tour. I was everywhere, doing everything, and I slept exactly one hour in four days. It all seems like such a blur now. I did a bunch more interviews that morning in Atlanta. I was running around, going from place to place for TV appearances, and I walked past a newspaper stand. I happened to look at the *USA Today* being displayed, and I was shocked to see my picture on the front of the paper.

"Hey," I said, "that's me." There were people all around and they started asking me for my autograph. That's when it started to hit me: I was famous. Or at least as famous as an amateur wrestler is ever going to get.

I was supposed to stay in Atlanta for the rest of the Olympics, but everything changed after I won the gold medal. The Rooney family, who own the Steelers, flew me back to Pittsburgh that day because they wanted to honor me at halftime of their preseason game at Three Rivers Stadium that night.

So I caught a flight back to Pittsburgh and it was kind of crazy because everybody on the plane knew who I was. I was passing my gold medal around for 200 people to look at and touch, and everybody wanted to talk to me about my experience.

The Rooneys arranged to have a limo pick me up at the airport. They're from Mount Lebanon, and some of their kids grew up with me, so they were always big fans of mine. But before I went to the game, somebody from Jimmy Buffett's band had set it up for me to play at his concert that night, too. I knew how to play the drums, so the limo took me to the concert at the Coca-Cola Amphitheater and I played drums for three songs. Then I was driven to Three Rivers Stadium, where the Steelers made a presentation to me at halftime of their game against the St.

Your American hero making his entrance at* RAW IS WAR *on April 16, 2001.

In Atlanta, Georgia, at Centennial Park soaking up the memories of the 1996 Olympics, where I won my gold medal.

★ ★ ★ ★ ★ ★ ★ ★ ★ ★ ★ ★

LEFT: *I married Karen on December 18, 1998, just after signing on with the WWE.*

BELOW: *Congressman Christopher Shays and his wife, Betsi Shays, along with me, Karen, and Linda McMahon at the 2001 presidential inauguration.*

OPPOSITE: *On location in New York during my 1-800-CALL-ATT commercial, which I filmed right before* WrestleMania *X-Seven.*

★ ★ ★ ★ ★ ★ ★ ★ ★

Slamming Chris Benoit to the canvas at WrestleMania *2000, my first* WrestleMania.

★ ★ ★ ★ ★ ★ ★ ★

ABOVE: *Your American hero trying to talk some sense into "Fat Bastard" (Paul Wight—The Big Show) on* SmackDown! *2000.*

RIGHT: *Applying the ankle lock and breaking Scotty 2 Hotty's ankle during a* RAW IS WAR *episode. Scotty would miss ten weeks of shows due to the injury.*

★ ★

After suffering a concussion during a match at SummerSlam against The Rock and Triple H, I cracked Triple H over the head with a sledgehammer and valiantly carried off his wife, Stephanie McMahon-Helmsley, to a destination unknown.

★ ★ ★ ★ ★ ★ ★ ★ ★ ★

Your American hero with a picture-perfect German suplex to foe Chris Jericho, aka Y2J.

★ ★ ★ ★ ★ ★ ★ ★ ★ ★ ★ ★ ★ ★

Your WWE Undisputed Champion making All-American Apple Pie on Live with Regis on October 25, 2000.

★ ★ ★ ★ ★ ★ ★

After soiling the Undertaker's motorcycle with milk, your American hero offers "the Dead Man" a sleek motor scooter as a peace offering. The Undertaker refuses with anger and swears vengeance.

★ ★ ★ ★ ★ ★ ★ ★ ★ ★

Louis Rams. They brought me out onto the field, and sixty thousand fans gave me a standing ovation. I had chills.

It was during that ride in the limo to the stadium that I put my head back and fell asleep for an hour—the first time I'd slept since the night before the gold medal match. From there I was up all night again, celebrating at home with friends and family, and the next day I was given two parades, one by the city of Pittsburgh and another one in my town of Mount Lebanon. It was nonstop for four days. I was riding the Olympic wave and loving every minute of it. As an amateur wrestler, you get used to being kind of anonymous, no matter how good you are. It's a sport America only pays attention to at the Olympics. Now I was a celebrity and I couldn't get enough. I guess that's why I refused to go to sleep for those few days; I wanted to soak in every possible second of that experience.

I flew back to Atlanta to be part of the closing ceremonies, and from there the Olympic committee flew the gold medalists first-class to Washington, D.C., to meet President Clinton. It was pretty cool, sitting there in the plane with some of the other gold medalists. Dan O'Brien sat in the row across from me. Michael Johnson was right in front of me. The female gymnasts like Kerri Strug and Dominique Dawes were there, too. When we arrived at the White House, they took us on a tour and then each one of us shook hands with the president. I was surprised because Bill Clinton knew each of our names. I walked up to him and he said, "Hey, Kurt Angle, great match, I really enjoyed it. You won the gold for our country."

Now, I don't know if he really watched my match or he had people telling him who everybody was. Either way, I respected him for making us feel like big shots. He made it a very personal moment for each one of us. I remember thinking, "Oh my God, he knows who I am."

After about a week of all this attention my head was spinning. It was more than I had ever imagined and I was enjoying every minute of it for days. But finally, about a week after I won the gold medal, I remember waking up one morning thinking a scary thought: "What the hell am I going to do with the rest of my life?"

My victory had made all the hours of training, all the years of sacrifice and dedication, worthwhile. But at the same time I knew I couldn't do it all over again in another four years. No way. My neck was still an issue, and I was completely burned out physically and mentally. I was done as an amateur wrestler. I was going out on top, and that's the way I wanted it. But I didn't know what I was going to do next. There was no million-dollar contract waiting for me at the next level, as there would have been if I had played football or basketball or baseball or hockey.

Or at least that's what I thought.

Actually, I did get a very lucrative offer within a few days from Vince McMahon and his wife, Linda, inviting me to join World Wrestling Entertainment. They'd seen me capture the hearts of America in the

Olympics and figured it would be quite a catch to land a gold medalist. My first reaction was to laugh at the idea because all my life I'd been told never to watch pro wrestling. It was garbage, everyone told me, and that was the unanimous feeling of anyone involved in amateur wrestling.

So, deep down, I knew I'd never accept their offer, but I have to admit, the money got my attention. I hated to waste their time, but I was curious, so I accepted their invitation for a tour of their facilities in Stamford, Connecticut. I was going to be in New York anyway because I was booked to appear with Regis Philbin and Kathie Lee Gifford on their morning TV show. That was a lot of fun. Regis put on a wrestling singlet and got on the mat with me so I could throw him around a little. He had the skinniest, whitest legs I'd ever seen, and he looked hilarious in that singlet.

When he came out I said, "I just want to know one thing, Regis: where's your microphone?"

He laughed and said, "You don't want to know, Angle."

When the show was over I got in a limo World Wrestling Entertainment provided and rode up I-95 to Stamford. I was impressed with the facility and I was impressed with the McMahons' presentation. As I left I said I'd have to think about it, but at the time there was a better chance that I'd join the circus. That's how strongly amateur wrestlers feel about the world of pro wrestling.

A lot of that feeling goes back to the days when pro wrestling tried to convince the public that it was giving the fans true competition. I think attitudes have changed in the last several years since Vince McMahon declared the World Wrestling Entertainment to be sports entertainment. The idea is to put on a spectacular show with scripted matches. Now I think people watch it just like they watch their other favorite TV shows, whether it's *NYPD Blue* or *Friends*.

But as I was growing up, there was tremendous resentment toward pro wrestling. You have to understand, the world of amateur wrestling gets almost no exposure. No media attention. And it's such a physically and mentally demanding sport that the people involved feel it deserves better. They become completely consumed by their sport and they develop a bitterness toward anything that diminishes their accomplishments. So they feel like they take a backseat to pro wrestling. As an amateur wrestler, you punish yourself every day to train and practice, and it would make you crazy when someone would say, "Oh, you're one of those rasslers on TV." You'd say, "No, I'm an Olympic wrestler, you idiot."

That feeling was ingrained so deeply in me at the time, right after the Olympics, that I couldn't imagine joining World Wrestling Entertainment. I had lived and breathed nothing but amateur wrestling for years. After high school I didn't even watch other sports. I had such tunnel vision that nothing else mattered. I watched *ESPN Sportscenter* at night, but that was about it. I didn't even watch the NFL, and I had always been a huge football fan.

But that's the culture of amateur wrestling; it breeds an us-against-the-world mentality. And at the time I was a symbol for the entire sport because I had won the gold medal and received all of that national publicity. Joining World Wrestling Entertainment at that time was unthinkable to me. When I took the McMahons' contract back to Pittsburgh and showed it to my agent, Ralph Cindrich, who is a well-known sports agent who represents a number of NFL players, he said, "You don't want to do this." And he tore it up right in front of me. I didn't give it much thought at the time. I had never watched World Wrestling Entertainment on TV and I wasn't about to start then.

Besides, I was an Olympic gold medalist. I didn't know exactly what the future held for me, but at the time I was sure there had to be a world of possibilities.

10

FAME IS FLEETING

For about six months my gold medal was an industry all by itself. Everybody wanted to rub elbows with a gold medalist, and they were happy to pay for the opportunity. So I was hustling my ass off, making as much money as I could. I had sponsors, commercial deals, motivational speaking appearances, whatever I could do to make a buck.

Sometimes I had as many as eight or nine appearances or meetings a day. I would start at seven A.M. and go to ten at night. I did a lot of motivational speaking at high schools. I'd hit as many as five schools in one day, driving from one school to the next. Within the first eight months, I spoke at two hundred and sixty schools and I really enjoyed that. I had a message I wanted to get out to kids. I was proof of what you could do if you dedicated yourself and made sacrifices. I told kids they shouldn't be afraid to put in long hours studying, training, whatever they needed to do to follow their dreams. The feedback I got was great, with one exception.

I agreed to speak to the Boy Scouts in Pittsburgh, but a conflict came up and I wasn't going to be able to make it. So the guy in charge asked me to make a tape. I videotaped myself speaking for about twenty minutes, and I sent some autographed photos with the tape. He watched it in his office and thought it was great. Then he rewound it all the way to the beginning, and that turned out to be a problem. I didn't realize it at the time, but when I taped myself I didn't rewind it to the beginning. I just started taping on an old tape that a buddy of mine had used in his video camera. I didn't know he had recorded video of some graffiti in downtown Pittsburgh that wasn't what you'd want six- and seven-year-old kids to see. Let's just say it was sexually graphic. And when they turned the tape on at the Boy Scout function, that's what came on the screen. I heard it took about fifteen seconds before anyone reacted and turned it off. They didn't know what the hell had happened. They never played the rest of the tape. The next thing you know, I was getting letters from angry parents and hearing talk about the Boy Scouts wanting to sue me. Nothing more ever came of it, but the whole thing was kind of embarrassing.

Other than that, I was enjoying everything about celebrity life. I did Jay Leno's show, and that was a big deal. When I went to New York for the Regis and Kathie Lee show, I went on Conan O'Brien's show, too. And I did an appearance at The Wiz with Joe Namath. He's an icon to everybody in western Pennsylvania because he's from Beaver Falls. He knew I was from Pittsburgh and we talked for a while. It was really cool.

But finally, after about six months, my fame started to fade. I wasn't in great demand anymore, so I started thinking seriously about an acting career. I had been taking some acting lessons, and I had made a few trips to Los Angeles. I hosted MTV's *Beach House* with Jenny McCarthy. I got to meet a lot of celebrities out there. I did an appearance at Niketown with Gabrielle Reece and Shaquille O'Neal. I played basketball at Garry Shandling's house. Ben Stiller was there, and I pissed him off quite a few times because I played more like a wrestler. They take their basketball seriously, but eventually I wore them down. I was in such good shape that they wanted to take breaks from me. I was starting to enjoy that L.A. thing, hanging out with celebrities, going to parties with them, going to their houses.

It was all because of Jimmy Miller. He and his brother, Dennis Miller, the comedian, grew up in Pittsburgh with my brothers, and Jimmy is a Hollywood agent. He represents Sandra Bullock, Jim Carrey, the Wayans brothers. He was really good to me. He got me back on the Leno show after they canceled me once. They were mad at the time when they found out I had gone on Conan O'Brien's show already. I didn't understand it, since both shows are on the same network, but they were all pissed off about it. It was the same way with Leno and Letterman. After the Olympics they both wanted me to come on, but they said they wouldn't take me if I went to do the other show first. I decided to do Leno, but I did Conan O'Brien's show first because I was in New York right after the Olympics. Anyway, Jimmy Miller has a lot of pull out in L.A., and he made a phone call and got me back on the show.

Then he arranged all of these meetings with production companies like Paramount and Fox. I was impressed that all these people would take time to meet with me. Jimmy was honest with them. He'd say, "Look, this kid doesn't have a clue as an actor, but he's got a great look. He's got great potential. You might want to consider him as your next action hero."

I was doing fifteen meetings every time I'd go out to L.A. Jimmy wanted me to move out there and I was thinking really hard about it. But then I got a call from some people from Fox-TV. They were launching an affiliate station in Pittsburgh in 1997 and they wanted me to be a weekend sports anchor for them. I was a little skeptical because they didn't ask me if I had any experience, or if I even had a college degree. But they offered me a guaranteed contract. And I knew there was nothing guaranteed about going out to Los Angeles. People were warning me that I could go out there and spend all the money I'd made hustling my ass off in the last six months, while trying to break into acting. So the more I thought about it, the more it made sense to try and get some experience in front of the camera for Fox, and then maybe go out there. I decided to try to establish myself in Pittsburgh first, kind of try to do the Howie Long thing.

Only it was pretty much a disaster. From the start I was nervous about going on TV without any real experience. Obviously, they wanted to take advantage of my status as a local hero to help give them ratings right away, and the people doing the hiring kept telling me, "Don't worry, we know you haven't done any broadcasting. We watched you on all these shows—you're intelligent, you have a lot of poise, you've got a great look. We'll teach you."

So I agreed. But I was still doing appearances at the time, still hustling to make a buck, and I probably didn't push the people at Fox as much as I should have for training. Before I knew it, the station was going on the air in January of '97, and I hadn't gone through any real rehearsal. Still, all I heard was "Don't worry, we'll work with you."

They flew me to the Super Bowl between the Patriots and Packers the first week on the job. There were six guys on the Patriots from the Pittsburgh area, and they wanted me to do a story on the local guys. So there I was, reporting live from New Orleans and I didn't know a damned thing about sportscasting. Those reports from New Orleans were horrible. I was more like a fan than anything: "Yeah, it's great down here. I'm having a good time."

I wasn't even talking about the game. But I got through it, and after the Super Bowl I flew back to Pittsburgh to begin my career as the weekend anchor. The producers gave me a crash course in broadcasting that sounded like a foreign language to me: "Kurt, listen to your news anchors, listen to the guy in your ear. Make sure you're looking from one camera to the other. Make sure you've got your scripts in order. Make sure you're reading the prompter."

I was like, "What?" I was panicking because I knew I'd be clueless. And I was right. The first Saturday night I did it, I would have given myself D– for a grade. I knew it was horrible, but the people there said, "Hey, that wasn't bad."

Then it got worse.

I was back the next night for the Sunday show. As the time for the sports segment approached, I was rushing, getting all my stuff together. I was trying to write my own stories. They had me learning how to take stories off the wire and edit them for TV highlights. But everything was going too fast for me, especially the time. All of a sudden they're calling for me in the studio. I got my scripts together while people were yelling at me to hurry. I ran through the door . . . and right smack into a camera. The scripts went flying out of my hands, and when I scooped them all up, I looked at them, and—oh, no—they were all out of order. Now people were actually pushing me toward the sports desk. One guy was putting a microphone on me while I was trying to get my sport jacket on. I reached the desk, looked into the camera, and the TelePrompTer went out. If I wasn't so panicked I would have sworn there had to be a hidden camera somewhere, and this was all a setup to make me look like an idiot for some celebrity bloopers show.

Unfortunately, it was all too unscripted. So now the guy in my ear was telling me, "Just introduce the first story and we'll get the prompter going."

I knew the first story was supposed to be about Duquesne University's basketball game that day. So I said, "The Duquesne Dukes, uh, they lost today. Let's go to the highlights."

I looked at my scripts and football was on top. So I'm whipping through the scripts, trying to find Duquesne while trying to narrate the highlights at the same time: "And there's a basket for . . ."

I never really watched much basketball, so I had no idea who played for Duquesne. Then, finally, I found the script, but just as the highlights were ending. So the camera came back to me and I said, "And at the Pro Bowl tonight, the AFC beat the NFC. Let's go to the highlights . . ."

And what came up on the screen? Goddamn golf.

By that point my news anchor and weather anchor were trying to help me get my scripts in order, and all you could hear were these papers shuffling while I was going "uh, uh" . . . and I swear it didn't get any better the rest of the segment. It was six minutes of hell, the most horrifying experience I could imagine. After about four minutes we kind of got the scripts together and I finished out the highlights. As I was wrapping it up, the camera showed a full shot of the three of us, and we were all sweating, and breathing heavy, while the scripts were spread all across the table. And I said, "That's the Angle on sports," because that's the tag line they wanted me to use. We went to commercial and I was in a state of shock. It was the most humiliating experience of my life.

Naturally, since it was my first weekend on the air as an anchor, it seemed like everyone in Pittsburgh had been watching. People were nice about it, but I had the feeling they had been laughing out loud watching me that night. And I wouldn't have blamed them. Meanwhile, the people at the studio were apologizing to me the next day. My news producer said it wasn't my fault, and Alby Oxenreite, the head sports anchor, said the TelePrompTer had never gone out on him in his fifteen years in the business.

But it wasn't much consolation. I felt like a failure. I knew that anybody with some experience would have been able to fake his way through the segment, even without scripts. So I started to come in late at night, after the news was over, and read the prompter, do some training. I didn't do as much as I could have, because I was still determined to do my speaking engagements during the day, make as much money as I could before the shine wore off that gold medal. As I look back, it's one of the few times in my life when I didn't dedicate myself to being the best that I could be once I committed to doing something. And that still bothers me.

I guess part of it was that I never felt comfortable at the station. I felt like no one there really cared what I was doing or whether I got better. Management wanted ratings, but I got the feeling that a lot of the people working there resented my presence. When I look back, I don't really blame them. I wouldn't have given me that job. In a way, it was like I was cutting in line, ahead of a lot of people in the business, to get that job, and there were bound to be hard feelings. But at the same time I did help them get good ratings for a while. I don't know if it was because of me or not, but we had higher ratings on weekends than on weekdays. At the beginning I'm sure some people wanted to watch me because they liked me after I won the gold medal and my name carried some weight. But they were probably also saying, "Okay, let's see how this kid screws up." And I did a good job of that. I think it became a comedy show to some people.

But I did get better as I went along. After about three months I was up to a D on my own grading system, and after six months I moved up to maybe a C–. Meanwhile, I took a pounding in the media. Some of the reviews, in newspapers and on radio, just buried me. And these were a lot of the same media people who had loved me as an Olympic athlete.

I remember reading one column about how horrible I was, and how no one's ever seen a sportscaster with a neck bigger than his head. Basically the guy was saying that I have more muscles than brains. Stuff like that. It kind of gave me a complex. I have a twenty-one-inch neck and I used to be pretty self-conscious about it. A lot of it went back to my freshman year at Clarion. Wrestling was big there and I got a lot of attention just for deciding to go there. So I thought I was a hotshot when I got there, but that changed when I went to a party my first week of school. This girl walked up to me and said, "What's your name?"

When I told her, she said, "Oh, you're the new wrestler." And I was thinking it was pretty cool. I was already a big man on campus. But she was just setting me up for a punch line.

"You know what you remind me of?" she said. "A thumb. That's what your head looks like."

And she stuck her thumb up, to show how the middle part of the thumb is bigger than the top. Everybody laughed at the party and started calling me "The Thumb." If I could have made myself disappear, I would have. At the time the incident made me feel terribly insecure about my neck, but I laugh about it now. I'm proud of my neck. It helped me become a great wrestler, and it gives me a certain look that projects strength and athleticism. It's just that seeing a columnist make fun of my neck, as if that had anything to do with being a good sportscaster, reopened some old wounds.

I stuck with it, though, and just when I was starting to feel somewhat comfortable in the studio, the Fox management decided to make me a reporter and put me out in the field, covering events. They thought I'd be upset, but I said, "That's what you should have done in the first place." The thing is, they wanted to cut my salary, too, and that's when I got mad. I said, "You're not cutting even one cent. You're the ones who wanted it this way." And they didn't cut my salary. I had a contract and they couldn't change it.

So I started working as a reporter. I thought I'd like that, going to games, talking to athletes like me. I knew a lot of the pro athletes in Pittsburgh from being on the banquet circuit after the Olympics. Some of them had made a point of telling me how much they admired what I did, things like that. So I figured this was perfect for me.

But I found out pretty quickly that once you cross that line and become part of the media, a lot of pro athletes never look at you in quite the same way. The more I worked, the more I'd go to games, the more I realized that athletes didn't respect me as much. I'd go in after a game sometimes and these guys would treat me like shit. I was just one more guy with a microphone who wanted to ask them why they struck out with the tying run on base, or why they let that receiver get deep for a game-winning touchdown.

It was hard for me. Only a year earlier I was voted the most popular athlete in Pittsburgh in the annual Dapper Dan voting, beating out Mario Lemieux, Steelers running back Jerome Bettis, and Pirates infielder Jeff King, and these guys were telling me how great I was. Every dinner I went to, I'd see some pro athlete who'd shake my hand and say, "Oh, Angle, you're awesome, I love you. I watched you in the Olympics, you're my idol."

Now a lot of these same guys were like, "Angle's just another pain-in-the-ass sports reporter."

After a while I was holding the microphone, thinking that I didn't like this career very much at all. People think it's a glamorous job, covering pro sports. It's a job a lot of people who love sports would love to have themselves, but I found out it's not all that glamorous, especially dealing with the athletes. I understand that it's not easy for guys to answer a lot of

questions after a tough loss, but it's part of being a professional. It's part of the reason they make big money. The fans are basically paying their salaries, and those fans have a right to read and hear what these guys have to say after a game, win or lose.

What hurt the most was the way some of the Steelers treated me. I had gotten to know some of them personally. Guys like Rod Woodson and Levon Kirkland. When I was training for the Olympics, they asked me ten thousand questions about my training. They were big fans, and they made sure to congratulate me after the Olympics. But now some of the same guys were giving me one-word answers when they didn't feel like talking. They knew I was just getting started in the business, and if I were them, I would have been more understanding. I tried to be sympathetic to them after a loss, but it didn't matter.

A guy like Woodson, he seemed like the nicest guy in the world when I was an Olympian. But he wouldn't give me the time of day when I became a sportscaster. When the Steelers wouldn't give him the contract he wanted that year, and he left to sign as a free agent with the Baltimore Ravens, I called him. I left him a message, explaining that I wanted to do a favorable story on how he felt about having to leave Pittsburgh. I wanted him to know I was supporting him. But he never called me back. As a matter of fact, he went to another station and gave them an exclusive interview, and it kind of hurt my feelings. I was trying to help him out and he just screwed me.

Now that I'm in World Wrestling Entertainment, the attitude has turned back around. It's amazing how many pro athletes tell me they watch World Wrestling Entertainment, and what big fans they are. But at the time I hated the feeling that I no longer had the respect of other athletes, and finally I decided I didn't want to do it anymore. So I left the job at Fox and started thinking about acting again.

At the time I also had a guy I was doing some work for in Pittsburgh, a friend named Dave Hawk, who later became my manager. Dave is a former professional bodybuilder who lives in Pittsburgh, and he came to me with an idea to promote a product called Ostrim. It's a beef jerky–like snack that is made from fat-free ostrich meat, not beef. He got me involved endorsing it, and after I gave up the Fox-TV job, it was the only paycheck I was getting for a while.

Dave was also trying to sell World Wrestling Entertainment on the idea of endorsing Ostrim. They didn't think it was the kind of thing their fans would buy, but Dave wound up working a deal with them on a beef stick. It was Dave who put the idea in my head that maybe I should take another look at joining World Wrestling Entertainment. He said he had talked to some of the people there and they would still love to have me.

I still didn't think it was for me. Besides my amateur wrestling bias, I had worked one night as a guest announcer for ECW, which stands for Extreme Championship Wrestling. It was about six months after the Olympics, and I came away from it with even more bad feelings about pro wrestling. Someone from ECW called me and gave me this pitch about how they were a new organization, trying to make pro wrestling more legitimate, and they were hoping I would help give them some credibility.

I thought they meant they were trying to be more like amateur wrestling, so I agreed. Actually, they were trying to sell themselves by being as outrageous and brutal as possible, but I didn't find that out until I showed up in Philadelphia one night to help them out. I worked one match and it was okay, but then they did a story line with Sandman and Raven that really troubled me.

First of all, they had a kid involved in the story, and I didn't think there was a place for that. The kid was only about seven years old, and he was supposed to be Sandman's son, but he had been kidnapped by Raven. In the match, Raven was beating up on Sandman, and then he pulled out a big wooden cross from beneath the ring.

Raven dragged Sandman over to the cross, and tied him to it, like Jesus being crucified. As he did that, the kid was watching the whole scene and cheering, as if Raven had turned Sandman's own son against him.

I thought the whole thing was pretty degrading. I was sitting there at the announcers' table thinking, "What am I doing here?" I was furious, really, because I felt I'd been tricked into being there. So when the match was over I went and found Paul E. Dangerously, who ran the ECW. Fortunately, the show wasn't on live TV. It was being taped to be shown a couple of nights later, so I told Paul E. there was no way in hell I could be part of that match, and I told him if they didn't take me out of it before it aired on TV, he'd be hearing from my lawyer about a lawsuit.

Paul E. swore he didn't know anything about the crucifixion. He said Raven and Sandman had decided to do that on their own, and he apologized. I didn't care. I left the arena right there thinking how badly my image would be damaged if people saw or heard me being part of that match.

Fortunately, Paul E. decided not to even show the match, and I just tried to forget I'd ever agreed to be there. I didn't see Paul E. again until he joined World Wrestling Entertainment as an announcer after Jerry "The King" Lawler resigned. He apologized once more, and again he swore that he had played no part in putting that whole thing together. Paul E. and I have a great relationship now, and we laugh about that experience to this day.

Now that I understand the whole concept of sports entertainment, I can see they were going for some shock value, trying to get people talking about ECW. But I still think that type of scenario was going too far, and at the time it convinced me there was no way I could ever be part of pro wrestling.

But Dave kept working on me, telling me World Wrestling Entertainment was the top organization in the business and I could be a star there. Finally, one night in October of 1998, I turned on *RAW IS WAR*, and nobody was being hung on a crucifix or anything. It was just great entertainment and more athletic than I'd ever realized. I was watching those guys, thinking, "Damn, these guys are good athletes. Why does everyone have a problem with this? I kind of like it."

So I started watching regularly, and after a month I was addicted. I saw how the matches were built around story lines to get people interested in the characters, not just in the matches themselves. The more I watched, the more I felt like I could make the transition and be good at it. For all of the problems I had on TV with Fox, I had some fun as a reporter. I didn't mind making fun of myself for a story. I did some on-camera gags when I was giving out our local Athlete of the Week award, and people thought I was pretty funny. So I knew I had the personality to entertain people and I started thinking I wanted to do that again. At that point it would have been hard for me to go back to coaching wrestling and walk away from the spotlight completely. I had become accustomed to being a celebrity, and I wanted to find a way to continue living that life. So I called World Wrestling Entertainment.

11

JOINING WORLD WRESTLING ENTERTAINMENT

The phone call to World Wrestling Entertainment didn't go exactly as I had hoped. It wasn't like they said, "Kurt who?" but the two years it took me to get back to them had definitely stolen some of my clout. When I got through to talent managers Jim Ross and Bruce Prichard, I tried to sell myself like it was still 1996, but they weren't buying it. They probably had a good laugh when I asked if that contract they had offered me two years earlier was still good. They told me I'd have to try out now and prove I deserved a shot.

"That's fine," I said. "As long as you understand, I'm an Olympic gold medalist. If I join I have to win. I don't lose for anybody."

At that point I'm sure they were rolling their eyes, thinking I was an idiot with a runaway ego. I didn't understand how the World Wrestling Entertainment worked at the time. All I knew was that I was the best wrestler in the world, and I wasn't about to come in and get my ass kicked in the ring.

"Sure, kid, sure," they said. "We'll be in touch."

Two weeks went by and I didn't hear from them. So I called back. They said they were very busy, but I was determined now to get my shot. I told them I really wanted to come up and try out. Finally, they agreed to bring me in for a look. They were having training camps one week a month in Stamford, Connecticut, where they're always looking for new talent. They get as many as two thousand calls a month from guys looking to break into the business. A lot of guys at these camps have been around for years, performing in independent shows around the country, looking for a break to get into the big time.

So I made plans to go to the training camp run by World Wrestling Entertainment talent coaches Tom Prichard and Dory Funk Jr., but as the time to go neared, I wasn't real comfortable about my decision. My manager, Dave Hawk, came with me to Stamford to ease some of the strain and advise me just in case they wanted to sign a deal. I didn't want an agent, but I wanted someone there that I trusted. The World Wrestling Entertainment doesn't like to work with agents and I don't blame them. They like to have a family-oriented business, where both sides work with a certain amount of trust. But I knew that Dave would make sure I was being treated fairly.

We roomed together in Stamford and though the other guys never told me at the time, they thought we were gay. Dave would run errands for me. It's funny as hell to think back on it, because Dave was running around doing everything for me there. He'd make protein shakes. He'd rub down my neck. He was doing my laundry. He just wanted me to feel better about being there because I was pretty uncomfortable about it. At the same time he was trying to work the Ostrim deal with World Wrestling Entertainment. So everybody thought Dave and I were gay, which would have come as quite a shock to my fiancée at the time, Karen, and Dave's wife, Tracey.

Dave didn't stay long, though. Even though everything was new to me—the bumps, the falls—I picked it up so quickly that I blew them away with my try-out. On my second day there, Jim Ross signed me to a five-year deal. I've been told they've never done that with anybody else. I'm sure the gold medal was a factor, but I know they saw a lot of talent in me.

So Dave went home and I went to Boston to be part of an untelevised show on my fourth day there. It's unheard of for someone to be put into a match after only three days in the business, but they let me do it because I picked up on everything so quickly. They couldn't believe how natural I was, not only with the moves but the selling—the way you react when you're taking slams, punches, and kicks. So, on the fourth day that I ever worked in World Wrestling Entertainment, they had me in a match with a kid named Christian, who's now one of the top World Wrestling Entertainment Superstars.

Before the match Christian and I were setting up our moves. I told him I was kind of scared about going out there live.

"I've never done this before," I said. "I don't know what to do."

"Don't worry," he said. "I'll talk to you."

Now, no one had ever said anything to me about talking in the ring. I had no idea what he meant.

"What do you mean you'll talk to me?" I said. "You're not allowed to talk to me. People are going to see you talking to me."

"No, they're not," he said. "Don't worry, you'll know exactly what we're doing the whole time. I'll even tell you a few jokes."

I was so nervous that I was thinking the joke was that I was going out in the ring to perform. I had no idea that these guys talked to each other during their matches.

I didn't understand the concept: the slower the match unfolds, the better it looks, the easier it is for the fans to digest the story of the match. So Christian would be punching me and he'd say, "I'll whip you in the corner, you move and throw a clothesline at me, and I'll duck it. Then I'll clothesline you." Something like that. Or he'd talk to me when he had me in a choke hold. Christian has long hair so he can talk freely and no one outside the ring ever knows it.

That night he was choking me and he said something that I didn't quite hear. As he left I said, "Wait a minute, wait a minute, what'd you say?" He's so experienced that when he heard me, he came back, started choking me again, and repeated the plans for the next move and to make sure I knew what was next before he left to continue the match.

I've had that trouble from time to time in the ring, because I'm basically deaf in my left ear. It's common in amateur wrestling to get what is called a cauliflower ear. Because guys are always grabbing you by the side of the head and tying up with you, or pushing you off when you shoot for a takedown, your ear can swell up. It became a problem for me because of all the years of wrestling. It would swell with fluid and I'd have to get the fluid drained. Finally, after I had it drained about eighty times, I said the hell with it, and I let the fluid harden and fill in my ear canal. I'll get surgery someday, probably when I retire from World Wrestling Entertainment, so I can hear out of it again.

I didn't tell anybody in World Wrestling Entertainment for awhile about my ear. So one night during *RAW IS WAR*, when I started doing TV shows, they had me doing commentary at the announcers' table during another match. I had headphones on and I could hear the director giving me instructions in my right ear. What I didn't know was the headphones are designed so that Vince McMahon could talk to me in my other ear. So during the match he was telling me things I should say about the match, and I didn't hear any of it. I got backstage and he was hot. He said, "Hey, did you hear anything I said to you out there?" And I didn't know what he was talking about.

When he told me he was talking into my left ear, I told him I was deaf in that ear. So now, whenever I do commentary, I have special headphones that I wear, and everything is channeled into my right ear.

The other guys know about it, but it still causes problems sometimes when we need to communicate in the ring. During the "Six-Man Hell in the Cell" match at *Armageddon* last year, when I was the WWE Undisputed Champion, I was choking Rocky outside the ring at one point. He said something to me and I had my left ear toward him. I said, "What?" He said it again and I said, "What?" He did it a third time and I still didn't hear him. Finally, he grabbed my head, turned it to the other side, and he said, "Throw me in the ring, you deaf son of a bitch."

Anyway, with Christian leading me through it, I got through that first match without any major problems. I got some good feedback from people who saw it. Jeff Jarrett, who was a four-time champion in World Championship Wrestling after leaving World Wrestling Entertainment, happened to be there. Afterward he told me he couldn't believe it was my first match. He said it looked like I'd been working for years. So right there I knew I made the right move by joining World Wrestling Entertainment. I just seemed to have a knack for it. After my brother Eric signed with World Wrestling Entertainment last year, he was training in Louisville for two months before he was ready for a match. And that's normal. To be in a match in four days, it just didn't happen.

So in some ways I was a natural, but I wasn't kidding myself. Without Christian telling me what to do, I would have been lost in the ring. I still had a huge transition to make.

In amateur wrestling you're taught to go by instincts that are ingrained in you through years of training and working on technique. When you go out on the mat you have a strategy, but from there, most everything you do is a reaction to your opponent. The faster you move, the better. Something happens— *bing, bang, boom*—you end up on top of your opponent. You're not even sure how you did it, but suddenly you've got the guy in trouble and you're trying to pin him.

World Wrestling Entertainment couldn't be more different. It starts with a thought process, a psychology about how the match will play out. Vince McMahon and the agents who set up the matches decide how the match is going to go, and after that it's mostly up to the two wrestlers to map out a path that will take them to the finish: "How do you want to start? How's the middle going to go? The comeback? The finish?"

You have to include the fans in your planning and you work with your opponent rather than against him. Speed is not an asset. You have to slow down so that people can digest what you're doing. Speed is everything in amateur wrestling; you do something extremely fast and people are impressed because they didn't see it happen. In the WWE it's just the opposite. They want the fans to see everything, including facial expressions. Are you scared? Are you mad? Are you in pain? In amateur wrestling you're taught never to show emotion that might give your opponent a psychological lift.

It was all so new to me. I was so fast at first that people were yelling at me to slow down. After a few days I knew my approach wasn't right. I knew I had to back up, relax, and forget everything I'd ever learned. It was the hardest thing in the world, to forget what I'd been doing for twenty years, go out there and let guys beat you up and throw you around. I had to learn how to get slammed. In amateur wrestling, anytime you get thrown to the mat you try to roll through the move and come up on your feet. In the WWE, you have to learn to get as high in the air as you can, then land flat on your back to create the loudest noise possible. And show the pain.

Once I committed myself to forgetting all my old instincts, I picked up the style quickly. I credit a lot of that to the coaching of Dory Funk Jr. and Tom Prichard, the talent coaches. They were teaching me and I was just listening, soaking it all in. By the third week they were putting me in tryout matches to go on TV. Nobody is supposed to be ready for TV in three weeks, and I don't think I was, but I was good enough that I could let a more experienced guy carry me and we could make it look like a hell of a match.

So I was improving quickly, and getting more and more excited about the WWE. Meanwhile, word was starting to get out back home in Pittsburgh, and the reaction was predictable. Nobody wanted me to go with the WWE, not even the people closest to me. My fiancée, Karen, was worried about the demands it would put on my body, which was still recovering from a variety of injuries I received during my amateur wrestling career. My mom was worried that the move would damage my reputation around town, and my brothers still had the traditional amateur wrestling attitude toward the WWE.

I think it was most difficult on Karen. She took most of the backlash from people at home. There were some letters, even some phone calls, from people upset that I was joining the WWE. They said I was selling out the sport of amateur wrestling. Karen took it personally and she got into a few confronta-

tions trying to make people understand that wrestling was my life—that I was following my heart. She would tell them, "He's the best in the world at something and he ought to be able to use that talent somewhere."

Eventually I think I won everybody over, and that was important to me. My brothers and my sister started watching on TV and they were amazed. They didn't realize how much more athletic pro wrestling had become from what they remembered as kids, watching it on TV on Saturday mornings in the 1960s and 1970s. They began to appreciate the athletic ability the guys showed, and they found themselves becoming interested in the story lines, too. It wasn't long before they were critiquing my World Wrestling Entertainment matches the same way they had done all those years in amateur wrestling. So they came around, and so did my high school and college coaches, George Lamprinakos and Bob Bubb. They were old-school guys, real traditional amateur wrestling guys who each put in thirty years in coaching. I'm sure they didn't like the idea at first, but they both watch me on the WWE all the time now.

Even Bruce Baumgartner has changed his feelings on the subject. Bruce is a legendary figure in amateur wrestling, the most successful American ever in international competition. He was one of the most dominant heavyweights who ever lived. He's a huge guy, about six feet one, 300 pounds. When we wrestled together on the USA team his calves were bigger than my thighs. He's just a mountain of a man, but he had great technique for a big guy, too. He medaled in four straight Olympics—two golds, a silver, and a bronze. When I won the gold in '96, he won the bronze at heavyweight that year at age thirty-six. He lived in Edinboro, Pennsylvania, about an hour away from me, and when I really wanted a workout, I used to go train with him. He was probably the only guy who could beat me day in and day out—he was that big and strong and talented. Once in a while I'd get the best of him, if I was really on, but there were days when he could just blow me off my feet. He was the only guy who could overpower me like that. It was frustrating to train with him because he gave me a lot of beatings. But when I did get the better of him once in a while, I was on top of the world; there are only a handful of wrestlers in the world who have ever beaten Bruce. He taught me a lot about how to wrestle in international competition, how to tone down my aggressive college style to be better in freestyle.

Bruce is a real family-values guy who has a job working for the U.S. Olympic Committee now, and he has the perfect image for that job. He was against me joining World Wrestling Entertainment and he said so. But when he started to watch the shows, he saw I was playing a character. When he criticized at the time I joined, he just assumed that it was still like the old days, when they tried to tell people it was real competition. Once he saw it was sports entertainment, Bruce said he had no problem with what I was doing. He thinks it's good for amateur wrestling, because people know me as a gold medalist and they see me wearing the USA stuff, so in a way I'm promoting our sport on national TV. Amateur wrestling needs that kind of exposure.

I've had a lot of honors come my way for my amateur wrestling career. I was honored in February by my high school, Mount Lebanon, which had a night for me to make me the first member of its Ring of Fame. It was really nice. About 3,000 people showed up. They set up a display case in the school with pictures of my accomplishments in high school, college, and the Olympics. They even named the gym after me. They told me it's not official yet, because they have to pass it through certain channels, but it's going to be called Angle Gym. And that's really an honor. It was an emotional night because it seemed like everyone from my past showed up: my former coaches, former teachers, ex-teammates, and friends. It was great to see all of them there.

I was already in the Clarion Wrestling Hall of Fame, as well as the Southwest Pennsylvania Hall of Fame and the Pennsylvania Hall of Fame. Then, in June, I was inducted into the National Wrestling Hall of Fame. That was a huge honor for me, especially since I was selected the first year I was eligible. You have to be retired from amateur wrestling for five years, the same as it is in baseball. And just like in other sports, there's a long list of guys waiting to get in. Some guys have been waiting years to get in there, and I got voted in on my first try. I knew that I had the credentials: I'm one of only four wrestlers ever to win wrestling's grand slam—the Junior Nationals, the NCAA Championships, the World Championships, and the Olympics. But I was glad to see that the voters from amateur wrestling didn't hold my move to the WWE against me.

It was nice because some of the employees from the WWE office went to the induction ceremony. A lot of them had been amateur wrestlers themselves, or they follow the sport. I know some people involved in amateur wrestling did have hard feelings toward me for a while, but actually, the president of the National Wrestling Hall of Fame, Myron Rodrick, is a big World Wrestling Entertainment fan. He enjoys it and he'd like to see other amateur wrestlers get into it because he understands it's another avenue for wrestling to get exposure.

Still, I know it was a shock at first for people in amateur wrestling to see me cross the line, and the hardest part was that Karen, my wife, had to deal with most of the hard feelings by herself because I wasn't home much. After going one week a month for a few months to the tryout camp, I was sent to Memphis for six months to perform for an independent wrestling organization, Power Pro Wrestling, which is sort of like the minor leagues for World Wrestling Entertainment. Karen and I had only been married for a few months, and this wasn't a great way to start a lifelong relationship.

I had met Karen a few months after the Olympics. She was working in sales for Iron City Beer, and I was making appearances for them after they named me their Iron City Athlete of the Year. It was Karen's job to escort me on some of the appearances, and there were sparks the very first time we were together. It's kind of funny because I was doing an appearance at

Hooters, with all of these waitresses running around in hot pants. Actually, Karen says she thought I was being a snob at first because I was kind of quiet. She's more outgoing and she says it wasn't until she hit on me that I opened up, and from there we got along great. Karen is a beautiful woman, and as we started dating I found out that she's also very caring. But there were always complications in our relationship.

She had an ex-boyfriend, and I had broken off an engagement not long before we met. Neither one of us was sure how serious we wanted to get in another relationship. We lived together for a while, but then we broke up, and each of us got back together briefly with our ex-partners. There was a lot of pain from all of that, but finally we decided we wanted to be together, and we got married on December 19, 1998.

The timing wasn't great for us as a couple, though. I had just gotten involved with World Wrestling Entertainment. At the time neither one of us knew what kind of demands that would put on my time. I was starting my training stint in Memphis, and I couldn't take time off for a honeymoon. Pretty soon I was spending most of my time in Memphis, and I was only getting home for maybe one day a week.

There was a lot of stress, and to make it worse, my family was dealing with a crisis right about then. My cousin, who was very dear to me, got in trouble with a friend and had to go to jail, leaving her one-year-old baby, Maria, at home. Her mother (my aunt) had just gone through a divorce and she was having a tough time with her own life. She didn't feel she could handle the job of caring for a baby at the time, so nobody knew what to do with Maria. That's when Karen volunteered to take care of her until my cousin got out of jail. I told her it was the nicest thing anyone could do for my family, but I didn't know if it was a good idea. I knew it would be difficult on everyone. I knew there were bound to be some hard feelings, with a young mother in jail, hearing about someone else taking care of her baby. But I agreed to let her try it. Then there was another factor, too. The baby was half-white, half-black. She's a gorgeous little girl. The racial part of it didn't matter to me at all. I'm not a prejudiced person and neither is my wife. But people can be cruel. People look at you funny. A lot of people know that Karen is married to me, and here she was, being seen in public with this baby who everyone knew wasn't mine. People, both white and black, would give her ignorant looks, and Karen was affected by it. Then again, sometimes she'd just tell them to stick it.

But the real hard part was the problem the situation caused between Karen and my family. Karen felt she needed full control of this baby to take care of her, and my family didn't want her to become too close to Maria because my cousin would be out of jail in a year or so. Karen put up with a lot of grief. She'd want to have a birthday party, have everyone over to celebrate. My mom and aunt didn't think it was a good idea—they felt my cousin would be upset, hearing about this party. Little by little the resentment grew on both sides. There would be times we'd give the baby to my aunt for a week. She was living in Virginia at the time, and we would arrange to meet

her halfway between there and Pittsburgh when it was time to pick up Maria. But she wouldn't show up because she didn't want to give Maria back. So there would be some harsh words exchanged on both sides. It wasn't fair to Karen, especially with me in Memphis.

Karen did a tremendous job with the baby, but after about eight months we decided it was just putting too much strain on everyone involved. So Karen gave her to my other aunt Ruth Ann, who took care of Maria for the next six months until my niece got out of jail. During that time Karen and my family patched things up. Now Karen is very close with my cousin, and everything worked out nicely. But at the time Karen admitted she missed Maria. She had become very close to the baby, and having her in the house helped fill the void caused by me being in Memphis. So now she wanted to start having babies. I knew it wasn't the time because I had to focus on my new career, and that led to some fights between us. It didn't help that there were always a lot of women around at the wrestling shows. Karen didn't know what might be going on. So things were going downhill fast. I didn't know if the marriage was going to work. We were thinking about breaking up. At one point Karen said she wanted to get a divorce, and if I had stayed in Memphis much longer, who knows what would have happened. But just about then the call came for me from the WWE. I was able to move home, and though I've been on the road an average of five days a week ever since then, I could still spend a little more time with Karen.

So we were able to work some things out and save our marriage. I started making more money. We bought a house in December of '99. I bought Karen a salon to run, and now she's taking cosmetology classes to become a beautician. We see Maria once in a while now, too. My cousin is out of jail and taking care of the baby. Looking back, I think it was a blessing for us that Karen took care of Maria. It taught Karen about parenting and it taught me about the sacrifices you have to make to be a good parent. We both realized that we need to spend more time together and continue to make our relationship stronger before we have kids. When you're married there has to be total trust, especially when you're apart 80 percent of the time. We broke that trust when we were dating and we've had a difficult marriage, but it's getting better all the time. Now when I'm home I spend as much time as I can with Karen.

She's a very giving person. When I met her she spent all the money she had on me. She'll give anything to you, but she's not always so good with money, although she's getting better all the time. She's teaching me about relationships and I'm teaching her the importance of our future. We have a good life, but it's real important to know that I can't do this forever. There is going to be a point where I'm going to retire and I'm going to need to be financially stable. Karen is a wonderful wife. Sometimes I'm guilty of putting my career ahead of my marriage, but that's the way I grew up, putting myself first all those years when I needed total dedication to become an Olympic champion. That's a problem, but it's real important for me to make an impact with my career. But now I'm starting to juggle my marriage and career better, knowing that I'll have Karen forever, while World Wrestling Entertainment probably won't always be part of my life when I'm older, although I wouldn't mind staying with the company in some form or another. I want to have kids, and lately we've been talking more and more about it. It was important to me to make a mark in World Wrestling Entertainment before I started a family, but I feel like I've gotten to the point where I can make it work now. And I know if she had kids, Karen wouldn't be as lonely when I'm on the road, so it might not be all that long before we have some little Angles running around the house.

At least we finally had our honeymoon. I'm going to take some time off from a couple of untelevised shows, and we're going to get away for five days. For two and a half years, I never had more than three days off in a row. That's just the way it is in World Wrestling Entertainment; unless you're injured, you're working. There are always shows to do all over the country, so there is no time for vacationing.

I'm not looking for time away from World Wrestling Entertainment anyway. I'm consumed by my work. I want to be the best at it, the same way I wanted to be the best in the world as an amateur wrestler. I don't really have any consuming hobbies away from World Wrestling Entertainment. The only thing I do to get away is go with my wife to a day spa outside of Pittsburgh every once in a while. It gives both of us a chance to just relax. My wife works hard, too, with her salon. She works hard with her business, our home, and our relationship.

So we'll go to the spa for a day. I'll get the full body massages. I'll even get a manicure and a facial treatment. I consider that stuff kind of girlie, but Karen sets it up and I say, "Oh, what the hell." If it's fun for her, it's fun for me. The most important thing is spending time with Karen because I only see her one or two days a week. So we'll go down there and enjoy each other's company.

Other than that, when I'm home we don't go out much. But we love watching movies. We've got a bad habit of buying DVDs. We've spent a small fortune on them, but it's a good way to relax at home. I love comedies. I love anything that Jim Carrey or Ben Stiller makes. I think I own every movie they've either made or starred in, like *There's Something About Mary* and *Ace Ventura*. I loved one movie that Ben Stiller directed and Jim Carrey starred in—*The Cable Guy*. It didn't get good reviews because it was a dark, sort of twisted comedy, but I thought it was great.

I think I enjoy comedies because when you're traveling five or six days a week, you don't get to laugh much. You try to make the best of it, but I'm always on the go, day after day. Between my training, our shows, interviews, and other things, it's a long day. From eight in the morning to midnight, I'm busy as hell on the road. So I like to relax and enjoy myself at home. I've always enjoyed laughing, I've always been a cheerful person. I like adventure movies and thrillers, but there's something about comedies that makes me feel better.

I even use them to help give me ideas to make my character work. Especially in my first year, my character was this caricature of my image as a gold medal winner, and I had a lot of fun with it. I didn't mind making fun of myself as long as the fans were responding, and watching actors do comedy helped me understand how to entertain people.

One way or another, just about everything I do right now is geared toward my career. In the World Wrestling Entertainment you're always on edge, because you never want to take a step back. I don't want to be like that forever, but right now I'll do anything to make sure my career continues on the rise. I travel an average of five days a week. Sometimes it's just doing appearances for World Wrestling Entertainment. It makes me feel good that they have enough confidence in me to be the name and face for the company at an appearance.

There are times when my Olympic background helps the WWE on the corporate end. As much as the fans love the badass characters, they're not always ideal for doing business. So the company uses me for a lot of promotional campaigns. This year they've had me do things like launch Kmarts and attend the *Gladiator* movie premiere. In certain settings I give the company credibility. I'm a gold medalist and I can talk pretty well.

Last year the New York Stock Exchange invited us to make an appearance. I was the WWE Undisputed Champion at the time. I was wearing a nice sport jacket, and so was Rocky. Then you had Stone Cold wearing cutoff jeans shorts and his "Kick Your Ass" T-shirt. Mick Foley was wearing sweatpants with a tuxedo jacket and a flannel shirt underneath. That whole rebellious image is what makes them so popular with the fans, but there are times when it may not look so good if you're representing the company.

So the WWE uses me for a lot of things. I know I'm taking time away from my family when I don't absolutely have to, but it's my decision. I feel it's important to do these things for the company I work for. That's the attitude I took from the first day I showed up at the WWE tryout camp, and it's the attitude I had during that long six-month stretch in Memphis.

It was a tough time, no doubt about it. I was living in this dumpy apartment complex in Memphis with another WWE signee named Steve Bradley because, with my wife living at home in Pittsburgh, it was all I could afford. The Pittsburgh *Post-Gazette* sent a reporter and a photographer to Memphis to do a story on my new career, and they took pictures of me at the wrestling arena and at my apartment, too. I found out later that they decided not to run any pictures of the apartment complex because they thought it looked like a crack den or something. That's how bad the place was.

But it didn't really bother me. I wasn't in Memphis to soak up the atmosphere. I never made it down to Beale Street to enjoy any of the famous blues clubs. I had the same mentality there that I had when I was training for the Olympics. I was determined to get to the top, totally focused on my job. So as difficult as things were between Karen and me during that time, I never took my problems to the arena. I was pumped about the potential of this new career, and I knew I needed to use the time in Memphis to my advantage. It was great there—I got a lot of experience for TV matches. During that time the Entertainment would fly me into different cities, either to promote me with an on-camera appearance of some kind or to wrestle in an untelevised match.

They didn't want me to be seen on TV until they were sure I was ready to make a big impression, but they wanted people to know I had signed with World Wrestling Entertainment. One night they had me sitting in the crowd in my hometown with my wife during a televised show. Tiger Ali Singh, one of the World Wrestling Entertainment Superstars, used to come around with the microphone between the matches and offer money to get people to do something stupid or disgusting. His character is from India and he was always trying to show that American people will do anything for money. So he came over to me and he made a big production of introducing me to the crowd. Then we did this bit that was set up during the show.

"I know you're a real American hero, Kurt," he said. "But I think even you have your price. So I'll give you five hundred dollars if you'll blow your nose in this American flag I'm holding."

"No way," I said.

Then he began raising the offer. He went to two thousand, and finally five thousand dollars. I hesitated and pretended like I was torn about the decision, then finally I said, "For ten thousand I'll do that."

Well, all these people who saw me as a hero started booing the hell out of me while Tiger danced around and said, "See, see. You Americans will do anything for money."

But as he turned around I put the American flag down and I grabbed the flag that he was holding. The Indian flag. And I blew my nose in his flag. When I did that, he came after me with the American flag and hit me with it. I came back, threw him a couple of times, and then he slipped out of the ring. I didn't think anything of it at the time. I figured it was an innocent gag. But I got slammed in the Pittsburgh media for blowing my nose in the Indian flag.

I went for an interview on the weekend *Today* show, and I had no idea we were going to talk about that incident. The woman anchor said to me, "You said when you joined World Wrestling Entertainment that you'd never do anything sexist or racial."

I told her that what I did was directed at Tiger, not his country. I wasn't showing disrespect for India, I was just mocking him. But the line of questioning caught me off guard, and I wound up having to apologize during the interview. I thought everybody was a little too touchy about something that was meant to be comedy, but it was a good reminder for me that as a celebrity, everything I did was going to be news, especially in Pittsburgh.

At the time I was still feeling a little uncomfortable about my transition to World Wrestling Entertainment, and that incident didn't help. When I'd show up to be part of these World Wrestling Entertainment shows, I didn't really know anybody, and I still had all those feelings from my amateur wrestling days to overcome.

The first guy to make me feel comfortable was Owen Hart, the Superstar who died two years ago in a terrible accident at one of our shows when he fell on the canvas as a cable was lowering him into the ring from the roof. Owen had been an amateur wrestler and he was excited when he heard that I was coming on board. He sort of took me under his wing and tried to teach me little things here and there.

Four days before he died, I had a match with him. A lot of people considered Owen to be the best in the business, as far as understanding the psychology of the match and how to work the fans. Owen wasn't on the regular card that night, so Vince set him up with

me in an untelevised match to give me my first loss. Between training camp and then Memphis, I had been working for about ten months, and all they had me doing was winning. By then I understood that losing was part of the business, but when I was told I was finally going to lose, I was still kind of upset. That old competitive fire surfaced immediately. But wrestling Owen made it easier to handle because I had so much respect for him. It turned out to be my best match to that point by far, and it was because Owen was such a pro. He put the match together, how it would go, then he carried me through it, and made it look so easy. Afterward I told him it had been an honor. He thanked me for the compliment and told me I had a lot of talent, that I was going to do real well. I walked out of there that night feeling great, and hoping I could be as good as Owen eventually.

The next time I talked to him was the day he died. It was a Pay-Per-View at the Kemper Arena in Kansas City. I remember that he looked nervous when I saw him a couple of hours before the show. He didn't like heights, but he was willing to do whatever it took to play his character. He was playing this role as the Blue Blazer, a superhero. It was kind of a corny thing, a character that was a little bit over-the-top, like my character. He was cabled down into the ring for his match, and I don't know what went wrong, but he hit the canvas so hard that it looked like a dummy. He bounced, then came down and bounced again. For about forty to fifty minutes, emergency medical workers tried to revive him. When they finally brought him backstage, I was standing there, and I couldn't help but look. Owen was lifeless, completely blue. It really rocked me. I started crying. I wasn't best friends with him or anything, but I really respected and looked up to him. He was the one guy I had connected with right away. The thing I really liked about him was that he was a team player, he was always willing to put his ego aside for the good of the show. I only knew him for a short time, but he taught me a lot about how to handle myself in the WWE. I wanted to be like him in and out of the ring, and I've tried to carry myself like him ever since he died.

That whole incident really shook me up, but it didn't change my feeling that I was on a path to a successful career. I continued to do the untelevised shows here and there, but I was still doing most of my work in Memphis. I had one problem there, though. A guy named Randy Hales was the president of Power Pro Wrestling, and he wasn't always letting me get the experience I thought I needed. I was down there not just to wrestle but to talk on the microphone, and he hardly ever gave me the chance to do that. In wrestling today, if you want to be a World Wrestling Entertainment Champ, a big-time Superstar, you have to talk. You have to cut a good promo before the match to help get the crowd riled up, and you have to be able to use the microphone to work the crowd during or after the match, too.

That's World Wrestling Entertainment these days: you have to be versatile. You need a certain look. You have to be a very good athlete. A good worker. A good actor. And you have to be able to cut good promos. That's the one thing I was missing when they called me up from Memphis to join World Wrestling Entertainment. I don't know what the problem was, but I didn't get my mike time down there. So I didn't know if I could be good at it. I had done my sports broadcasting, my motivational speaking, but it's completely different out there in the World Wrestling Entertainment environment. You have to get a response from the fans, you have to be able to grab their interest. It's very hard to go out in front of fifteen thousand or twenty thousand people, and know that seven million people are watching on TV, and you have to cut this promo right the first time.

I never had to worry about that when I was trying to win a gold medal. And when I got the word that I would be making my World Wrestling Entertainment debut, the idea of bombing on that microphone was my only real fear. Fortunately, Vince McMahon took care of that my very first night in the ring.

12

DEBUTING IN WORLD WRESTLING ENTERTAINMENT

I made my debut at *Survivor Series* in November 1999 against Shawn Stasiak. World Wrestling Entertainment had been promoting the match for weeks on their TV shows, building up a sense of anticipation about the Olympic gold medalist. They'd have someone interview me for a TV spot and I would talk about my three I's—intensity, integrity, intelligence. That was the idea that Vince McMahon had for me, to bill myself as smarter and better than anybody else in World Wrestling Entertainment.

So I'd talk about how all my life I'd gone after this dream, and I reached it, which makes me an American hero—a role model for kids. But right away they were giving me kind of an odd twist. Vince wanted me to rub people the wrong way. He wanted them to say, "There's something about this guy, he's always talking about himself."

And I was. Me, me, me. My three I's. I do this and I do that. And I'd drive home my point with my catchphrase: "It's true. It's true."

That was something I used to say to people when I was doing motivational speaking after I won the gold medal. Whenever I talked to groups of people, or high school kids, I talked to them about how to improve their lives, how they needed to make sacrifices to achieve a goal. I'd say that if you put your mind to it, dedicate yourself, you will succeed eventually. And I'd always say, "You will. It's true. It's true."

So it was something I said naturally, and it sort of took on a life of its own when I got into World Wrestling Entertainment. Whether I was talking about myself or making fun of the city we were in that night, I'd finish by saying, "It's true, it's true."

And now everywhere I go, fans are always yelling it at me. It's perfect for my character.

Right from the start Vince wanted me to talk about how great I was, how smart I was, until people got sick of it. I'd say, "You people should look up to me. I'm here for you. I'm going to make a big impact; all these athletes will look up to me."

And it worked out beautifully because Vince wanted to break me in as a heel, a guy the fans would love to hate. And the centerpiece in the plan was my gold medal.

Personally, I wanted to get away from the gold medal. I figured this was a different career and I wanted to separate myself from what I'd done in the past. I didn't understand that World Wrestling Entertainment people saw it right away as a valuable tool to turn people against me. I remember Tom Prichard talking to all the wrestlers in the WWE training camp one day, saying that I could be the biggest heel in the business because of my gold medal. And at the time I'm sitting there thinking, "This guy's crazy. I'm a role model. People are going to love me."

So at the start I didn't want them bringing the gold medal crap into it. I'm thinking, "I don't want to rub people the wrong way. I want to prove I can do this without that." But they wanted to throw the gold medal in people's faces.

So, on my first night, I was matched up with Shawn Stasiak. The fans had never seen me in the ring, so they couldn't really identify with me, and a few minutes into the match people started chanting, "Boring. Boring. Boring." That's the one chant you never want to hear because it means you're not entertaining the fans. But Vince had prepared me for this type of reaction and he had given me a plan of attack if it happened.

Within a few minutes of the chant starting, I started to beat the heck out of Shawn. Then I went and grabbed the microphone and stared defiantly at the crowd.

"You do NOT boo an Olympic gold medalist," I yelled, trying to sound pissed as hell. "You do NOT say an Olympic gold medalist is boring. I'm the best wrestler in the world."

And on and on and on. All of a sudden the boos for being boring turned ten times as loud into real hardcore boos for being an arrogant ass. People were screaming back at me, gesturing and everything. And I was thinking, "Hey, what the hell just happened? Maybe I've got something here." A few minutes later, I hit Stasiak with my Angle Slam, and pinned

him to win my first World Wrestling Entertainment match.

Vince was waiting for the response, and it was exactly what he wanted. It was something new for me, after being such a hero to people, but it didn't bother me because I never took it as a real-life, serious approach. They wanted me to play a certain character, and to me it was like being in a movie or TV show. When I got that response, I thought it was amazing that I could make people react to my character with such passion.

So from there I started playing the role to its fullest. When I'd walk out for my match, I was the all-American role model—the golden boy who doesn't drink, doesn't smoke, and lives his life by the three I's. I'd smile this goofy smile and wave. Like, "Hey, I'm your Olympic gold medalist."

Boy, does that piss people off. They're like, "Look at this freakin' idiot."

I was walking down the aisle, saying, "That's right, I'm here, I'm here."

I was shaking kids' hands, introducing myself for all to hear: "Kurt Angle, Olympic gold medalist. Kurt Angle, Olympic gold medalist. How are you tonight?" And this was all before I even stepped into the ring.

My character development stemmed from what happened with The Rock a few years earlier. Rocky was a big-time college football player and World Wrestling Entertainment brought him in to play the role of an all-American athlete. They thought he was a natural as a babyface, a guy the fans would love.

But at the beginning the fans turned on him—they couldn't identify with him. These fans aren't idiots. You have to work to gain their acceptance, their approval. Plus, the fans are into the rebellious Superstars now. They want to see Stone Cold flip off his boss, because that's what they'd like to be able to do. These days the good guys don't go by the rules. In the eighties, if you went by the rules, you were a babyface. But since maybe the early nineties, the rebels have been the babyfaces. Rocky was an all-American babyface who went by the rules, and the fans turned on him. They would chant, "Rocky sucks! Rocky sucks!"

Now The Rock is one of the most popular babyfaces of all time. But only three or four years ago people were chanting that he sucks. At the time, instead of reacting to the chants, World Wrestling Entertainment ignored it. They tried to push him through that barrier, but it took longer than anybody expected. So I didn't go out there as an all-American hero expecting cheers. Fans responded the same way they had with Rocky, but the difference was that I responded to their response, and it worked perfectly. So, the next night, my second show ever with World Wrestling Entertainment is in Pittsburgh. It was my first night on *RAW IS WAR,* and I'm in my hometown. I remember Vince coming up to me and saying, "These people are going to boo the hell out of you."

I said, "Vince, this is my hometown. They're not booing me. No way. These people had two parades for me. They gave me a standing ovation at a Steelers game. I did commercials here. I did appearances here.

I was the Iron Man of the Year for Iron City Beer. I was everything here. There's no way they're going to boo me."

Vince just smiled and said, "Oh yes they will."

I was wrestling the Godfather. His character is a pimp and the fans love him because he brings girls out with him. So I cut a promo before the match that was played on the scoreboard in the arena. In the promo I attacked the Godfather. I said, "I'm here to clean up the World Wrestling Entertainment. To make it legitimate. We don't need people like the Godfather in World Wrestling Entertainment. You don't cheer a pimp who has prostitutes! You people should cheer me and boo him. Your children finally will have somebody to look up to."

I laid it on pretty thick. Fans do not like to be told what to do, and the people booed. My people. Because the fans don't want to hear that. They love the rebels, and I was just the opposite. My character would kiss Vince McMahon's ass on TV. I was this goody-goody and people hated me, even in my hometown. I actually took it as a compliment. They were responding to my character. A bunch of my family members were in the arena that night, and it was hard for them. Actually, a couple of my brothers almost got in fights. People were yelling, "Angle, you sucked as a sportscaster, and now you suck as a wrestler."

My brothers didn't want to hear that. They were telling people, "I'm gonna kick your ass if you don't shut up."

Mark took it a step further. He brought his teenage daughters to the show, and he understood that people would be yelling things they might not like. He told me later that he didn't say a word when some guys behind him were yelling at me, calling me gay, things like that. But when his oldest daughter finally said she was going to "tell these guys to shut up," that was all Mark needed to hear.

He turned around to them and said, "If you guys don't shut up, I'm gonna rip your goddamn throats out." He said they shut up after that.

So it was a little rough on my family at first. They know what to expect now and they're good about it, although there are still some nights when my wife gets a little too worked up and starts yelling at people. But the thing is, even their reaction to what was happening told me I was onto something. If the act worked in Pittsburgh, I knew it could work anywhere.

From there, little by little, World Wrestling Entertainment started giving me more to say. Before I knew it I was cutting two-minute promos, three-minute promos, until eventually I was doing nine- and ten-minute promos. That was big because in World Wrestling Entertainment 80 percent of the guys don't talk, they just wrestle. They don't get the opportunity to use microphone skills. Vince McMahon wanted me to do it, and I was able to live up to his expectations, so I became a big part of his plans. Within two months I won my first title, on February 10, 2000. I won the European Championship from Val Venis, who's very good. That was great. It meant I had direction, I was being utilized.

Not long after that, Vince set up a match with

Chyna, and it caught me by surprise. I remember thinking, "They want me to wrestle a woman? Why?"

I had a lot of respect for Chyna for what she did in the ring. She was strong and tough, but she was still a woman. The agents told me that I had to be careful, that I shouldn't punch her. So I was kind of confused about how to go about wrestling Chyna. People were telling me to be careful with her, but then I was watching her kick ass in the ring.

The idea behind the match was to help build my character as a heel. Chyna was such a great personality, and she was so big as a babyface that it was a perfect way to get people to react to me. When we got into the ring the crowd was cheering for Chyna, so I took the microphone and I stirred up the crowd, demanding to know why the fans were booing me.

"First of all," I said, "this is a woman. A woman has no business wrestling a man. Second of all, she's a freak. She's two hundred pounds of muscle . . . and she's a woman? You prefer to cheer her over an Olympic hero?"

The people went for it. They were trying to boo me out of the arena. Then we went on to have a really good match. I realized that it didn't feel any different than wrestling a man. She was very tough; she could hold her own. I wasn't so careful. We had such an intense match that I forgot she was a woman. Some of the bumps I gave her were pretty brutal. I gave her belly-to-back suplexes. I did punch her a few times when a spot didn't work right and I had to fill in as a transition to our next move.

After the match I had more respect for Chyna as an

athlete than I did beforehand. When she won the Intercontinental Championship, as I was just starting in the business, it was a big breakthrough. I didn't think it was such a good idea, but it wasn't my place to say anything. I just didn't feel it would legitimize that title.

But after I saw how she proved herself, I wasn't so against it anymore. It helped me understand the sports entertainment side of it—that a title doesn't always have to be legitimized, as long as the people enjoy it. I was kind of a male chauvinist before I wrestled Chyna, but she proved me wrong in a lot of ways. The match made me realize that you can make anything look legitimate in the WWE if it's done the right way.

It was good for me because, coming into the business, I had a lot to learn. I understood that I was going to get beat, but I also knew that I was one of the best athletes in the WWE, and if it came down to it, I could protect myself and hold my ground pretty damn well against anybody, whether it be a wrestling match or a fight.

But taking on Chyna in a match where she got the best of me, it gave me a better understanding about how to sell yourself in this business. It made me realize that I'd have to take the beating sometimes. Although it was a little bit humbling, it makes you understand that there's a job that has to be done, and if you do it the right way, both of you can look strong. Both of you will win in the long run.

Chyna beat me around pretty hard in the match. But I didn't lose my European Title because I didn't get pinned. Instead, I was disqualified for knocking her out with the belt. I was real nervous about doing that because I didn't want to ruin that pretty face. Chyna does a lot of acting. She's done a *Playboy* centerfold. One wrong shot and you're scarring the girl for life. So it was a lot of pressure, but we pulled it off pretty well. And it gave me more heat as a heel, since it looked like I had to hit her in the head with the belt to keep from losing my title.

Eventually I won the Intercontinental Title, not from Chyna but from Chris Jericho, who is one of the crowd favorites in the WWE. At that point I held the European belt as well, so I went around saying I now held the Euro-Continental Title. Very seldom do you see someone hold two titles at one time. But Vince had this concept: let's see how much gold we can throw on this kid. It was funny, that first night I came out in Pittsburgh, the night after my debut in *Survivor Series '99,* Vince said, "You got any medals at home?"

I said, "Yeah, a bunch of them."

"How many can you get here?" he said.

I said, "As many as you want. How many you want, four or five?"

"No," he said. "More like twenty."

So I had twenty-one medals around my neck the first night in my own hometown. He wanted me to look like an egomaniac—like, "Look what I won!" And that drew heat from the fans right away. So every night I'm coming out with these medals on. Plus I've got two championship belts in three months. I'm the man with so much gold, I look like I belong in a vault somewhere.

For a while I was wearing my Olympic gold medal into the ring for every match, along with the other medals. I thought it was important to have the real thing. But I stopped doing that after someone stole it one night in Baltimore. It was after a match at the Baltimore Arena. I was outside, signing autographs in the parking lot. Security wasn't good there, and people could walk right through the lot where we parked our cars. I put my bag down next to me, and I was signing for fifteen or twenty minutes when I looked down and noticed that my bag was gone. I started screaming, "Some asshole stole my gold medal and I want it back!" I was hot. I was freaking out.

"Call security!" I yelled. "Call the police! Call Vince!"

I figured that if anybody could get it back before it showed up at a memorabilia show somewhere, it was Vince. He has a way of getting what he wants from people. Earlier that night someone from the crowd threw a baseball at Stephanie as she was walking up the ramp after her match, and it hit her in the thigh. It didn't really hurt her, but it shook her up. And Vince was pissed. He sent security guards into the crowd to find out who did it. When they couldn't find the guy, Vince had someone go out and start offering tickets to the next show. Then another show. Then another show. Finally, about four people pointed at a guy and said, "He did it!"

Fortunately, I didn't end up needing Vince, at least on that night. As I was standing there yelling my head off about someone stealing my bag and about calling the police, I saw this young kid coming through the crowd of autograph seekers carrying my bag. I opened that bag and fortunately my gold medal was in it. The kid told me he found the bag on a bus.

I was relieved but still agitated. I didn't know what to think and I sure wanted to strike out at somebody.

The kid acted pissed and said, "Hey, shouldn't you thank me for finding this?"

I was so riled I wanted to smack someone and would have even lashed out at him, but I thought, If I take a swipe at this poor kid, that is really stupid and I will get myself into trouble. So I calmed down and said, "You're right, thank you."

As you might expect, that was the last time I brought my gold medal with me to a show. I wear these other medals now, and on TV it still looks like I am wearing my Olympic medal.

But anyway, the gag with the medals works perfectly with my character, and I thought the idea was hilarious. I was really starting to love my character because it was so over-the-top. They had me doing these TV spots where I'd walk up to security guards backstage and just start babbling about the greatness of me:

"Hey, you see my two titles, my two belts?"

And I'd explain to them what they were in this convoluted way, talking real fast:

"The European Title, that means I represent the countries of Europe. The Intercontinental, that means I represent the countries of North America. And you know, I weighed both belts. This one weighs five ounces more than the other. Probably because more countries represent the Intercontinental than the European."

And I'd just keep going on. People were like, "This guy's really out of his mind. He weighs his belts and he's actually got a philosophy about them." So now the fans saw that I was just into winning gold, which drew more heat on me.

A month later, at *WrestleMania,* I wrestled a Triple-Threat match against Chris Benoit and Chris Jericho, and I put up both of my titles. I lost them without getting pinned. They each won titles, but I never lost, because they pinned each other for their titles. That gave me a reason to complain and sound like a sore loser:

"This is a conspiracy," I moaned. "I didn't get pinned and I lost my titles." People were like, "Oh, God, somebody shut this guy up."

So I was getting the response from the fans, and I was always giving them more reason to hate me. Then one of the talent managers came up with the idea to have me insult the crowd in a personal way by making fun of something about the city we were in that night. World Wrestling Entertainment writers and I began reading the newspapers in every city to find something that makes for an easy target. Usually it has to do with sports. But it can be anything that will make people react.

Once in a while we'd do a show in Arkansas, and there was nothing easier than making fun of Bill Clinton. Of course, Jay Leno and David Letterman were telling jokes about Clinton every night on TV, but the trick for me was to turn it around on the people at the show. I'd blame them for making this guy a governor, and call them the biggest idiots in America, things like that.

It was never hard to find ways to tweak people. I remember in New York one time, I picked up on the comments that Atlanta Braves pitcher John Rocker made. He created that big controversy by talking about all the "weird, disgusting people" you see on the number 7 subway train that goes to Shea Stadium. I got on the microphone at Madison Square Garden and I said, "John Rocker was wrong about what he said."

And people started cheering. Then I went on:

"Yeah, he was wrong. You don't have to get on the number 7 train to see crack addicts and murderers. You can look out the window and see them all over New York City."

It was great. You set them up and then stick it to them. There's an art to it.

I think the most reaction I ever got was one of my first shows in Pittsburgh. At the same time I'm never afraid to be the butt of a joke myself. One night when I made fun of Mario Lemieux during a show in Pittsburgh, The Rock jumped into the ring and told the fans he had a little surprise for me that might make me want to stop before I insulted anybody else. Then, on the video screen, they played a tape of this really bad pizza commercial I made for a local place in Pittsburgh after the Olympics.

The day before, one of the WWE talent managers had asked me if I had anything like that so that The Rock could goof on me, and I gave it to him. I didn't really want anybody to see it, it was so bad, but I figured what the hell. I knew the fans would love it, and they did. They roared when they saw it, and that was great.

I understood that it was important to get the fans to react to me. Crowd reaction is what dictates how far you go in this business, and I was getting a lot of it. I didn't mind making myself sound like a goof, and as the reaction grew, World Wrestling Entertainment kept making me look ridiculous.

The next big match was at *King of the Ring*. When you win that, you get the honor of sitting on the King's throne. They give you a crown and a cape, which is just what my character would love. I was proud to wear it, not realizing I looked like an idiot. No one else would ever wear it, but I waltzed around in all my glory as people booed. It was funny because all my life

I'd lived for the cheers that came with winning as an amateur wrestler. The idea of being booed would have devastated me at an earlier time. But now I was loving the idea that I could make people react like this to a character who was so different from the real me.

And I was moving up the ladder fast. I won *King of the Ring* after seven months in the WWE, and no one else had ever done that. It was a huge feat, because when you win *King of the Ring,* that pushes you to main event level. You're doing angles with the top guys in the business—The Rock, Stone Cold, Triple H, Undertaker, Kane, all those guys. That's what *King of the Ring* is for, to escalate one man to main event. Six months into the business, that man was me.

But as fast as I was progressing, it wasn't like I won every match. When I first started, one of the ways I annoyed people was by keeping track of all my matches and reminding everyone that I was still undefeated. I won something like twenty-five straight matches when I started, and I was bragging about it: "I'm undefeated. No one's ever done this. I'll never lose."

I went to *Royal Rumble* in January, still undefeated at 27–0. Most of the matches I won, I'd either cheated or someone had helped me out. I didn't always win straight up, but I always said I did. That drew more heat. At *Royal Rumble* I wrestled Tazz, who had been the ECW Heavyweight Champion for more than eight months. They wanted to give him a very good push coming in, so they had him match up against me, because I had so much heat on me. They knew he'd be a babyface coming in because people could identify with him as someone who had been in the business for ten years. That first night, we had a great match. It ended when Tazz got me in a submission hold, a choke-out. He choked me out, won the match, and ended my undefeated streak. But you're not allowed to choke in World Wrestling Entertainment. So I complained that I never lost.

"Illegal hold!" I screamed at anyone who would listen. I complained night after night and maintained that I was still undefeated. "No one's beaten me, it was an illegal choke hold, it doesn't count," I protested. I even supposedly called the Olympic Committee and got a favorable ruling on my appeal. That drew even more heat from the fans. So you can understand how, as I made the progression every episode, more people started to hate me. There was a domino effect and I was getting more and more notorious as a heel.

The first time I legitimately lost, if I don't count Tazz, was right before I won the Euro Title. On January 31, 2000, on *RAW IS WAR* in Pittsburgh, I wrestled The Rock and he defeated me for the first time. It was kind of neat. The fans went nuts. They wanted to see me lose and see my undefeated streak come to an end. They wanted to see me run out of excuses, and The Rock beat me straight up. Even the reaction to losing told me my profile was becoming bigger and bigger in the eyes of the fans.

But my big test was proving whether I had the presence you need at the main event level. My win at *King of the Ring* put me there, and then it was up to me to prove I was ready for it.

13

AT THE MAIN EVENT LEVEL

Vince McMahon likes to say the fans decide which Superstars are on top in World Wrestling Entertainment by the way they react to our performances, night in and night out. And he's right. If they don't react with some passion, either for you or against you, then you're not going anywhere in this business. But getting to the top takes more than good chemistry with the fans.

It's important to earn the respect of the guys you work with or they can make life tough for you. I'm sure there were some hard feelings when guys saw me start advancing so quickly, but I always made a point of showing everyone respect. I always want my opponent to look good when I have a match, and I think guys could see that I wasn't a phony. I felt it was really important for me to get along with everybody, because I was learning all the time, and there were some moments when my inexperience showed.

Right after *King of the Ring*, I wrestled a guy named Bob Holly. Hardcore Holly. Bob is considered one of the better workers in the business. He's respected by the athletes and the fans. I'm not known to be a highflier, but in our match we decided that I would do a moonsault off the top rope—a backflip where I splash on top of him on the canvas. I'd never done one, and I didn't really know where to set him down on the canvas. When I did it, I set him out a little too far, and I came up short. So instead of landing on him with my chest and stomach, my legs landed on him. He brought his arms up to protect himself and caught the full force of my knees and feet. You could hear the crack as the impact broke three bones in his left arm. I didn't know that at the time, but I could see that he was in a lot of pain. From that point I was carrying him through the match, but he still had to use his arm as we carried out our moves.

Finally, we finished the match, and I took him to the hospital. I went into the X-ray room with the doctor, and saw that the bones in his arm were completely severed. All three bones were sticking in different directions. I went back to see him and he started saying that he thought maybe it wasn't so bad.

"Bob," I said. "The bones are broken in half."

I felt so bad. You never want to hurt someone. We know the risk is there. It can be dangerous out there, because we're going hard and fast and aggressive in the ring. But you never want someone to get seriously hurt. Bob was out for nearly six months. They had to put screws and a plate in his arm. Considering how bad the injury was, I'm still amazed that Bob made it through that match. Usually, if a guy gets hurt like that, he'll let his opponent know, "I'm hurt, I'm hurt. Just pin me." And they find a way to end it quickly.

But Bob worked six more minutes with his arm broken in half. I knocked him down eight or nine times, and other times I was taking the hand of his broken arm and whipping him off the ropes. Every time I'd grab it he'd scream. But he went through with the whole move. He was in so much pain that he couldn't remember anything, so I had to talk him through the rest of the match. It was good for me because I'd never done that before. Before the injury Bob was the "general," meaning that he was calling the shots as we went along. But afterward I had to take over as the general and talk us through the match.

More than anything, Bob proved how tough he was that night. I don't know how he was able to take the pain, but he wanted to finish the match and I give him a lot of respect because we had a tremendous match. Still, I ended up taking six months of the guy's career. I felt bad for him and I was a little nervous about how people would look at me. You don't want to get a reputation for being dangerous. But if there were hard feelings, Bob never let me know. He was cool about it. He said, "Kurt, it's not your fault. You didn't mean to do it. It was a mistake."

Later I even kidded him about it. One night I hit a moonsault perfectly on Triple H. When I came backstage I said, "Bob, how'd you like my moonsault?" He laughed and said, "You bastard, why couldn't you have done that one to me?"

But right after it happened, I was worried about what the other guys in the locker room would think. If they think you're dangerous, nobody is going to want to work with you. If you get that type of repu-

tation, you're going to see your chances of winning a title or working with the top guys dwindle.

And actually, guys were nervous about me trying my moonsault on them after my match with Bob Holly. I couldn't talk anyone into letting me do it for months. Finally, eight months after that happened, I was talking strategy with Triple H for our match that night and I tried to convince him to let me try it.

"I swear I'll land it right this time," I said.

"You know what, Angle," he said. "I'll do anything."

And that's the great thing about Triple H. He'll do anything for the business. By letting me land a moonsault on him, and doing it right this time, he kind of opened doors for me. The other guys saw that he let me do it, and he's our most valuable guy. So since then guys have been open to the idea when we thought it would be good for the match.

But after I broke Bob's arm, everybody tested me right away in the locker room. This business is crazy, anyway. There's a lot of ribbing between the guys. You're on the road with all these guys, and at times we act like children, and at times we pick on each other and you have to learn to be part of the give-and-take. If you don't have the personality for it, if you react the wrong way, they can make your life tough. They won't back off. They'll get nastier or they'll just freeze you out. Then you're an outsider and you've got big problems.

So the best thing to do is to laugh it off. "You're right, I'm dangerous," I'd say.

Guys were ribbing me left and right: "Angle, I

heard they banned that moonsault from the Olympics because you were hurting too many guys." Or, someone would hit a moonsault and they'd say, "Angle, you see that? *That's* a moonsault."

And it was constant—fifty times a day for probably a month or two. They want to make you laugh, but in a way they want to see how you react to it, because, you know what, you did screw up. And you better take responsibility for it. You better not get pissed off. Basically they're saying, "You better take this abuse because you broke one of our best guys' arms."

I think I handled it well. I'm pretty easygoing, anyway. I get along with the guys. I probably get picked on the most. Like Triple H once said, "You're an easy target, Angle."

Triple H gets me good every once in a while. One time I had a tag-team match with him where we were taking on Stone Cold and The Rock. At the time Vince had a story line going to set up one of the Pay-Per-Views where Triple H and Stone Cold had each signed a contract stipulating that neither one could lay a hand on the other.

So in this match anytime they were in the ring at the same time, one of them had to tag out. It was a great match and I finally got pinned by Rocky at the end. Rocky and Stone Cold were posing in the ring as the TV portion of the show ended. Usually we end up giving the fans in the arena a little something extra after we go off the air, and this time Triple H grabbed me outside the ring and said, "The hell with that contract. TV is over. Let's go back in there and kick their ass."

"You sure?" I said.

"Yeah," Triple H said. "You go after Rocky and I'll go after Steve."

"All right," I said. "Let's do it."

And we both started running for the ring. As I slid in, Triple H stopped cold. I got up ready to go, and I looked around, and there's Triple H, laughing at me outside the ring. Meanwhile, Rocky and Stone Cold started pounding on me, and they were laughing at me, too.

Finally, we ended the show and I went backstage and everybody was cracking up, including Vince.

"Triple H is right, Angle," Vince said. "You *are* gullible."

And I am. I can be a little spacey sometimes. Everyone likes to pick on me. They know I'll laugh. That's what they like most about me: that I may have come in as an Olympic gold medalist, but I never acted like I was hot stuff. I had a good attitude, I was willing to learn, and I didn't think I was better than anyone else. That's why everyone took a quick liking to me, and that's the way I feel. I don't think I'm better than anyone else. Sure, I was the best amateur wrestler, but I would never say that in sports entertainment because all the best guys are right here. And when you reach the main event level, it's important to prove you belong with the very best.

By the time my win at *King of the Ring* pushed me up to that level, I'd already proven I had good chemistry with The Rock. Then, in my first Pay-Per-View as a main event Superstar, I had a match with the Undertaker. He basically beat me up, but I'd always wanted to work with him. He's so famous. People

love him, and he's one of the best workers in the business. We had a good match and I proved to the office I had good chemistry with the Undertaker, which is important. My next test was Triple H. I think he's the very best in the business. These guys are all good, but Triple H has a good sense of the psychology of making the matches work. He's very intelligent. In a lot of ways he's like Vince McMahon. He has a real feel for the business.

I did an angle where I was trying to steal Stephanie McMahon-Helmsley from Triple H, and it worked beautifully. The fans really responded, and that was important because it proved that I could be a major player in the World Wrestling Entertainment and handle just about any kind of role they wanted me to play.

But the night I think I really won everybody over came at *SummerSlam* in August. It featured a Triple-Threat match for the title—Triple H, Rocky, and me. It was a huge moment for me. These guys were already proven champions, and here I was, just nine months into World Wrestling Entertainment, in the main event with them at *SummerSlam,* which is the second most popular Pay-Per-View of the year, behind *WrestleMania*.

I was still after Stephanie, whose character is Triple H's wife. I went out to the ring first, and Triple H followed. He started beating the hell out of me because I was trying to steal his wife. He took me over to the announcers' table, put me on the table, and set me up for the Pedigree—his finishing move. When he does the move, he bends you over, puts your head between his legs, tucks your arms behind your back, and locks them there. Then he jumps up, you jump up, and you land face-first on the mat. Only this time I was going to land on the table. The story line called for me to get a concussion, get knocked out, but come back later.

The idea was to let Rocky and Triple H have a great match and I could come back later, after I shook off the cobwebs. But as we started the move, the table gave out and I crashed to the floor. I didn't have time to react, and my head hit the concrete four feet below, knocking me out for real. I wound up with a major concussion. After about fifteen seconds I came to, and I tried to jump up like everything was fine. When you take a move like that you're supposed to sell it like you're out. But I didn't know where the hell I was.

Triple H knew we were in trouble. He was yelling

for the trainer. So then Rocky came out, and Triple H and Rocky started going at it. They took me backstage, and I was really woozy. But I was trying to pull myself together. In the story line, Stephanie thought we were just good friends and she was supposed to talk me into going back out there, to help Triple H. I was supposed to say, "Only for you, Steph, I'll do it for you." We were getting ready to do the line for the cameras backstage, and I looked at her and said, "What am I saying again?"

She told me and we got ready again. And just then I said, "What am I saying?"

I was lying there on a gurney, which is what the script called for, and I was still out of it. World Wrestling Entertainment gave me a tape later that included all the backstage stuff that wasn't shown on TV. They record everything in case they want to use it for a videotape or a documentary later, and it was kind of weird watching it because I didn't remember any of it. You could see that I had this vacant look in my eyes, like the lights were on but nobody was home.

I actually thought it was kind of funny, seeing it myself. At least six times I sat up on the gurney and said, "So what am I saying?" My wife watched it with me and she got mad at me for laughing. She thought it was scary and she didn't think I should have finished the match. But that's just the way I was raised, to be tougher than everybody else.

So I kept telling everybody I wanted to finish the match. But when I kept asking Stephanie what I was supposed to say, you could see everybody sort of starting to panic. Vince didn't know what to do. He

was thinking about pulling me out, but he wanted to finish the story line. Finally, we did it live and I managed to say the words and make it work. I don't even remember doing it, but when I saw the tape you could tell I didn't know what I was saying.

Anyway, after we did the scene backstage, I was going back out for the end of the match. But we had another fifteen minutes to go. I looked at Stephanie and Vince and said, "I don't know what I'm supposed to do."

I didn't even know where I was. I didn't know I was in Raleigh, North Carolina. So Vince said, "Are you sure you're okay to go back out there?"

"Yeah, yeah, I'm okay," I said, "but I don't know what I'm doing."

So he said, "Don't worry, the guys will lead you through the rest of the match."

Now I was really nervous. I didn't even know what the finish was as Stephanie was pulling me out there. The next thing I remember, I had an oxygen mask on and I was being taken to the hospital—for real. I don't remember anything about the match, but amazingly enough, I went out there and pulled off one of the best matches I'd ever had. We were using a sledgehammer. We were using false finishes. I finished the match like I knew what I was doing, and they talked me through the whole thing. I'd never believe it if I hadn't seen a tape of it later.

I walked back out to the ring, and I managed to remember that I was supposed to grab Triple H's leg, pull him out, and whip him into the steps, and then jump into the ring. From there, when I got into the ring, Rocky was telling me what to do. The match ended up being so incredible that Vince McMahon thought the world of me. He told people, "This guy's really a player. He proved himself when he didn't know what he was doing."

Maybe it was dangerous, but that's just the way I am. Just like when I wrestled in the Olympic trials with a broken neck. Something inside of me won't let me walk away. I always believed that my heart and toughness is what won the Olympics for me, and in a way this was my chance to show that kind of heart at World Wrestling Entertainment level. When I watch that tape it doesn't bring back the slightest memory. But the match was so good that I told people maybe I should have a concussion every time.

And it showed just how good guys like Triple H and Rocky really are. They never made me look weak. I looked strong, which is what I needed because I wasn't quite at their level yet. I needed to look like I belonged out there, and those guys carried me. That shows you what this is all about, working as a team. If they can make me look strong, it makes them look stronger. If they stomp me, it just looks like I'm a wimp. But if I'm fighting back, holding my ground, it makes them look stronger, more heroic, when they finally beat me.

When I got to the hospital after the match, the doctors did CAT scans to determine how bad my concussion was. I must have hit my head pretty damn hard because it bothered me for about six weeks. I continued to wrestle, and sometimes when I'd hit the canvas, I'd see a quick flash of light. I'd black out for just a second. Then I'd pop up and I wouldn't remember anything. The guy I was working with would have to tell me what we were doing the rest of the match. It really became a concern after a couple of weeks because I wasn't getting any better. They took me off the shows that weren't being televised so I could rest more. After about three weeks they lightened my TV schedule, too. I was only making short appearances until finally everything cleared up. Fortunately, I didn't have any more problems, and when I look back, that match was definitely the turning point of my World Wrestling Entertainment career. It allowed me to step into that main event level and get respect. Not just from the fans but from the guys. A lot of fans don't even know that I got hurt that night. But the guys do. And that counts for a lot in this business.

* * *

I may pride myself on my toughness, but I do worry about injuries. I had serious knee and neck injuries in amateur wrestling, but World Wrestling Entertainment is tougher on my body on a day-to-day basis. All that hitting the canvas and flying around in the ring takes a toll, especially when you have matches an average of five days a week. I get up and go work out every day, no matter what city I'm in, to stay in shape and sometimes just to shake off the soreness from the night before. Usually I feel like if I don't work out, I'll be too stiff to wrestle that night.

It's hard to get out of bed some mornings, though. The injuries are starting to catch up with me. I've had surgery twice on my knees, and one time doctors told me I'd never wrestle again because I hurt my knee so badly. That's another reason I work out; I need to do a lot of lifting with my legs to keep the muscles around my knees strong. It's the only way I can do what I do in the ring every night. But the knees aren't my only problem. I've got bad shoulders. My neck has been a problem since that amateur tournament in 1996 when I cracked two vertebrae. I had a few broken noses during my amateur career. I can't hear in my left ear because of all the fluid buildup over the years when guys would squash my ear with their hands as they tried to fight off my takedowns. I have nerve damage in my face because I got kicked there real hard accidentally during an amateur freestyle match.

I got kneed in the face one time in a tournament and blood came gushing out of my nose. The trainer guessed that I lost eight ounces of blood. They had to close my nose shut at the hospital because a capillary had broken. I also broke both of my hands in amateur wrestling. One time a guy brought his knee up to kick out of a takedown attempt, and the force of his kick broke a bone in my hand. The other time I had my arms around a guy in a gut wrench, and we both wound up falling on top of my hand, which was caught in an awkward position.

If you're involved in amateur wrestling long enough, there's no way to avoid injuries. You're always putting so much stress on your joints. You have to learn to work around injuries. A lot of guys would quit training; they'd just wait until they healed. I couldn't do that. When I had a broken hand, I'd lift weights for hours with my other arm. I don't know if it's true, but I've always heard that there's a transfer process from one arm to the other because the body has a way of equalizing the muscles. Maybe it's crazy, but it gave me a reason to work even harder. And when the doctors told me I had to wear a cast for six weeks, I cut it off after three and a half.

Still, I know there could be a long-term effect from all my different injuries as I get older. That's why I have to think about how long I want to stay in the business. When I joined, I told my wife I'd get out after five years. But I've been so successful that now I want to go much longer. My wife says I'll be in a wheelchair in ten years, and I do worry about it because I want to raise a family someday and be active with my kids. My body has taken a lot of abuse over the years and I'm still abusing it. I'm always hitting the canvas with a lot of force in my matches, and like I said, it takes a toll.

I know now that the one thing you can't take chances with is your head. When I got the concussion, I couldn't think straight. I was always in a daze. When I did promos I was repeating myself six times before I could finish my sentence. I shouldn't have continued to wrestle, but I treated it just like every other injury I've ever had, which means I thought I could work right through it.

I had the worst match of my career because of it, too. It was two days after I had my concussion. I was in a match against Eddie Guerrero. I still had a lot of cobwebs in my head. Eddie used this move on me called a "flying head-scissors" where he jumps up, puts his legs around your head, then arches his back and flips you over onto your back. It looks brutal, like he flops you on your head. If you flip and roll, you actually land on your back and you're fine. But I really did land on my head this time, before I rolled over, and when I came up I didn't know where I was. I saw a quick flash of light and I experienced some dizziness. I lost my bearings, so I said to Eddie, "What are we doing?"

From that point I was pretty much out of it, and everything started going wrong. There were so many timing moves in this match, and I wasn't able to make them work. Everything was off just enough to make the rest of the match messy. Thank goodness it was a *SmackDown!* show that we taped two days ahead of time, because the TV people were able to clean it up a little with some editing and make it look decent. But the people in the arena had to be wondering what was going on. Basically I shouldn't have been out there wrestling at all, but that was my choice. I told the World Wrestling Entertainment people I was ready when I really wasn't.

It's just my nature, the way I was taught by my brothers. Toughness is what counts most. So finally, when Triple H asked me a few weeks later if I would do the table slam again, I reluctantly agreed. I really wanted to say no, because I was kind of spooked by the idea that I could get another concussion. But finally I said yes. I was willing to do it for the sake of World Wrestling Entertainment, and this time it went perfectly. The table collapsed when Triple H and I came down on it, and so while it looked like I took another vicious shot, this time I was able to protect myself and land without getting hurt.

It was good to do it again and get over the fear of another concussion, and it helped raise the intensity between Triple H and me even higher as we fought over Stephanie. More than anything, I think that's probably why I went ahead and convinced myself to do it again. When you're involved in the hottest story line in World Wrestling Entertainment, you don't want to leave everybody hanging. And I didn't want to mess with a good thing because I was getting a lot of recognition by playing the role of a wife stealer.

The agents and writers had come up with the idea a few months earlier, partly as a way of bringing more heat on me. I had become so entertaining with some of the comedy-type stuff that people were starting to like my character, and the office thought I was too valuable as a heel to have me turn into a babyface.

So they decided to go with the wife-stealing angle. There are certain things that people are always going to

hate you for, and one of them is going after another guy's wife. But they still let me have fun with it. The story developed so that Stephanie was helping to manage me. We did a pretape for TV where she was explaining why she was being so helpful to me, and all three of us were in a room together. Triple H didn't like it, but Stephanie was telling him she was just my friend.

So then I spoke up and said, "Yeah, Triple H, she's just my friend. We're just friends." Then, when Stephanie would turn away from me to look at Triple H, the camera would show me with this smirk on my face, like I was laughing at Triple H because I was getting away with this.

Stephanie was wrestling a mixed tag-team match that night, so at one point she said to Triple H, "I need a partner for tonight's match. I don't know if I want Kurt or you."

Now Triple H was furious.

"Are you serious?" he said. "You'd rather go out there with this idiot than me?"

"I don't know," Stephanie said. "I just think Kurt just might be the smarter choice right now."

Finally, Stephanie decided to flip a coin. She's got a quarter and she's about to flip it, when I break in and say, "Hold on a second. Wouldn't you rather use a real American coin?" And I take the gold medal off my neck.

Now Triple H wanted to kill me. But he had to hold his temper because he knew he'd lose Stephanie if he went after me. So I won the coin toss and I was behind her, jumping up and down, where Stephanie couldn't see me. I was pointing at Triple H, laughing, like, "Go on, get out of here." But then, when Stephanie would turn around, I wouldn't be doing anything, playing real innocent. It was great because people thought I was such a snake.

We went with that for about three months, and it won Storyline of the Year in the wrestling publications. It kept building toward the night when I kissed Stephanie. During that time Triple H and I would be teaming up in tag-team matches because my character was pretending to join forces with him and Stephanie. One night on *RAW* we won a match against the A.P.A., and Triple H walked out of the ring and up the runway out of the arena as they were beating the hell out of me. He was happy to watch me get pounded.

Then on *SmackDown!* we were partnered again in a rematch with the Acolytes, but early in the match Stephanie accidentally got knocked out while she was outside the ring. While I was in the ring, Triple H picked her up and carried her backstage, leaving me on my own again. Then, on the video screen in the arena, they showed Stephanie regaining her senses backstage, and asking Triple H to go back and help me.

"Don't leave Kurt alone," she pleaded.

So Triple H came back, and they started beating the hell out of him in the ring. This time *I* left *him* out there and went back to see Stephanie. Once again the video screen was showing the scene from backstage. Stephanie is lying on a couch. She's still groggy, half knocked out, and I'm putting the moves on her.

"You don't know how much I care about you," I said to her.

And then I kissed her. Earlier that day I called my

wife at home and told her I was going to have to kiss Stephanie. She was cool about it. She said she understood it was part of the job and told me not to worry about it. But I was very uncomfortable with it. We did it live, during the match, so we had to make it look good. Vince McMahon and his son, Shane, were both in the room at the same time, which made it more nerve-racking.

It turned out to be about a twelve-second kiss, long enough to sell it to the audience. It seemed a lot longer than that when I was doing it, and on TV it was pretty convincing. Too convincing, in some ways.

At home in Pittsburgh people were feeling bad for Karen. They started bringing gifts to her salon for her. Karen had to explain to them that it wasn't real, it was like being an actor in a movie. And they were like, "Oh, yeah, right, but anyway, we feel bad."

It sounds hokey as hell to think that people want to believe it, but I guess it's like a soap opera. People get wrapped up in the stories. Actually, it goes a step further than a soap opera because anything can happen. You've got guys flying all over the ring, beating the hell out of one another. It's not trick photography, or action scenes done by a computer, like you see in the movies. We're live, and what you see is what you get. That's the beauty of sports entertainment.

So I was in the middle of that story line when I got my concussion, and I kept wrestling because we had to bring it to a conclusion. The writers didn't want to take it any further with Stephanie and me, because Triple H's character was such a hard-ass that it wouldn't have been realistic to have him take her back if she had an affair. A month before *No Mercy,* where I won the title, Triple H and I beat the hell out of each other at the *Unforgiven* Pay-Per-View in September 2000. At the end, we were both lying in the ring, exhausted. Stephanie came into the ring and Triple H said, "You have to choose between him and me right now. Right now."

So Stephanie looked at me, then looked at him, and finally she kicked me in the groin. That energized Triple H, so he got up and put me in his finishing move to end the match. And that ended the relationship between Stephanie and me. We remained friends, but there was no more messing around on my part. I was no longer a threat to break up their marriage. From there the story line fizzled out. To me it would have been more interesting to take it a little further, but I understand that our characters have to be protected. Triple H wouldn't take back someone who had an affair, and to be honest, I wouldn't either, so I guess that was as far as we could take it. But it was such a hot story line, you might see it down the road again.

When I finished that showdown with Triple H, I had gone against all the main event Superstars and I'd taken my lumps, but I also showed that I belonged with them in the ring. I had taken the abuse in the locker room and proved I was one of the boys. I was getting better and better on the microphone, getting people to react to my insults about their sports teams or whatever. So that's when Vince McMahon decided it was my time.

14

WINNING THE BELT

The referee's arm slammed to the canvas, officially making me the WWE Undisputed Champion and shocking an arena full of people expecting to see The Rock walk away wearing his championship belt. I had just pinned the People's Champ, and you could feel a jolt of electricity go through the crowd.

The fans were stunned. It was like, "What happened? Angle's the champ?"

And then the booing started. World Wrestling Entertainment fans love to be surprised, but they love The Rock even more. And they love to hate me. So as the result sank in, at *No Mercy* in Albany, New York, in October 2000, people were booing from every corner of the arena.

It had taken me less than a year in World Wrestling Entertainment to go all the way to the top. And I did it in style. I pinned The Rock, the most popular Superstar in the business. And I had to go through Rikishi, The Rock's 400-pound cousin, to do it. I finished them both with my Angle Slam, my trademark finishing move, and now as I stood over them in the ring in

Albany, holding the championship belt, I soaked up the fans' reaction and took their boos as compliments.

I even rubbed it in their faces. Just for fun I dropped to my knees, crying, like I did when I won the gold medal in Atlanta in 1996. And the fans booed even louder, which only confirmed that Vince McMahon was right in deciding my time had come.

You don't get that kind of response unless you've established a distinctive personality, either as a babyface or a heel. I'd become champion in eleven months, more quickly than anyone in the history of World Wrestling Entertainment, and, I have to admit, it happened faster than I thought it would, and a lot faster than some people probably thought it should have. But what do you do with an Olympic champion who can talk on the microphone, who can make the fans react to him, who can excel in the ring and make his character seem so real? What do you do with somebody who has all the ingredients to be a champion—and has already proven he *is* a champion?

What do you do with this guy? You can't hold him back. It's not realistic to have an Olympic champion in the WWE and let other guys step all over him. I'm not saying I'm better than the other guys in the business. I have all the respect in the world for the other guys in the World Wrestling Entertainment, and I'm always trying to learn from them, especially the other main event Superstars like Rocky, Triple H, Stone Cold, Rikishi, Kane, and the Undertaker. But I do feel like I belong. I crossed a barrier, coming over from the world of amateur wrestling, which has always resented pro wrestling. And my earlier career carried some weight when I got here.

I still had to prove myself, though. And I did. I put in my time training in Memphis, and once I started I worked hard to learn from the other guys as I moved up the ladder. I took my share of bumps and bruises. And I swallowed some pride to make my character work. I made him this milk-drinking dork that people love to hate. I play the fool sometimes, and not everybody is willing to do that. Some guys say, "I ain't getting laughed at," but I don't mind because it's good for World Wrestling Entertainment and it's good for me. In other words, it's good business.

So the bottom line is that I was ready when Vince McMahon decided I should own the title, but I was still kind of stunned when Rocky told me about it a few days before the match. We were sitting down together to go over our setup match about five days before *No Mercy*. We had been building up to the championship match for about four weeks. We were making sure we made all the right moves to hook the fans and make them believe I had a legitimate shot at winning. I'd thrown Rocky around enough that people wanted to see him kick my ass. Of course, they want to see The Rock kick everybody's ass, but they also want to know he's got a match on his hands.

So I remember Rocky sitting me down, saying, "Listen, on Sunday I'm going to be giving you the Strap." That's what we call the championship belt. The Strap.

And I was like, "What?" I was so elated. "Man, that's awesome, I can't believe it."

He said, "You deserve it, man. You deserve it. Now's your time, Kurt."

Vince McMahon had told Rocky of his decision, and Rocky wanted to explain the game plan. We tried to keep it as quiet as possible, but we were discussing our match for that night, the *SmackDown!* before *No Mercy*. There's a certain psychology leading up to the Pay-Per-Views. Usually the heels need to get heat on the babyfaces, which basically means the bad guy beats up on the good guy. It gives the rivalry a little more juice and it creates some suspense. Maybe I'll sneak up behind Rocky and beat the hell out of him, to make it look like he's at a big disadvantage for the match that's five days away. It leaves the fans with the question of whether Rocky's going to be strong enough to shake it off and come back and beat me.

So Rocky was explaining all of this, about how I would be taking over the title. And he said to me, "When you have the Strap, you need to take your whole game to another level. You're the champion. You're representing us and you're representing yourself. You want to carry that ball so that they have as much confidence in you being champion as me."

In other words, he was telling me, "Don't drop the damn ball."

I took it to heart and I did raise my game. I had the title for almost five months, the longest anybody had held it in the previous three years. And I did pretty damn well with it. Looking back, I think I could have been a little more aggressive. But when you're a heel in the business, it's hard to be aggressive through the whole match. You can be aggressive at certain moments, but you're prone to being bumped around, which means taking most of the beatings. When you're a babyface champion, you usually do the ass-kicking, knocking the other guy around.

Anyway, when I was champion I always remembered Rocky's message. He wanted me to understand that the champion needed to carry himself a certain way. That day, he told me he didn't mind giving up the Strap, but "only if we have a great match. I want to have one of the best I've ever had." I was honored to hear Rocky put it that way. He was already a five-time WWE Undisputed Champion at the time. And you know what—we had an incredible match. It might have been *the* best match I'd ever had to that point. We'd only been working together for a few months, and obviously, when you have a long-running feud with somebody, like he's had with Triple H, a match like that is going to be a little more emotional.

But Rocky and I have always worked well together. I have good chemistry with a lot of guys, but with Rocky, there's something there that works. We really complement each other's moves. Everything looks so real. When he hits me with a Rock Bottom, I'm not going to dead-ass him. I'm going to get five feet in the air and I'm going to make it look like he put me through the floor. He loves that. He's like, "Man, you got it." And he does the same for me.

The way we do it, the way we sell it, the way we tell a story, we probably have the best chemistry of anyone. We're very similar because we're both so athletic, but our characters are totally different, and I

think the contrast helps sell the drama. We're both funny in our own way, but he's hip and I'm square. He's cool and I'm the nerd. It works.

So after Rocky told me that I would become the champion, I went out that night and pounded on him in the *SmackDown!* match to set up *No Mercy*. People were thinking he'd get his revenge in a big way on the Pay-Per-View. But by then they knew they had to take me seriously because I'd been winning so much and moving up the ladder so fast.

So we went into Albany five days later and I was walking on air, knowing I was going to win the championship that night. It was so different from my experiences in amateur wrestling. I found myself thinking about that as I went to the arena. As a wrestler on the USA national team, I won tournaments all over the world, but no matter how many times I won, those final hours before a big match, especially a final match, were always nerve-racking. I used to get this tingling feeling throughout my body. It was a nervous feeling, and it would get to the point where I felt like I was paralyzed. All because I had such a major fear of losing.

I've always been motivated by that fear of failure more than anything else in wrestling. That's what drove me to work out eight hours a day for two years leading up to the Olympics.

Before just about every match the worst scenario would run through my mind: what if I lose here? But the more scared I got, the better I wrestled. I don't know if I needed to feel that way to make the adrenaline kick in or what. But I remember the times when

I wasn't as nervous, I didn't perform as well. I guess there's a fine line between being scared of losing and being afraid to compete. It's weird, because most people will crack under pressure. But the more pressure there was on me, the more I produced.

The stress wore on me, though. Sometimes I wouldn't be able to sleep the night before a big match. All through my career in amateur wrestling I felt that stress. After the Olympics I took a two-year break where I didn't do much of anything competitively, and I needed that break. I was finally able to relax.

Now I still get worked up for my World Wrestling Entertainment matches, but we already know what's going to happen, so it's not quite as stressful. You still want to perform your best. The hardest part is that you're always thinking about what you're supposed to do. You can't just rely on your athletic instincts, the way I did in amateur wrestling. You're playing a part. You're basically an actor, doing acrobatic stunts. But this way was easier on my stomach. I didn't have to deal with that fear of losing. So for that championship match I was able to enjoy the night from start to finish like nothing I'd ever experienced.

And Rocky and I did bring down the house with a wild match. There were Superstars flying all over the ring at times. Stephanie—who just a few weeks before had agreed to become my "business partner"—ended up on the receiving end of a "Rock Bottom." Before the match, Triple H had warned me that if anything happened to Stephanie, I would pay. So Triple H came out looking for blood. My character was still trying to steal Stephanie at the time, so he wanted to pound on

me. Then Rikishi, The Rock's cousin, came out and got into the mix, too. Rocky and I were getting knocked down by everybody, but we kept fighting back against each other. There were some great false finishes that made it look like the match would end before it really did. You want to keep the fans guessing.

Finally, the ending was set up to help The Rock save face. Rocky was beating me up in the corner, when Rikishi charged the corner to squish me with his patented move—The Stink-Face. I pulled Rocky in the way and Rikishi slammed into him. We both bounced out of the corner, and when Rikishi saw that he had hit Rocky, he started fuming. He tried to super-kick me, but I ducked and he kicked Rocky right in the chin, knocking him down. Now Rikishi was standing there, stunned that he'd decked Rocky. He turned toward me and I hit him with my finish, the Olympic Slam. Right then Rocky bounced up and I slammed him, too. Now they were both down and I jumped on Rocky and pinned him for the title.

The ending gave Rocky's fans a reason to believe he'd gotten a raw deal. The way they saw it, Rikishi just got in the way and messed everything up. Either that or, as the story line would show over the next few months, he was just cheating for me because he wanted Rocky out of the way himself. I had a different view of the match, of course. In my eyes I'd beaten the hell out of two main event Superstars and left them both lying on the canvas. But whatever way you wanted to interpret the finish, there wasn't any doubt about how the fans felt seeing me take the Strap from Rocky.

There was an initial roar, just because I think the ending caught the fans by surprise. I'm sure they expected Rocky to kick out of the pin and get up and beat me. So when the ref counted out the pin, people reacted loudly, which was a tribute to the match. In fact, one of the World Wrestling Entertainment talent managers paid me a great compliment that night. Sometimes he goes out and sits in the audience to gauge the reaction of the fans, because that can dictate the direction of our story lines. He was out there that night and he told me afterward he couldn't believe how much buzz there was in the crowd as we were throwing each other around in the ring. He said the match was so intense that finally he stopped paying attention to the fans and got caught up in watching us himself.

"You guys reminded me of why I became a fan of World Wrestling Entertainment in the first place," the manager said. "I knew what was going to happen and I was still on the edge of my seat."

That made me feel good. That's the whole idea, to put on a show the fans walk away talking about for days.

So I became the champion that night. I can't say my life changed the way it did when I won the Olympic gold medal, when I became an instant celebrity. As a main event Superstar, I had that celebrity status before I won the belt.

But I did notice that everywhere I went around the country, people were taking notice of me more and more. I was already signing a lot of autographs, but the demand became greater. As much as we travel, we're constantly in situations where we're accessible to our fans. So when I became the champ, World Wrestling Entertainment assigned a full-time security guard to me, to be used however I felt necessary.

Usually I'll have the guy meet me at the airport when I fly into a city. He'll take me to the show and back to the hotel. It's kind of nice because then he can be the bad guy sometimes. I like to sign autographs, but in certain cities the demand can be overwhelming. You have to be somewhere and you don't have time to sign one hundred autographs. Or let's say you're going to a hotel after a show, and everyone knows you're staying there, which happens sometimes. So there are three hundred and fifty fans waiting for you at midnight, and you've gotta get up at six in the morning to catch a flight for the next night's show. To be fair, that's not the time to ask me to sign three hundred and fifty autographs. I never feel good about having to say no, but that's when a security guard can make the situation easier for you.

Then, once in a while you find yourself in potentially dangerous situations. People lose touch with reality, and maybe they want to test you as the character you play. I've been in that situation every so often, and that's where it helps to have a security guard step in and tell the fan to back off.

It doesn't happen often. The vast majority of our fans are great. When they tell you they love your work, that's a great compliment. What I hear most often is, "We love the way you entertain us." And that's the highest compliment anyone can give me.

Unfortunately, there's a very small percentage that doesn't get it. They can't seem to separate the character from the person outside the ring. A lot of times it's rebellious-type people who think Triple H and Stone Cold are cool, while I'm this dorky, establishment-type guy they hate. A couple of times people have challenged me in public, but nobody has ever gotten to me. Usually it's when I'm leaving the arena. I had a girl jump on my car and try to punch through the windshield one time in St. Louis. Another time, in Chicago, a guy punched the driver's-side window as I was pulling out of a parking lot. Then there was a time in Minneapolis when a guy reached into the car, got his hand on me, and told me he wanted to kill me.

There was also that time in Indianapolis when a kid told me he wanted to "kick my ass" and then he spit in my face. Big mistake. That was the only time I actually got out of my car. Although I was really angry and wanted to do something in retaliation, I realized as a celebrity I could not.

It wasn't done in a joking manner, either. It was kind of scary, to the point where it pissed me off. Usually I don't let anything bother me. I know that part of being a heel is dealing with fans who take your character to heart, and I can laugh off insults. But when somebody gets their hands on me or spits on me that's a different story. Fortunately, I had a security guard to grab the guy and back him off, and I let it go. But I was hot both times.

It does bother me sometimes that people think I'm this character in real life. You can't have everyone playing the role of Stone Cold or The Rock or the Undertaker. I've added a different dimension that other people have never seen before. When you match me up against Stone Cold or whoever else, it makes them shine in their character because we're complete opposites. People should appreciate that I'm the one guy who has enough courage to put myself over the top and make myself look like a fool here and there. That's harder to do than being a badass, but it's good for World Wrestling Entertainment. We can't be so one-dimensional where everyone is the same. As it is, I'm one of the few guys who wears any color but black into the ring. I wear the red-white-and-blue Olympic colors and it sets me apart even more. That's why I like my character so much, because there's nobody else even close to it.

Anyway, having a security guard is definitely helpful. It's not like we travel as a team in World Wres-

tling Entertainment, like a baseball team or a football team, where you always have teammates around if there's a problem.

I usually travel by myself. If I travel with anyone, it's with Edge and Christian, or Chris Jericho. Those are my closest friends in the business and they're rising stars themselves. Edge and Christian are without a doubt the most successful tag team in the history of World Wrestling Entertainment. They've won the tag-team championship seven times, which is an all-time record, and I think each of them has the kind of poise and promise to be a main eventer in the near future. And Jericho is a former European, Intercontinental Hardcore and Tag Team Champion who is really talented, and getting more and more popular with the fans all the time. I don't think there's any doubt he'll win the World Wrestling Entertainment title someday, because he has that kind of presence.

I've become close to Stephanie and Shane McMahon, too, and Chyna is a good friend as well. But for the most part, I've found that guys tend to go their separate ways away from the arena. It's kind of a strange life, in a way. You go on the road with these guys, you work together, and they're your friends. But when you go home, they're not really included in your life. Am I going to keep in touch with these guys ten or fifteen years from now, after I'm out of the business? Maybe not. That's just the nature of the business. We spend a lot of time together at the arena, but we live in different places around the country, and we all have our own lives. Don't get me wrong: It's a great life. I love it. I love what being in World Wrestling Entertainment has done for me. I don't mind all the time on the road. I don't like being away from my wife, but that's the life of a performer in any business.

World Wrestling Entertainment gives me plane tickets every week for the cities where I'm doing shows, but other than that, I'm on my own for my travel arrangements and expenses. When I first started, I was on a pretty tight budget. I stayed in a lot of Motel 8s, those types of places that cost $50 or less a night. As I began to move up the ladder and make more money, I moved up to Fairfield Inns, La Quintas, then the nicer chains like the Marriotts, the Hiltons. When I became a main event Superstar, I started staying in more exclusive hotels, mostly because of the service they provide. They know who I am, they'll do things like keep the kitchen open so I can get something to eat when I get back from a show late at night. They have security to help with the fans, if necessary. Basically they wait on you hand and foot. Obviously, it costs a lot more, but it's always nice to be catered to, especially since I usually don't have a lot of time to take care of the little things I might need on the road. I can call ahead and ask them to take care of something, and they do it.

It was the same with renting cars. I started out renting economy size. Now it's full size or luxury style. It doesn't look real good for the WWE Undisputed Champion to drive to a show where a lot of fans might be waiting, and pull up in this little economy car. There's an image you want to project as a World Wrestling Entertainment Superstar, and especially when you're the champion. It's the same thing with flying. World Wrestling Entertainment pays for me to fly first class because that's the image they want their Superstars to have. What are people going to think if they see Kurt Angle crammed into a middle seat in coach? They assume you're making big money, so you better spend it.

But even when you spend top dollar, it's not a glamorous life. At least not as glamorous as people probably think. You're traveling to a different city every day. Usually you're going to bed late and getting up early, because we don't stay in one city for more than a day, except for *WrestleMania,* where we do about four days of appearances beforehand.

So a lot of days you're dragging. But you have to put on a good show when the lights go on. Mentally, physically, spiritually, you better kick it into gear even if you don't feel up to it. No matter if it's a televised or nontelevised show, you owe it to the fans to give them what they want to see. Sometimes we're working in small arenas in places like Jonesboro, Arkansas, or Wilkes-Barre, Pennsylvania, doing shows that aren't for World Wrestling Entertainment but for independent organizations. The office asks you to do a favor and work a show for a minor-league operation like the one in Memphis that helps train new wrestlers for them. There might only be four thousand people or less in the seats, but you've got to remember they've paid to see you perform and you better have enough pride to deliver a top-notch show.

What most of us do, to get the day-to-day soreness out and stay in shape for five shows a week, is go work out at a local gym somewhere during the after-

noon before a show. I'll do some cardiovascular training, some weight work, and it helps work out the kinks and get you ready to go again that night. I try to work out just about every day of the week, even when I'm home. It makes me feel better, it keeps me from getting edgy.

After I got started in World Wrestling Entertainment, I did an interview with a Pittsburgh writer named Jim O'Brien, and when I told him about my schedule on the road, he wrote a story about how I was missing an opportunity to see the world. I knew what he was saying, but I don't think he understood how busy my schedule is. On a typical day, I get up, catch a plane, get to the next city, eat lunch, go work out, and go to the arena. I spend the next eight hours there doing promos and interviews, and rehearsing matches and any other story lines I'm in that night. After I have my match, I usually get back to the hotel at midnight, grab a late-night snack, and catch six hours of sleep before doing it all again the next day.

So when do I have time to go see the sights in a city, to try and enjoy the finer things in life on the road? There's no time. This isn't a luxury cruise where I get to travel around the world. When I was in amateur wrestling, I did try to take advantage of my traveling overseas. I'd get up, hit my two-hour workout, and go see the city because I had three or four hours of free time. Usually I was in the same city for four or five days while competing in a tournament. I don't have that luxury now. You're in and out, in and out. It's a grind, but you get used to it. You take it for what it is. You're a gypsy and you learn to live that lifestyle.

Some guys like to go out, drink beers, go to nightclubs, talk to women. I don't see how they do it with the schedule we keep. It's not my lifestyle anyway. I don't have time to break my body down that way, and make my days even longer. I'm driven to succeed in this career the same way I was driven as an amateur wrestler. I only have one thing on my mind, and that's being the best.

It is different now as far as my goals are concerned. I'm not looking for gold medals or titles. My focus is to be one of the best in the history of World Wrestling Entertainment. I want to make such an impact that people will remember me forever as an entertainer. If I can be considered one of the best in sports entertainment, that's what I'm shooting for. I want people to say I gave them a great show. I know that I'll go down in the record books as one of the best in amateur wrestling history, and that's what I want to do in sports entertainment. It's just measured differently.

I'm not going to kid you, though. Part of my motivation is to make as much money as I can, just like any other professional athlete. What I like about World Wrestling Entertainment is that you're rewarded if you produce. You have money incentives in your contract, based on how and where you're being utilized in the show. So people are guaranteed that they're getting our best efforts. I think that's important, especially these days when people are turned off by pro athletes in other sports who sign huge contracts that are guaranteed, no matter if they have a great year or a lousy year.

Here you've got a chance to make big money, but you've got to earn it, depending on whether you can move up to the main event level. In my first year my contract called for me to make a modest amount, but because I moved up the ladder so fast, I made significantly more. My goal for my second year was to double that. It's like anything else, you have to be willing to work hard to succeed. And no one appreciates it more than me. I only have to talk to my brothers when I'm home to be reminded that I'm lucky. They bust their asses in blue-collar jobs, and they come home just as tired as me, maybe more so, but they'll never have a chance to make the kind of money I'm making. That helps me keep this celebrity life in perspective, and be grateful for it even on the days when the hotel wake-up call comes awfully damn early.

5

MY REIGN AS CHAMP

I don't think anybody expected me to hold on to the WWE Undisputed Championship very long. Especially since I was wrestling the Undertaker the very next Pay-Per-View after I beat The Rock at *No Mercy*. Nobody in the business has a more intimidating look than Taker. He's about six feet ten, he's got a hard look to him, and he's got the whole biker image going. I've gotta admit, the first time I wrestled him I was a little intimidated myself. He still kids me about it because the first time he went to punch me, I sort of closed my eyes and made a face like I was bracing myself to get knocked out. I knew he wasn't going to hit me, at least not hard, but I guess something about him made me a little nervous. We ended up having a great match, but he beat me up pretty thoroughly that time.

So I'm sure the fans thought I'd lose the belt to him at the *Survivor Series* in November. The match marked my one-year anniversary in World Wrestling Entertainment, and I stopped to think about what a remarkable year it was for me. I never could have imagined I'd win the World Wrestling Entertainment

Title my first year, so I would have been happy to turn it over right away if that's what Vince wanted. But he had other plans, and this match made it clear that I wasn't going to replace The Rock or anybody else as the People's Champ. I was more like the Weasels' Champ.

I pounded away against the Undertaker in that match. It was a little like David vs. Goliath, because he's that much bigger than me. It was like chopping down a tree. But that's what makes it interesting, when you've got different styles in the ring: big guy vs. little guy, babyface vs. heel, it's all designed to stimulate reactions from the fans. That's the psychology of sports entertainment. So I was chopping away, but gradually he began to overpower me toward the end of the match. Finally, he knocked me out of the ring. Now I was on the run, like I was trying to get away because I was getting pounded by him. So I slid underneath the ring, out of view from the fans. The Undertaker reached in, grabbed my foot, pulled me out, and then threw me back into the ring.

He jumped in and staggered me with a punch to set up his finish—the Last Ride. He lifted me up over his head and slammed me on my back. I hit the mat and stayed down, while Taker covered me for the pin. The referee started to count, "One, two . . ." and suddenly he stopped. "Hold on a second," he said. "That's not Kurt Angle."

Undertaker jumped up, got in the ref's face, and backed him into a corner. "What the hell do you mean, that's not Kurt Angle?" he said.

Well, it wasn't. My brother Eric had been hiding

under the ring, and that's who the Undertaker pulled out and slammed in the ring. So just then, I slid out from beneath the ring and jumped in while the crowd was trying to figure out what the hell was going on. I ran up behind the Undertaker while he was still stunned, and I rolled him up for a one-two-three pin. And before he knew what hit him, I jumped up and ran out of the stadium, leaving my brother lying there. The fans didn't know how to react at first. They didn't know who my brother was, they just knew he looked like me. And they knew that whoever the guy was, I had cheated my way to victory. I looked like an all-time coward. So they booed like crazy as I waved good-bye going up the runway.

It was my favorite finish while I was the champ, because it caught everybody by surprise, and we pulled it off perfectly. None of the other guys, besides Taker, knew about it because we kept it real quiet. Vince wasn't even planning on that type of finish until my brother happened to show up in Columbus, Ohio, where we had a show five days before *Survivor Series*. Eric had just signed with World Wrestling Entertainment after a tryout, and he was going to start his training in Louisville for an independent show. He decided to come see me and maybe meet a few people.

I was talking to Vince when Eric showed up. I said, "Hey, Vince, you remember Eric?"

Vince started looking Eric up and down and he got this smirk on his face. I thought it was kind of strange at the time, but I found out later what it was all about. He came up with the idea for the finish right there, but he didn't want anyone to know. He had his son, Shane, call me the day before the Pay-Per-View and tell me to fly Eric in for the show. I still didn't know what he had in mind, and I was a little nervous because Eric didn't have any training. But Vince explained it the day of the match, and it worked beautifully. That's where Vince is really sharp. He's always coming up with ways to surprise the fans, and that's part of the reason World Wrestling Entertainment has been so successful. The shows never get old. The fans never know what to expect.

So I was still the champion, but obviously I wasn't a dominating champion. And more and more, I was becoming this hypocrite. I was always preaching the three I's—intelligence, integrity, and intensity—and yet I had no integrity in the ring. But at the same time I continued to parade around as the good-guy gold medalist. I wouldn't admit I was a worm, and the fans were dying to see somebody kick my ass.

The odds were pretty good that somebody would do it a few weeks later at *Armageddon*. Vince decided to put together the first-ever six-man Hell in a Cell match, with the top six main event Superstars. Usually, when you get six guys in the ring, or an enclosed steel structure in this case, it turns into a traffic jam of guys all pounding on one another. But this one worked out well. There was a lot of pairing off, in the cage, outside the cage, even on top of the cage, so we didn't get all jammed up together.

We didn't have that much planned, except the finish, so we did a lot of improvising and we pulled it off. It was a wild match. We had a little bit of everything. Rikishi even took a fifteen-foot drop off the cage into the back of a pickup truck. I don't know if there has ever been a more explosive match. There was so much hitting of heads on poles, and raking of heads on the cage, that by the end every one of us was drenched in blood.

We knew, going into the match, it would be brutal and bloody. So I was ready for it, unlike the other time I got cut, when Chris Jericho hit me with the Intercontinental belt last year. He didn't mean to draw blood, but he clocked me pretty good. I needed sixteen stitches in the top of my head, so it was a pretty big gash. You see guys get hit with belts all the time, but there's a trick to it.

The trick didn't work. It happens sometimes. I knew I was gushing blood, so I wanted the camera guy to make sure he got it. I wasn't worried about how bad it was, I just wanted to make sure we got it on camera so we didn't waste it. It's good TV, it's good for the business. I know some people will say that's going too far, but sometimes it's good to give people a taste of reality; let them know you can really get hurt doing this stuff, just in case anybody gets any ideas about trying it at home. We say it all the time: The stuff we do isn't something you want to do for fun in the backyard.

We only draw blood once in a while. For the "Hell in a Cell," Vince and the agents decided we needed something like that. They wanted it to be one of the most brutal matches ever. By the end of the match, everybody had taken a shot that made them bleed. Guys don't mind. I think the boys actually are excited

when they get to do it, because you don't get to do it very often. You don't want to do it often because it lessens the impact.

The brutality of the match almost made the ending anticlimactic. But I won again, and I did it in sort of a lucky way. At the end everybody was hitting finishes on everybody, and we were all down in the ring. Rocky was the last one to get knocked down, and I just happened to be lying next to him. I came to, rolled over, and covered him. The ref counted "one-two-three" and it looked like I just happened to be in the right place at the right time.

So I was still the champion, and I was still annoying the fans by the way I was winning. By that point Vince was looking for ways to make my character even sappier. He'd already used my brother Eric at *Survivor Series,* so at Christmas he decided to have an Angle family Christmas on *RAW.* He knew that my other brothers had all been amateur wrestlers and good athletes, so he decided to fly them to Chattanooga for our Christmas show.

It was just the kind of thing my character would do. I was just nerdy enough that I would have my family come into the ring with me and sing a Christmas song. It was funny because my brothers, my big, bad brothers, were nervous that day as they were waiting around for the show to start. They might be tough guys, but they were out of their element now, having to sing in an arena with 15,000 people watching, and millions more on TV. It was a great way for me to get back at them for the years of abuse they used to inflict on me.

I was in the ring for the first segment of the show, and I invited them out on the microphone. They walked down the runway wearing Santa hats and light-up wreaths around their necks. It was pretty funny. The creative team of World Wrestling Entertainment had them wearing Olympic-style sweatsuits, like me, and my character was so proud. We stood there, all of us, waving like idiots to the crowd. Vince wanted to find ways to be over-the-top with my character and this was definitely over-the-top. Edge and Christian were out there, too, because they were my character's buddies. And Stephanie McMahon-Helmsley was "business partners" with my character at the time, so she was out there. And we all stood together and sang "Walking in a Winter

Wonderland." I think my brothers—and my nephew Markie, the three-time All-American wrestler—were a little embarrassed. They didn't know what they were getting into and I could see them looking at me, like, "Do you know how much abuse we're going to take back home for this?"

But they were good sports about it. We did a pre-taping where I was walking around the arena, showing them what we do. I ran into K-Kwik, the rap singer and World Wrestling Entertainment Superstar. Being the nerdy guy I am, I said, "Hey, brothers, I want you to meet a fellow Superstar. His name is K . . ." and I pretended I didn't remember his name. That's how my character is, kind of oblivious to everybody else.

K-Kwik reminded me and I said, "Oh, K-Kwik, that's right. Guys, say hi to K-Kwik." And they did this big wave of the hand like I was doing and said "Hi, K-Kwik." They played the role of nerds like me, and I was thinking, "Man, they must really love me to do this for me. And they're going to kill me afterward." But when they got home to Pittsburgh they were sort of famous for a day because everybody had seen them on TV, so they wound up getting a kick out of it.

We even got my brothers involved in my six-man tag-team match that night. They were sitting in the front row, and when I knocked Chris Jericho out of the ring, he went over to my brothers, swore at them, and got into a little bit of a scuffle with them. My brothers had never pulled a punch in their life, so they didn't have much finesse. Jericho had to kind of cover up and protect himself, because my brothers were throwing all these reckless punches. Then the Dudley Boyz, who were teaming up with Jericho, came over and started punching my brothers, and it became a big slugfest. It was kind of funny because afterward you saw all these red marks on everyone's faces from punches landing. My brothers didn't mean to hurt anybody, but when they got a little rough, so did the Dudley Boyz.

One guy, Buh-Buh Ray Dudley, actually kind of stunned Mark with a shot to the head. Mark was smart enough not to retaliate with any real force. He knew this was my thing. I was glad he used his head because I knew his instinct was to fire back at Buh-Buh Ray. Put it this way: if it happened anywhere else, Buh-Buh Ray would have had his hands full. He's a tough guy, and I'm not saying he couldn't handle himself, but I don't know anyone tougher than Mark. Fortunately, Mark was professional enough to let it go. The Dudleys are real aggressive, kind of like me. They're not trying to hurt you, but sometimes they're going to lay into you just because they're going so hard in the ring and they want to put on a great show.

Pulling your punches is something that takes a lot of finesse. It's kind of an art to make your punches and kicks look real without actually hurting your opponent. Most guys are pretty good, but you're going to get people who lay into you. They get caught up in what's going on. If you don't have great finesse, you're called "stiff" by the other guys in World Wrestling Entertainment. I'm considered one of the stiffest

guys in the business, which isn't necessarily a compliment. I'll put it this way: a high percentage of my punches are going to land. I try not to, but I'm naturally aggressive. When I do a clothesline or a suplex, I do it with force. Not to the point where I'm going to hurt anybody, but when I do something, I don't like it to be hokey or fake. I would rather someone lay into me to make it look real than do something that looks completely fake.

It's tough to do, especially when you first start out. It takes time to do it effectively, make it look good, and eventually establish your own moves that give you an identity. I think I've improved 1,000 percent, especially with my punches and my kicks, but when that adrenaline starts flowing, sometimes I go a little harder than I should.

The stiffest guys in World Wrestling Entertainment are the A.P.A. They're tough guys out of the ring, too. Their gimmick is what they are in real life. They both played as linemen in the NFL. Faarooq's real name is Ron Simmons; he was a star defensive lineman at Florida State who finished in the top eight in the Heisman Trophy voting in 1982, losing out to Herschel Walker. And Bradshaw, aka John Cayfield, played for the Oakland Raiders for a while. So they're both tough SOBs, and when they hit someone with a clothesline or another move, they want people to say, "Wow! That was real."

I remember thinking that very thing a couple of years ago. It was March of 1999, and I was still working in Memphis. But World Wrestling Entertainment had me come to a match to do some promo-type spots. I was sitting in the front row of seats, watching the matches. By this time I had been training in Memphis for a couple of months and I was ready to come in and kick some ass. So now here came Public Enemy out to the ring. They were a tag team that had come from the WCW. They only lasted with World Wrestling Entertainment for a short while, mainly because they didn't fit in. That's the best way I can put it. They weren't fitting in with the company's style and the way we go about doing things.

So they didn't know it, but this was going to be their last match. And for whatever reason, it was with the A.P.A. Was it a coincidence? People can judge for themselves. But the A.P.A. came out and beat the hell out of Public Enemy. They were clotheslining them in the face and taking these vicious swings to hit them with chairs. Once one of the A.P.A. picked up the stairs by the ring and slammed them into the head of one of the Public Enemy guys. Coming from amateur wrestling, I was ready for just about anything in the ring, but when I saw this I looked at my wife and I said, "If they want me to do this shit, they're crazy."

I didn't know what was going on at the time. I thought the A.P.A. were just out of control, but later I found out they were sending a message to Public Enemy that their World Wrestling Entertainment career was over. The A.P.A. are the go-to guys in World Wrestling Entertainment. If there's any trouble at all in the ranks, somebody can go to them and they'll take care of it. At that time I just remember saying, "Wow, I never want to wrestle these guys."

I did end up wrestling them, though, and I found out they're not really out of control. They're very skilled. But they're still the stiffest guys in World Wrestling Entertainment because they want that image for their characters. When they come out, people say, "Okay, someone's gonna get their ass kicked."

So you better be prepared for a physical match when you go against them, and that was fine with me. I love the contact. I had good matches with them, and when they laid into me, I laid into them. That's just the way it is with some guys. There are no hard feelings unless somebody gets a little too carried away and really smashes you. But guys usually take care of that in the ring. If someone gets hit too hard, they'll hit back with real force just to let you know, "Hey, you went too far. Don't do it again."

And guys always get the message. This business is tough enough on our bodies. Nobody wants to hurt anybody. You get beat up as it is, being in the ring five nights a week, and everyone needs to protect themselves and we need to protect one another, too.

That is, unless you have a mutual agreement like I had with Chris Benoit at *WrestleMania*. We agreed beforehand that we were going to treat it about as close to a real wrestling match as you can and still be called sports entertainment. We both said, "Hurt me, beat the hell out of me, don't worry about it, I'll be fine." Guys like Chris and me, we get into the match and our intensity flares and we don't feel anything anyway. Then there are guys like Triple H and the Undertaker; they look like they're intense and kicking ass, but their heart rates hardly get above fifty

when they're in the ring. They just have a way of staying relaxed. It's an old-school thing. In the old days, those guys barely even laid into each other. That's how it was. Now the matches are a little bit stiffer, and there is more athletic movement. But those guys are very good at making it look like they're laying into you when they're really not.

Some guys in the business just have more finesse. Somebody like Rocky has so much finesse that he's never going to lay into you, and he's more professional than some other guys, too. If you happen to land one on him, he'll let it go. Guys like the Dudleys, you lay into them, they're going to lay into you right back. And sometimes they're going to lay into you anyway, because they don't know any other way. My brothers found out about that, especially Mark. I knew that Buh-Buh must have clocked him because afterward Mark said to me, "That SOB got me good. He's lucky we were in this arena."

But the show went well overall. My brothers came away with more appreciation for what I do. They saw how much work went into the show, and they couldn't believe how many things I had to do before the match. There were promos, pre-taped interviews, the planning for my match. The hours can add up quickly. I had been doing more and more stuff like that after I became champion. I didn't mind. I figured the more they wanted to use me, the better. But sometimes it could be a little much. I remember one match in Louisville, we had ten segments during the show and I was in every segment. Every one of them. I did a promo at the beginning, I had pretapes in other segments, I had a commentary of a match where I jumped The Rock, and I had another match where I ran in and beat up on Triple H. That was all before my own match at the end of the night with Stone Cold Steve Austin. I think I was one of a very few to ever be involved in every segment, and I guess it's because I had the different skills to handle it. But it was a little overwhelming. I remember Stone Cold was kind of irritated because every time we tried to get together to talk strategy for our match, somebody would pull me away for something I had to do. He said to me, "Man, they've gotta stop this shit. You don't need to do all this stuff."

And he was right. But to me it was a challenge. I wanted to prove that I could be effective doing as much as they wanted me to do. So my brothers saw all that work I put into it. And they saw me perform under pressure. They found out it's not like playing a sport, where you just let your instincts take over in the heat of the moment. It's going out there and playing a character—being sharp, hitting your lines, and working the match to make sure it comes out the way you planned it. In sports, you play on instinct: you fake one way, you go the other, and after it works you say, "What the hell did I just do?" Here, if you're gonna fake one way and go the other, you better have it set up that way or somebody's going to get hurt real bad. Because it's not about instinct. It's about doing your work, being prepared, and then concentrating so that you make everything look good in the ring.

After the Angle Family Christmas show, the holidays passed and I started the year still holding the belt as World Wrestling Entertainment Undisputed Champ. I had no idea how long I'd hold on to it, but I was enjoying my status. People were starting to wonder when I was going to lose. With each win I was becoming more and more legitimate as the champion. Up next was *Royal Rumble* in January and another big step for me.

I wrestled Triple H, who I think is the best in the business. At the time he was the top heel in World Wrestling Entertainment, and so he thought I should take on the role of babyface for our match. Nobody knows the psychology of the business better than he does, but in this case, I think he underestimated how much the fans appreciate his character. When two heels go at it, the fans usually cheer for the guy with the higher World Wrestling Entertainment profile. Hunter had been established as a main event Superstar for years, while I was still relatively new. But he was convinced he could make the fans turn on him. So we went out there and I'm bumping him around, playing the babyface role. I knocked him out of the ring and I was screaming for him to "get back in here," and people started chanting, "Angle sucks! Angle sucks!" I tried to tell Triple H that would happen because I knew people appreciated him more than me. But it turned out okay because we had such a wild, hellacious match that the fans started reacting to everything.

In the end, once again I had help in winning the title. Stone Cold had a feud going with Triple H, and he snuck into the ring and stunned Triple H from be-

hind just as Triple H was ready to finish me off. I had been knocked down and out, but now Triple H was down, too. As Stone Cold walked away, I came to, I saw Triple H down on the canvas, and I crawled over and pinned him.

So once again I made it out of Pay-Per-View as the champion. It was just another way to get under the fans' skin. Because the next night on *RAW* I was bragging that I had beaten the best in the game. It was the second time I had beaten Triple H, so I was telling the fans that without a doubt, I was the best in the business. The fans were booing, cursing at me for being such a weasel. And I loved it.

LOSING THE TITLE

As the year 2001 began, I knew my time was running out as the World Wrestling Entertainment Undisputed Champ. Nobody holds the belt very long anymore, that's just the way it is. Fans want change. It's a remote-control world these days—people don't like what they see, *zap,* they move on to something else. Besides, it was clear I wasn't a dominating champ. I was pulling out title matches with shaky wins, after I'd been battered around in the ring. Or else I always seemed to have some trick up my sleeve to help me win, somebody to help me. Basically people thought I was a cheater.

I think that's probably why I kept the belt as long as I did. Every time the title was on the line, people were figuring I had to lose it this time, but I'd pull off some stunt to win again. It kept them guessing, which is a big part of the business. If it gets predictable then the fans get bored.

But then it was decided that The Rock would take back the title at *No Way Out* at the end of February, setting up The Rock and Stone Cold as the featured match for *WrestleMania,* our biggest event of the year. And I understood that. At that point I'd still only been in the business for a little over a year, and it takes time to become a legitimate main eventer for *WrestleMania*. I felt like I'd proven I belonged as a main event Superstar, but I knew I probably needed another year to be ready to headline *WrestleMania*.

So I didn't care that I was losing the title, but how I lost it would be very important. I knew it was critical to my future that Rocky "made me," which is the term we use when your opponent makes you look good, even in a loss—like you should have won but you didn't. It was real important in my case because of my image with the fans. In their eyes I'd been lucky to win the title and even luckier to hold on to it for five months. But if I looked like a killer against Rocky, even while I was losing, it would establish me as a legitimate threat to win back the title.

It's part of the process of building a reputation with the fans, which is crucial. The top guys understand that. I remember Triple H talking to me a few weeks before *No Way Out*. He said, "Listen, you've got to make sure that they make you in that match with The Rock. He's going to take that title and go to *WrestleMania* as the top card, but what's going to happen to you? It all depends how you look in that match."

So that was my mind-set going into *No Way Out,* and we pulled it off. Rocky was incredible. With his experience, he made me look tremendously strong. Pat Patterson, the agent of our match, set up a great match. We had exciting false finishes all over the place. There were belt shots, chair shots, moonsaults off the top rope. Rocky and I were really in sync, making all the right moves. And the fans were eating it up. It was perfect . . . until the end.

We had set up the finish just the way we wanted. After each of us had kicked out of all sorts of false finishes, Rocky finally hit me with his Rock Bottom. I got up high in the air and came crashing down to the canvas. And I went limp. I was ecstatic about the way the match had gone, and so now I just sort of let all the air come out of me. Rocky covered me and the referee started his count.

"One . . . two . . ." but instead of slapping the mat for the third time, he stopped his hand, the way he would if I was going to kick out. Only I didn't kick out. The ref didn't realize this was the finish. So he looked at us, then he looked at the announcers' table where the bell was, and he knew he had messed up. He should have just said, "It's a fall. The Rock wins."

But I guess he thought it would look bad, since he hadn't finished the count. So he said, "No fall. The match continues."

And Rocky and I were like, "What the hell? What are we going to do now?"

The fans knew something wasn't right. They were booing, chanting "Bullshit, Bullshit" as both of us scrambled to get up. But I think they probably thought the ref was just cheating for me, that it was just another one of my schemes.

Still, I didn't know what to do. Fortunately, Rocky said, "Come here." He was smart enough to give me another Rock Bottom, with a lot of force. I went crashing to the canvas again, and Rocky covered me again, and pulled my leg real tight into a pinning position. He looked up at the ref and snarled, "Count the goddamn finish."

This time the ref counted it out, and The Rock was the champ again. Afterward both of us were upset because we'd set up the finish so perfectly, and we were worried that it looked bad, but later we watched the tape and it didn't look bad at all on TV. Because of the camera angle at the time, people watching couldn't really tell if I kicked out or not. The announcers, Jim Ross and Jerry Lawler, covered it up by saying, "Oh my God, Angle kicked out again." In a way, it made me look stronger for fighting Rocky off one more time.

So, mistake and all, the match did "make me" the way I had hoped. And since then I think the fans have looked at me differently, like I belong at the top. They don't look at me as this guy who doesn't deserve the title. They look at me as a threat now. It has a lot to do with that match and it may have something to do with the change in my character.

For a few weeks before that match, my character began to show a meaner side, to make sure that fans continued to hate me as a heel. I was becoming more cynical in the way I talked, and more vicious in the ring. It was almost like I had a screw loose. I was into breaking bones all of a sudden, and knocking people out cold. It wasn't very all-American, but it was a natural progression for my character. The goofy smile was being replaced by this crazed intensity in the ring.

Vince wanted me to develop that mean side, and it was probably something I needed. When you're a champion heel like I was, the best way to make people hate you is to get your ass kicked in a match and still squeak out a win and retain the title. But after I lost the title I could be more vicious, more aggressive, and use a lot of my wrestling moves. I came up with my own submission hold, the ankle lock. Kenny Shamrock, who is an Ultimate Fighting Champion now, used to use the ankle lock in World Wrestling Entertainment, and when I adopted it as my signature move, it did wonders for me.

Mostly it gave me a certain identity. Whenever I grabbed someone's ankle and locked it in, the fans would go wild. I'd yell at my opponent and get that crazed look on my face, and people thought I was going to snap the ankle, especially after we made it look like I really did break Scotty 2 Hotty's ankle one night. And the way we did that shows you the creativity of the people doing the story lines for the World Wrestling Entertainment.

Scotty had been having neck problems for a while. A week or so before that match a doctor checked him out and told him he needed about eight weeks of rehab. At the same time World Wrestling Entertainment was trying to come up with a way for me to grab the fans' attention with my new move. I hadn't made anyone tap out yet with the ankle lock; I'd only used it as a threat. So they decided to have me take out Scotty with an ankle lock.

This was the week after *No Way Out,* when I was screaming at every opportunity for a rematch with

The Rock. I was on the first TV segment, doing a promo, talking about how I should be in the main event at *WrestleMania* instead of The Rock and Stone Cold, and how I should still have my title. So they both came out and beat the hell out of me. As I was lying there, we cut to commercial. When we came back from commercial, I was still standing next to the ring, protesting. Our commissioner, William Regal, came down and said he was going to let me wrestle The Rock later that week for the title.

"If you win, you're in the main event at *WrestleMania*," he said.

I said, "I want him tonight."

And I was still talking when the music started for

Too Cool, Scotty and Grand Master Sexay. I was kind of in the middle of a rage, so when they got in the ring, I jumped in and beat them both up. I showed everybody what happened when they disrespected me by putting their music on and coming down while I was talking. I jumped them when they weren't looking, threw Grand Master out of the ring, and whipped him into the stairs.

Then I jumped back in and got Scotty down. We had practiced this all afternoon. I had to pull his shoe halfway off, to a point where I could turn the shoe and make it look like I snapped the ankle and it would stick. We were kind of laughing about it because it could have looked funny. It was tough because if you pulled it too far off, the shoe was coming off. If you didn't pull it far enough, I really was going to break his ankle. We were practicing it and it was hard to get it right. But that night it worked really well. I pulled it halfway off and clamped my move in. Then, at just the right time, I loaded up and I rotated the shoe to make it look like I snapped it. It stuck there perfectly and the fans actually thought I broke his ankle. I got serious heat for that.

People asked me at home if I really snapped his ankle. I guess some of them wanted to believe it. World Wrestling Entertainment made it look convincing. They brought the paramedics down and put Scotty on a stretcher, then wheeled him up the runway. On TV they showed a close-up of his feet and one was angled in to make it look like it was broken.

Later that week I was on a radio call-in show, and

one guy called up screaming at me for breaking Scotty's ankle. Now, overall our fans are awesome, and if they want to believe that everything they see is real, that's fine. But sometimes you get a few who take it a little bit too far. And the thing is, you're not quite sure if they're messing with you. You're not sure how to take it or react. This guy on the call-in show was screaming at me, saying he wanted to break my ankle. I said, "If you want to try, I'll give you my address, buddy." Then he started screaming louder and the station cut him off. After they cut him off, I explained to people the whole story, about how Scotty needed time off for his neck. If the guy was still listening, he must have felt like a real idiot.

But obviously, I was selling the move. After that, whenever I would grab that move, people thought I was going to snap another one. It's great to see people respond like that. It's what Vince was hoping for. I remember when I put the ankle lock on Rocky at *No Way Out,* and I made it look like I wanted to rip his foot off. I was so intense that it looked like the veins in my forehead were going to pop. People told me later that as Vince was watching it, he said to the guys backstage, "Angle has arrived."

And after losing the title, I found it was easier to play the role that way. I wanted the belt back and I was ready to do anything to get it. The story line had me constantly trying to challenge Rocky, Stone Cold, or anyone else in line for a title shot. I was still a big part of things, as a threat to those guys, and that felt good. It's not like I was put on the shelf after I lost the title.

I like playing the role that way even more. I can be a lot more aggressive. I can use more of my suplexes. I don't have to bump all the time, let guys beat me up. I've got a harder edge to me now. My nickname before among the fans was "Crybaby" because I was always whining and crying, and I was scared to wrestle certain guys. I remember for my first match with the Undertaker, six months into the business, my character was scared to death of this guy, to the point where I was supposedly losing sleep. I didn't want to face the guy because he was a killer—a seven-foot, 330-pound animal. And even though I was an Olympic gold medalist, the script called for me to run from him whenever I could.

Well, after *No Way Out* I didn't run from anyone anymore. I was a legitimate main event Superstar who could beat anybody. But I was still a heel. I still had a way of making the fans hate me. Instead of just wearing people out with the Olympic gold medalist routine, I was becoming more and more devious.

I teamed up with Chris Benoit in a handicap match against The Rock. Before the match we'd do promos and I'd be telling Chris, "Let's rip this guy in half." But then in the ring I'd be sneaky and make sure Chris didn't look too good. In one match Chris put Rocky in his trademark hold, his Crossface. It looked like he was going to make Rocky tap out, so I snuck around and put Rocky's foot up on the rope. That forced the referee to make Chris let go of his hold.

Chris didn't see me do it, but the fans saw it. They

were hollering at me for being a backstabber. The idea was that I wanted to be the one to get the glory. Well, I ended up getting pinned by Rocky, and at that point Chris jumped into the ring to stick up for me. He and The Rock started going at it, and Rocky reversed him and put him in a Sharpshooter—another one of his submission holds. Now, you'd think I'd get up and come to Chris's rescue. Nope. I got up, looked at Chris being pummeled, and I just started smiling as I left the ring and walked up the runway, leaving my partner in the ring. Now, that's cold.

It also helped set up my match with Benoit at *WrestleMania* as well as this year's rivalry to determine who the "best technical wrestler" is in the World Wrestling Entertainment. Chris doesn't have any real experience as an amateur wrestler, but he is known for being really smooth and athletic in the ring. We both have our trademark wrestling moves. He has the Crippler Crossface and I have the ankle lock, and before *WrestleMania* both of us were saying to the world, "I'm the best technical wrestler in the World Wrestling Entertainment."

In reality, there isn't any doubt who would win if we actually held an amateur-style match. I think everyone in World Wrestling Entertainment knows what I can do if I want to. I've always been pretty humble about my ability and I'm easygoing in the ring. Whoever I'm wrestling, I want both of us to feel good about the match and I'll go out of my way to make the other guy look good. I let guys throw me around. I don't have an ego about that, but the guys know.

I've had about fifteen of the boys challenge me to wrestle in the hours before a show, just because they wanted to see what I had. Let's just say I'm undefeated. I've had fun with it, but I let them know pretty quickly that I can do anything I want with them in a real wrestling match. Some of the guys wrestled in high school, but that's about it. None of them has been able to give me any kind of match. Not the big guys, the 300-plus-pounders, and not the smaller guys, the 200-pounders. Usually they're shocked by my quickness. That's what opens their eyes more than anything. Before they know it, I shoot on them, take them down, and tie them up in knots. Or I spin behind them before they can blink and take them down that way, putting them on their back. Or I'll hit them with an arm throw or a fireman's carry. Afterward they say something like, "Damn, Angle, I didn't know you were that quick. I didn't think you could pick me up and throw me on my back." I've done that to guys as big as 350 pounds, just to show them what I could do. It's an explosion thing. If you have certain positioning, you can throw anybody.

I never do it to show off, but if a guy wants to see if I'm for real, I'm happy to show him. It's fun because it's all the stuff I don't get to use in World Wrestling Entertainment. You'll see my wrestling mentality come out once in a while in the ring, when something happens and I have to react. But I never want to show anyone up out there. The only time I think I surprised somebody with one of my amateur wrestling moves was in a match with Triple H.

It was during the story line where I was trying to steal Stephanie from him. I was in the ring doing a promo, talking on the microphone about my great friendship with Stephanie, and Triple H came running down to the ring and got in my face. We weren't wearing match gear, but we ended up going at it and he beat the hell out of me, then threw me out of the ring. When he threw me out, the music was supposed to start in the arena for Mick Foley, who was the commissioner then and was going to come down to put an end to our flare-up. There was a mixup in production, and the music didn't start. So Triple H and I were stuck, on national TV, standing there looking at each other, like, "What do we do now?"

So Triple H took his shirt off and gestured for me to

come get my ass kicked. Well, at that point I wasn't going to get punked out, especially after I just got thrown out of the ring. So I took my sweat top off and said, "Okay, let's go." The music still didn't come on, so I slid into the ring, got up, and charged him. This was one time when my instincts took over and I hit him with one of my old wrestling moves—a double-leg takedown, where I shot for his legs, jacked him up, and knocked him on his back real quick. I started punching him and he had this look on his face like, "What the hell just happened?" So I told him to roll on top of me and start throwing punches at me. Finally, somebody started the music and Mick Foley came out to stop us. At the time I think I shocked Triple H with my quickness. He didn't know what to do when I went for his legs. We made it look good, though, when he rolled me over and started pounding me.

And afterward we laughed about it. "Angle," he said, "what the hell was with that double-leg? This ain't the goddamn Olympics."

I do think there's room for some of those amateur wrestling moves in the World Wrestling Entertainment. It adds another dimension. But you need two guys who can pull it off, and that's what Chris Benoit and I did at *WrestleMania*. We had given people a taste of it a few weeks earlier, and the fans seemed to love it, so we decided to build our *WrestleMania* match around that true wrestling style. We were a little nervous because we knew it wasn't what fans expected, and we were worried they might not really understand what we were doing and start giving us the "Boring . . . Boring" chant.

But the fans really got into it, probably because they never see it anymore. People see the kicks and the punches, and the high spots off the ropes in just about every match, but we were doing some of the old wrestling moves that people hadn't seen in years. It was about as close to Olympic-style wrestling as you could ever see in World Wrestling Entertainment. We were both shooting for takedowns, then doing reversals and putting each other in our submission holds.

Of all the matches I had in my first eighteen months in the business, that had to be my favorite because it gave me a chance to showcase my amateur wrestling talents. It wouldn't have worked with a lot of guys, but Chris was perfect for it. He never did much amateur wrestling, but he helped the match flow and look so real that it kind of scared me. I think if Chris had a year of work as an amateur wrestler, he could be really good. I initiated most of the moves, but I'd leave him openings to counter me, and Chris picked up on them and used them perfectly. We actually wrestled for about six minutes. Then we made it look like I got frustrated because Chris was countering all of my Olympic moves, and I cheap-shotted him from behind to knock him down. At that point we shifted gears into the pro-style part of the match, and finally, I pinned Chris by pulling his tights while he was on his back. Another cheap win for your Olympic hero.

When it was over we were both blown up, which is our way of saying we were dead tired. I was actually shocked at how tired I was. I never get blown up during a regular match, but this was like going back to my old days, only I'm not in that kind of superior condition anymore. After the match I was lying down in the locker room thinking about those days when I was working out eight hours a day, wondering how I put my body through all that for as long as I did.

The reaction in the World Wrestling Entertainment to our match was great, too. Vince McMahon liked it so much he actually gave me a hug backstage, which is something he hardly ever does. And the agents, the old-school guys like Jack Lanza, Pat Patterson, and Gerry Brisco who do most of the planning for the matches, they were ecstatic. Gerry was my agent for my matches the first six months I was in World Wrestling Entertainment, and he couldn't wait to tell me how proud he was of me.

"You did something nobody else could do and you brought back something we need," he said. "Some old-school wrestling."

The match was such a hit that we carried the story line between Chris and me into the summer and built a new rivalry out of it. The fans might get to see more of that in the future, too. In the last year we've signed a few more amateur wrestlers who are in World Wrestling Entertainment development camp. A couple of them are national champions, so they're obviously very talented. I think I've made it easier for other wrestlers to make the move to World Wrestling Entertainment, and in turn World Wrestling Entertainment sees how well it's worked out with me. One time Vince said to me, "I wish I had ten more like you." It felt good to hear him say that. It's because I caught on so quickly and because I've never had an ego about coming in as an Olympic champion. It's all about having a good attitude and being a team player.

But that's what is great about our locker room. You don't see big egos. Everybody looks out for themselves, that's only natural, but there's definitely a feeling that we're all trying to do what's good for the company, too. That's the difference between World Wrestling Entertainment and some organizations from the past. They have guys who won't do jobs, which means they won't get beaten in the ring to help raise another guy's profile in the company. They've got guys walking around saying, "I'm not getting pinned. No way, not me." The only way they'll agree to lose is if there is interference from other wrestlers, so it looks like the guy had no chance.

To be honest, I think everyone is protected too much, even in World Wrestling Entertainment. Most of the top guys hardly ever do straight-up jobs. There always has to be some kind of twist when a guy gets pinned. Usually it's a chair shot when the referee isn't looking. Or a couple of guys who are helping the heel will come storming into the ring to help beat the babyface. To me, I think it'd be more legitimate to see everybody get their butt whipped once in a while. When you watch football or baseball or basketball or hockey, or even amateur wrestling, you see that no-body is unbeatable, and that's because it's so competitive. I'd like to see it that way in World Wrestling Entertainment as well. If The Rock beats me straight-up on *RAW*, with no interference, then on *SmackDown!* that same week I should be able to beat him the same way to gain back some respect. Suspense and great competition is what fans want to see in any sporting event, and I think that kind of give-and-take would be proof of how competitive the top Superstars are in World Wrestling Entertainment.

I understand the psychology of the heel needing to cheat to win, because it dramatizes the difference between the characters and it raises the level of emotion with the fans. I just don't think it always has to be that way. Of course, that's just my opinion, and as a heel I feel like a middle linebacker some days, always chasing the babyface quarterback.

But from what I've seen and heard, the egos in other organizations can get out of control. Some of these guys are living their characters. That's the problem sometimes with this business. Guys get into their characters and they start to believe that's who they really are. We've had guys from the other entertainments come over with some of those attitudes, and if they don't check their egos at the door they don't last very long.

In World Wrestling Entertainment it's simple: Vince lays down the law. Everything has to go through him. He lets people know the way it's done here. That's why he likes me. I trust him, so I'll do whatever he wants and I don't have a problem with it, even if I have to look bad. Jim Ross, our announcer, felt the

same way about me when I joined. He's got a lot of influence in the company. He helps train the newcomers, and he saw that I had talent but I didn't have a huge ego. He knew I'd mesh well with World Wrestling Entertainment.

Not that you'd know it by watching my character, but that's the fun of it. I've always enjoyed playing the heel, and I've enjoyed it more since they made me a little nastier after I lost the belt. I'm getting better and better at it and letting that nasty side come out in the ring. Stone Cold Steve Austin turned heel this year, and he is probably the number one heel now. If you're next in line behind him, you're doing fantastic, but I would like to be the number one heel eventually. I've always been that way. My goal is to be the very best in the business. So I listen to everybody in the business and I ask questions. When the matchmakers and the writers are talking, I'll interrupt them and ask why they want to make the match go a certain way. I want to know the psychology of it as well.

After *No Way Out,* I started getting even more response from the fans when I would make my entrance into the ring. Anytime a big main eventer walks out, good guy or bad guy, the first response is a big cheer because the fans want to see one of the top guys. Triple H gets it more than anybody. He gets the loudest pop when he comes out, then people start booing because he has been the top heel in the business for so long. People love to hate me, too. If anything, I became more popular after I lost the title.

And I reached the point where Vince McMahon started looking to me to start helping some of these guys and be a leader. After *No Way Out* I had a match with Test, a young guy with a tremendous look and a big future. He's six feet seven, 280 pounds, he's real athletic, and he's going to be a main event Superstar in the near future. He already gets a big response from the fans. But sometimes he gets a little too excited in the ring and starts doing everything real fast. It was up to me to slow him down at the right times, to pull back the reins and let the crowd respond to the action before we moved on to the next part of the match.

We had a great match and I handled the flow of it pretty well. As I walked up the runway and went backstage, Vince seemed to be happy. He gave us both a thumbs-up, and that's all I needed to see to know I'd done a good job. Vince left it up to me to make that match look phenomenal, and I did. It told me that I was really coming into my own, where I understood the business enough to work with the psychology of the crowd.

Some guys don't always seem to get that part of it. It's not really something that's taught when you break into the business. When I started I was taught a bunch of moves, but I wasn't taught the psychology. A lot of these guys have some great moves, but there's no selling. There's no story. And the story is critical to making sports entertainment work. It's what makes it interesting to the fans.

To me, the moves are the easy part. The hard part is doing the right thing at the right time and telling a story, and doing it in a short period of time for TV. I've learned a lot just by watching some of the main event Superstars. Triple H—his matches are works of art. Whether he's doing the attacking or his opponent is attacking him, Triple H is going to sell it the right way. He's going to show it on his face and in the way his body reacts. He's going to know just the right time to grab the crowd. The right time to cut the other guy off. When to make a comeback. When the finish should be. He can feel it. Just watching him, it's a beautiful thing.

I see the satisfaction on his face when he's done. He knows when he has that crowd. He knows how good it was. A lot of guys are worried about "How did it look? How did my moves look?" Well, who cares how your moves looked? Did you grab the crowd? If not, then you've got a problem. I'm learning that more and more each time I work. It's a rush when I'm out there and I'm feeling the crowd. By the spring of this year I'd be out there thinking, "Oh, I've got these people. I can feel it."

It was like that at *No Way Out*. At one point Rocky hit me with the belt and I was down on the canvas, he covered me for the pin, "1, 2 . . . ," and I barely kicked out. I started to get up, and Rocky jumped on me, pounding away: *bang, bang, bang.* But then I cut him off—I surprised him and nailed him with my finish, the Angle Slam. So he was down and people thought it was over for him. I did it with just the right timing, right out of the blue, and the fans were stunned. When I started slowly crawling on Rocky for the cover, I could hear them screaming for

Rocky because they thought he was finished. Then the count goes 1, then 2, and at 2⅞ Rocky kicked out and the place erupted with noise. We continued on with great emotion and false finishes.

And I was looking at Rocky like, "Do you feel it? We've got these people. Let's keep it going."

That's what it's all about in this business. I love entertaining people this way just as I loved competing for all those years in amateur wrestling, and I feel blessed the way my dreams have come true for me. Even what seemed like a bad time for me, the Fox-TV job in Pittsburgh after the Olympics, turned out to be a blessing because it gave me on-camera experience that helped me when I got into the World Wrestling Entertainment and had to use the microphone.

So the only question now is how long I can do this without permanently damaging my body. My wife and I plan to start a family soon, and I don't want to be so beat up physically in ten years that I can't get out there and play with my kids in the yard, or maybe coach them in a sport.

I love being part of this business more every day, especially since I had what I call my bonding moment with Vince McMahon. It happened in May of this year during our trip to England for our annual Pay-Per-View, and what an experience it was.

Since I started with the World Wrestling Entertainment I've always had a friendly relationship with Vince, but until the trip to London I never felt like I was as close to him as most of the other main event guys. I had great respect for him as the boss, but I guess I was somewhat intimidated by him, even though other people in the business told me it was important to develop a strong one-on-one relationship with him. Also, I wanted to be careful not to step on the toes of guys that I knew were very tight with Vince. So I kept my distance.

But all of that changed on the charter flight back from England. Vince was moving around, talking to different people, and eventually he came over and sat down on the armrest of my seat. We started talking about World Wrestling Entertainment, and my match in England, and then we started talking about his years in amateur wrestling. He told me that his dad sent him to a military school in Virginia for his high school years, and that he had been a runner-up to the state champion among private schools. From there we started talking about the time when Vince took me down in the ring one night on *RAW IS WAR*. It was set up where he snuck behind me, lifted me up in the air, and took me down, then jumped out of the ring, yelling "two" for the takedown.

The whole thing was Vince's idea, and I think he came up with it just because he wanted to take down an Olympic champion. But anyway, on the plane he was teasing me about that, saying he was the only one who ever took me down in the wrestling ring. It was all in fun and we had a good talk for about an hour or so. Finally, as he stood up to walk away, his last words were, "Remember, Angle, I'm the only one who's ever taken you down."

Well, at that moment something made me decide to have a little fun with the boss. When Vince got up to walk away, I attacked him from behind, knocked him down, turned him over, and pinned him right in the aisle. There were about eighty World Wrestling Entertainment people on the plane, and everyone was howling. Everyone except the Undertaker, anyway.

I think he must have been sleeping, and woke up when he heard the commotion. He told me later he saw Vince on the floor and couldn't tell who was on top of him. Vince and I had been on the floor for about thirty seconds as Vince struggled to get me off of him, when the Undertaker came over and put a choke hold on me. He clamped me so tight that he actually choked me out and I blacked out for a minute. When I came to, Vince was standing up and he had this big smile on his face. I think he just loved the idea that he was wrestling with an Olympic champion, and he decided it wasn't going to end there.

In fact, he turned it into a competition for the next four hours on the plane. Any chance he had, he tried to take me down. He'd attack me from behind. He'd wait until I came out of the bathroom. Half the time I wouldn't see him. He'd pop up from behind a chair and jump on me, or leg-dive me. He'd do whatever he could to try to take me down. One time he hit me hard, knocked me backward off my feet. I hit my face on the ground, then got up and attacked him. I took him down, held him down for a while, and then we got up and hugged each other.

One thing about Vince, he's a strong guy. He hasn't been involved in amateur wrestling in nearly forty years, so you'd think I could take him down in two seconds. But he was so strong that he was fighting me off, pushing me back, and then I'd have to come after him again. He's fifty-five years old, he weighs 250 pounds, and I couldn't believe how strong he is. I had to do some finessing, fake and wait for him to react, then spin him around. I couldn't just outmuscle him.

So we went back and forth for the rest of the flight, and everybody seemed to be getting a kick out of it. The Undertaker said to me, "You'll never see Bill Gates doing this with any of his employees." He's not kidding. But that's Vince's relationship with the guys.

He lives to bond with us, kind of like a brotherly thing.

I figured the whole thing was over when we had to return to our seats for the landing at Newark Airport. But then, I was sitting there, strapped in as we were about to land, and I saw this figure in the dark, crawling up the aisle. The flight attendants were already strapped in, but there was Vince, trying to sneak up on me one more time. I turned around and said to Chris Jericho, "Do you believe this?"

Vince was still in the aisle when we landed, and when I got up out of my seat he attacked me again. This time he knocked me into his wife, Linda, who fell on the floor. I said, "Oh my God, I just knocked over Linda McMahon." But she was a great sport about it. She knew Vince was having a good time, and she probably recognized that it was his way of bonding with me. So we went at it one more time, and finally, when we got off the plane, Vince said, "This isn't over."

It sure made the trip home livelier than anyone expected, but it also moved my relationship with Vince to a different level. I think he wants me to be one of the leaders of this company eventually, and from that point on I felt I could go to Vince and talk about anything. That's the relationship he has with guys like Stone Cold, Triple H, Rocky, the Undertaker, and a lot of others, and that's what I wanted. Until then I'd go to the writers if I had any suggestions, but since then not only do I go to my writers like Brian Gewirtz, I talk to Vince or Shane if I have ideas for my match or really for anything with World Wrestling Entertainment. Vince has an unbelievable knack for knowing what works and what doesn't, but if he likes what you have to say he's always willing to listen. Since then I've felt more involved in the inner workings of World Wrestling Entertainment, and that makes me want to do well for Vince as well as for myself and my family.

So who knows how long I might be able to do this? I want to make as much money as I can so that my family can live comfortably when I do retire from the World Wrestling Entertainment. I don't want to have to work after that, but I also know that I'll never be one to sit by the pool all day. As an athlete I've always been driven to achieve, and I'm sure I'll always want to feel like I'm doing something productive.

If TV or movie opportunities come out of being in World Wrestling Entertainment, I'll probably try some things. I don't think I'll ever be an A-plus actor, but if I could do some movies, that would be another kind of achievement. Whatever else I do, though, I know I'll always make World Wrestling Entertainment my home base.

Whenever I finally retire, I know at some point I'll want to do some coaching for amateur wrestling because the sport has done so much for me. Right now the only thing I do to help amateur wrestling is volunteer to put on wrestling clinics a couple of times a year for a high school wrestling team coached by Jerry Brisco, one of our ring agents in the World Wrestling Entertainment and a former All-American wrestler for Oklahoma State. His brother Jack was a two-time NCAA champion and former NWA pro wrestling champ. Those clinics help me brush up on my teaching technique, and the kids are great, so it's very rewarding.

But as much as I enjoy teaching the sport, I don't have much interest in high school or college coaching because I don't think I want to deal with all the off-the-mat responsibilities that go with those jobs. It's very stressful. I don't really want those two A.M. phone calls telling me that one of my wrestlers was arrested for being drunk and disorderly, or something like that. And I don't want to have to be a hard-ass, pushing kids if they aren't committed to wrestling the way I was or worrying about if they can stay eligible in school. I'd prefer working with younger kids at the midget wrestling level, because there it's about teaching the sport and making it fun for the kids.

Wrestling is a dying sport in our country because kids don't seem to want to pay the price it takes anymore. They'd rather go play video games. Unlike sports such as baseball or soccer, wrestling isn't quite as fun. More kids tend to loathe it than love it because it's so physically and psychologically demanding. But I feel I've got a knack for teaching it, for making it fun for kids.

At the same time I'd also be interested in coaching at the Olympic level. That's more voluntary-type coaching, so they're always looking for good people, and I know at that level I'd be working with athletes who are completely dedicated. I just feel like I've got a lot to offer, and at some point I'd like to give back to wrestling because of what the sport has done for me.

But right now that all seems too far down the road

to think about very seriously. What I am thinking about, though, and I'm sure this will surprise some people, is making a comeback for the 2004 Olympics. I know that might sound like a contradiction to a lot of what you've already read, especially in terms of committing myself to my old conditioning regimen again.

But the deeper I got into writing this book, the more I started thinking about how much I missed the competition. And if I did come back, it's not like I'd be in training for years and years, like I was in the past. Basically I was in amateur wrestling for twenty years straight, and after '96 I was done. I needed to get away. Now the hunger is coming back. I figure it would take a year of dedicated training to be ready for the Olympic qualifying tournaments. I'd take a year off from World Wrestling Entertainment, and I might even be able to stay in it part-time until the last few months before the Olympics. What a story that would be, to be off for eight years and then come back and win the Olympics again.

It sounds almost impossible, but believe me, I could probably do it. At thirty-four, thirty-five years old, I'm still going to be young enough at that time. I could give 110 percent for a year. I've got the knowledge, I've got the technique, and I know I've got whatever it takes to be there. I've done it. Since I last competed, a couple of weight classes have been consolidated, including mine. The 220-pound class and the 198-pound class have been combined to form just one 213-pound weight class. Since I always wrestled underweight anyway, I think that would work to my advantage. I'm up to about 230 pounds now, but if I spent a month on the wrestling mat I'd be down to 215 easily. I still can't imagine doing the training I did for a long-term period, but for a year I could do whatever it took.

If I do it, a bunch of guys in my weight class will get scared in a hurry. There probably will be some young stud at the top of the weight class by 2004, but you know what? He might just have to wait another four years to make the Olympic team. Why not? I see other guys doing it. Mario Lemieux came back, and Michael Jordan did it more than once. Those guys are my idols and I understand what they're feeling. I walked away when I was on top, just like those guys did. It's hard not to wonder if I could still be the best. Maybe I'd find out I'm over-the-hill, but I don't think so.

What really prompted serious thoughts about a comeback was a comment from a guy we signed for World Wrestling Entertainment, an NCAA champion heavyweight wrestler named Brock Lesner. He's a young guy, a tremendous athlete who is going to be great in World Wrestling Entertainment when he finishes his training, probably sometime next year. He's six feet three, weighs 300 pounds, and one day one of the guys asked Brock how he would do against me in a wrestling match.

"Well, he's a little guy," Brock said. "I don't think he'd be able to handle my size."

What he doesn't know is that I used to torture guys his size, so when I heard he'd said that, it wounded my pride a little. He was a great college wrestler, but he's not on the Olympic level, and that's a huge difference. He doesn't know what he's dealing with when he talks like that.

Naturally, the boys in the locker room started ribbing me when they heard about it. So a few weeks later Brock was at one of our shows to be part of an untelevised match. And the boys started egging me on: "Angle, he's here. Why don't you get him?"

At first I said no, I didn't want to start any trouble. But then I was sitting around with Jerry Brisco while guys were going over their matches. Brock and another former college wrestler, Shelton Benjamin, who joined World Wrestling Entertainment, were standing nearby, and Jerry told them he wanted to invite them to the wrestling clinic that I help him put on every year for his team.

I decided this was my chance to tweak Brock a little bit.

"Jerry," I said, "these guys don't know technique."

Brock looked at me and said, "What do you mean we don't know technique?"

I was trying to get a reaction and draw him into the ring.

"You guys don't know real technique," I said.

We went back and forth a little bit and finally I said, "You know what? Show me." And I climbed into the ring.

"No," Brock said. "I've got sandals on."

"Hold on, I'll take my shoes off," I said. "Let's go."

But he wouldn't bite. All the boys were standing there, and he wouldn't wrestle me. I just wanted to show them I could handle a guy who weighs 300 pounds. I'm not taking anything away from Brock. He's a national champion and I give him all the credit in the world. He's a superior athlete. He's an NCAA champion, maybe one of the best college heavyweights in years, but he's not an Olympic champion. Not that I'm arrogant, but I'm confident. Even though I've been off the mat for five years, I know I could beat him.

It's all good-natured fun between Brock and me, but we may have to settle this eventually. One of the guys asked him later that day why he didn't take my challenge, and Brock told him, "Oh, man, I could kick his ass."

So we'll see. I think the reason he wouldn't get in the ring with me is because, deep down, he knows how good I am. I don't take it lightly when anybody challenges my reputation in amateur wrestling. When it comes to that sport, I don't care how big a guy is, I don't lose. I don't care if I've been out of that sport for five years, or even ten for that matter.

I guess Brock's comments lit a match to my old competitive spirit, and more and more I started thinking, "Wow, I really was that damn good. I used to take guys like Brock and eat 'em alive."

It's only natural to miss that feeling of superiority. Maybe it will pass as the time to make a decision on a comeback gets closer, but I don't know. I've got the urge again to shock the wrestling world and do something spectacular, something that would rank with the greatest feats in Olympic history. I'm just wondering, though . . . Do you think they'll let me use my ankle-lock submission hold in the Olympics? Stay tuned.

★ CAPTIONS

Page xiv: Wrapping up Y2J for another pinfall.

Page 8: Using some amateur wrestling skills on another World Wrestling Entertainment foe.

Page 14: A picture of your Olympic hero's most beloved grandmother *(front)*, mom, and dad.

Page 21: My father before I was born, 1966.

Page 27: Mom and Dad leaving church in Davidsonville, Maryland, while visiting relatives.

Page 30: My brother Eric *(right)* and me on my sixth birthday.

Page 35: Eric and Kurt flexing some muscle during Christmas 1977.

Page 52: Senior football season 1987.

Page 61: The Angle kids celebrating the Olympic gold medal. *Left to right:* John, Eric, Le'Anne, Kurt, David, Mark.

Page 68: Holding the Golden Plaque after winning my second national title in college. Oklahoma City, Oklahoma.

Page 81: Attacking a competitor from Iowa State at the University of Wisconsin in 1991.

Page 84: Man on a mission: My third win of the five matches I had at the Olympics, against a Ukrainian wrestler, Sahid Murtazaliyev.

Page 90: A snapshot of Kurt and his mother, Jackie, at Kurt and Karen's wedding, December 18, 1998.

Page 92: On location in London, with Shane McMahon before the *Insurextion* PPV. May 5, 2000.

Page 100: In Moscow, at the Sport Hotel with USA teammate Jack Griffin, 1994.

Page 105: Applying the leg lace for a two-point turn against Mark Coleman, June 1994.

Pages 108–109: Kurt with former wrestling greats *(left to right)* Jeff Ellis, Gus De Augustino, and Pat Santoro.

Page 116: A cold stare at yet another World Wrestling Entertainment victim for your Olympic hero.

Page 122: The incredibly intelligent, talented, and often goofy legend of amateur wrestling, Dave Schultz.

Page 130: 1992 trials, John du Pont comforts me after a heartbreaking loss in the semifinals.

Page 142: Team USA's four world champions at the 1995 World Championships. *Left to right:* Terry Brands, Bruce Baumgartner, Kevin Jackson, and Kurt Angle.

Page 149: With a busted eye, your Olympic hero focuses on a win at the 1995 World Team trials.

Page 159: Kurt with Coach Bob Bubb at his induction into the Amateur Wrestling Hall of Fame, June 2001.

Page 168: The 1995 World Championship finals: Kurt Angle fighting off 1994 World Champion Arawat Sabejew (Germany) for a win.

Page 174: Your Olympic hero celebrating a win in the finals of the 1995 World Championships at the Omni in Atlanta, Georgia.

Page 177: Kurt and football legend Joe Namath at the grand opening of the Wiz in New York City. August 1996.

Page 179: Realizing the dream, on the podium at the 1996 Olympics. *Left:* Abbas Jadidi (Iran); *right:* Arawat Sabejew (Germany).

Page 182: Showing the excitement after winning the 1995 World Championships.

Page 186: Kurt with manager Dave Hawk—former Mr. World, Mr. Universe, Mr. USA, and bodybuilding champ.

Page 194: Good friend and loyal amateur wrestling fan Garth Brooks invites your Olympic hero to a concert at the Civic Arena in Pittsburgh.

Page 198: Putting a choke hold on "the Deadman"— the Undertaker—*Fully Loaded 2000*.

Page 202: Kurt and wife-to-be, Karen, attend an ECW event prior to signing with World Wrestling Entertainment.

Page 204: The most "celebrated real athlete," making his patented entrance into the ring at *Smack-Down!* 2000.

Page 213: Kurt Angle, in *King of the Ring* 2000, is about to show Rikishi why he won a gold medal in 1996.

Page 221: Kurt and wife, Karen, with little Marie.

Page 230: Kurt relaxing in the sun with Owen Hart and Prince Albert before a *SmackDown!* event in Orlando.

Page 234: Your Olympic hero celebrating yet another win.

Pages 238–239: World Wrestling Entertainment Undisputed Champion, Kurt Angle, celebrates his big win at *No Mercy* 2000 over The Rock at *RAW IS WAR*.

Page 244: Kurt takes the sledgehammer to Triple H, a much-hated foe at *SummerSlam* 2000.

Page 248: The very few fans who show loyalty to their Olympic hero, Kurt Angle.

Page 252: Kurt is about to degrade yet another city he considers to be beneath his standards.

Page 256: Your Olympic hero is working over Y2J at *No Way Out* 2000.

Pages 260–261: Kurt is taking his opponent Chris Jericho down for a pinfall.

Page 265: Kurt Angle pleading his case as to why he should be the number one contender at *WrestleMania* X-Seven, during *RAW IS WAR*.

Page 268: Kurt lays a big Olympic hero kiss on Stephanie during his feud with her husband, Triple H.

Page 275: Kurt is frustrated and confused as to why the fans could turn against a true American hero. January 4, 2000.

Page 280: After capturing the title from The Rock at *No Mercy*, Kurt explains why he deserves to be the champion for years to come.

Page 286: Kurt with wife, Karen, in Washington, D.C., at the presidential inauguration. January 2001.

Page 289: Kurt enters the arena with friend and manager Stephanie McMahon-Helmsley on *RAW IS WAR*. October 23, 2000.

Pages 294–295: Celebrating another title defense against Triple H at the *Royal Rumble* 2001.

Page 299: Accompanying CEO Linda McMahon, Kurt Angle, the honorary chairman of SmackDown Your Vote!, is about to announce his own inauguration.

Page 302: King Kurt, the King of the Ring 2000, flaunts his crown and cape.

Pages 308–309: Kurt, along with family members and Stephanie, celebrates an "Angle Christmas" on *RAW IS WAR*. December 25, 2000.

Page 311: Kurt and buddies Edge and Christian have fun with the fans before tagging against Rikishi and Too Cool at a *RAW IS WAR* on June 5, 2000.

Page 314: Making his first main event on *Fully Loaded* 2000, Angle works on the Undertaker's knee.

Pages 318–319: Kurt and Triple H fight over Stephanie.

Page 323: Kurt finds a new manager, Trish Stratus, after capturing the title.

Page 324: Having fun with the crowd in Buffalo after imitating a missed field goal attempt in the Super Bowl by Scott Norwood, the Buffalo Bills goal kicker, on *SmackDown!* May 6, 2000.

Page 330: World Wrestling Entertainment goes public at the NYSE in New York City as Kurt and Stephanie entertain the thousands of fans outside. May 6, 2000.

Page 336: Stephanie is trying to calm your Olympic hero down after Triple H makes fun of his win at the Olympics by matching his celebration tears.

Page 342: Kurt is preaching his three I's—intensity, integrity, and intelligence—on *SmackDown!* September 7, 1999.

Pages 346–347: Kurt is pleading his case to Commissioner Mick Foley and his assistant Debra as to why he shouldn't have to defend his title that night.

Page 351: Kurt and Shane-O-Mac aren't happy with Mr. McMahon's decision to keep Kurt from defending his title.